Modelling with AutoCAD Release 2000

Bob McFarlane
M.Sc, B.SC, ARCST, C.Eng, FIED, RCADDes, MIMechE, MIEE, MIMgt, MBCS, MCSD, MILog

CAD Course Leader Motherwell College
AutoDESK Educational Developer

OXFORD AUCKLAND BOSTON JOHANNESBURG MELBOURNE NEW DELHI

Butterworth-Heinemann
Linacre House, Jordan Hill, Oxford OX2 8DP
225 Wildwood Avenue, Woburn, MA 01801-2041
A division of Reed Educational and Professional Publishing Ltd

ℛ A member of the Reed Elsevier plc group

First published 2000

British Library Cataloguing in Publication Data
A catalogue record for this book is available from the British Library

Library of Congress Cataloguing in Publication Data
A catalogue record for this book is available from the Library of Congress

ISBN 0 7506 5056 7

Produced and typeset by Gray Publishing, Tunbridge Wells, Kent
Printed and bound in Great Britain by The Bath Press, Avon

Modelling with
AutoCAD
Release 2000

Book

Other titles from Bob McFarlane

Beginning AutoCAD   ISBN 0 340 58571 4

Progressing with AutoCAD   ISBN 0 340 60173 6

Introducing 3DAutoCAD   ISBN 0 340 61456 0

Solid Modelling with AutoCAD   ISBN 0 340 63204 6

Starting with AutoCAD LT   ISBN 0 340 62543 0

Advancing with AutoCAD LT   ISBN 0 340 64579 2

3D Draughting using AutoCAD   ISBN 0 340 67782 1

Beginning AutoCAD R13 for Windows   ISBN 0 340 64572 5

Advancing with AutoCAD R13 for Windows   ISBN 0 340 69187 5

Modelling with AutoCAD R13 for Windows   ISBN 0 340 69251 0

Using AutoLISP with AutoCAD   ISBN 0 340 72016 6

Beginning AutoCAD R14 for Windows NT and Windows 95   ISBN 0 340 72017 4

Advancing with AutoCAD R14 for Windows NT and Windows 95   ISBN 0 340 74053 1

Contents

Preface

This book is intended for the AutoCAD Release 2000 user who wants to learn about modelling. My aim is to demonstrate how the user can create 3D wire-frame models, surface models and solid models with practical exercises backed up by user activities. The concept of how multiple viewports can be used to enhance drawing productivity will also be discussed in detail, as will the paper space options which are new to R2000. The user will also be introduced to rendering.

The book will provide an invaluable aid to a wide variety of users, ranging from the capable to the competent. The book will assist students on any national course which requires 3D draughting and solid modelling, e.g. City and Guilds, BTEC and SQA as well as students at higher institutions. Users in industry will find the book useful as a reference and an 'inspiration'. The book will also prove useful to the Design/Technology departments in schools who are now becoming more involved in computer-aided design.

Reader requirements

The following are the requirements I consider important for using the book:

- the ability to draw with Release 2000
- the ability to use icons and toolbars
- an understanding of how to use dialogue boxes
- the ability to open and save drawings to a named folder
- a knowledge of model/paper space would be an advantage, although this is not essential.

Using the book

The book is essentially a self-teaching package with the reader working interactively through exercises using information supplied. The various prompts and responses will be listed in order and icons and dialogue boxes will be included where appropriate.

The following points are important:

- All drawing work should be saved to a named folder. The folder name is at your discretion, but I will refer to it as **MODR2000**, e.g. open drawing MODR2000\MODEL1 or similar.
- Icons will be displayed when the command is used for the first time.
- Menu bar selection will be in bold type, e.g. **Draw-Surfaces-3D Face**.
- Keyboard entry will also be in bold type, e.g. **VPOINT, UCS**, etc.
- Prompts will be in typewriter type, e.g. First corner.
- The symbol **<R>** will require the user to press the return/enter key.

Note

All the exercises and activities have been completed using Release 2000. I have tried to correct any errors in the drawings and text, but if any error should occur, I apologize for them and hope they do not spoil your learning experience. Modelling is an intriguing topic and should give you satisfaction and enjoyment.

Any comments you have about how to improve the material in the book would be greatly appreciated.

Chapter 1

The 3D standard sheet

To assist us with the models which will be created, a standard sheet (prototype drawing) will be made with layers, a text style, dimension styles, etc. This standard sheet will be saved as both a drawing and a template.

1 Start AutoCAD R2000 and:
   prompt Startup dialogue box
   respond **pick Use a Wizard**
   prompt Startup (Use a Wizard) dialogue box
   respond **pick Advanced Setup then OK**
   prompt Advanced Setup dialogue box
   respond select the following to the various steps:
       Step 1   Units: Decimal; Precision 0.00; Next>>
       Step 2   Angle: Decimal Degrees; Precision 0.0; Next>>
       Step 3   Angle Measure: East(0); Next>>
       Step 4   Angle Direction: Counter-Clockwise(+); Next>>
       Step 5   Area: Width 420 and Length 297 (i.e. A3); Finish.

2 A blank screen will be displayed.

3 *Layers*
   Menu bar with **Format-Layer** and make the following new layers:

name	colour	linetype
MODEL	RED	continuous
TEXT	GREEN	continuous
DIM	MAGENTA	continuous
OBJECTS	BLUE	continuous
SECT	number: 96	continuous
0	white	continuous

   NB: other layers will be added as required.

4 *Text style*
   Menu bar with **Format-Text Style** and make a new text style:
   Name: ST1
   Font: romans.shx
   Height: 0; Width factor: 1; Obliquing angle: 0
   Apply then Close the dialogue box.

5 *Units*
   Menu bar with **Format-Units** and:
   Units: Decimal with Precision: 0.00
   Angle: Decimal Degrees with Precision: 0.0
   Drawing units for DesignCenter blocks: Millimeters.

6 *Limits*

Menu bar with **Format-Drawing Limits** and:

prompt   Specify lower left corner and enter: **0,0 <R>**

prompt   Specify upper right corner and enter: **420,297 <R>**.

7 *Drafting Settings*

Menu bar with **Tools-Drafting Settings** and set:

Snap: 5 and grid: 10 – not generally used in 3D

Polar snap: off

Object snap: all clear – will be set as/when required.

8 *Dimension style*

Menu bar with **Dimension-Style** and:

prompt   Dimension Style Manager dialogue box

respond **pick New**

prompt   Create New Dimension Style dialogue box

respond 1. New Style Name: **3DSTD**

2. Start With: ISO-25 (or similar)

3. Use for: All dimensions

4. pick Continue

prompt   New Dimension Style: 3DSTD dialogue box

respond **pick Lines and Arrows tab and alter:**

a) Dimension Lines

1. Baseline spacing: 10

b) Extension Lines

1. Extend beyond dim lines: 2.5

2. Offset from origin: 2.5

c) Arrowheads

1. both Closed Filled

2. Leader: Closed Filled

3. Arrow size: 3.5

4. Center Mark for Circles: None

then   **pick Text tab and alter:**

a) Text Appearance

1. Text Style: ST1

2. Text Height: 4

b) Text Placement

1. Vertical: Above

2. Horizontal: Centred

3. Offset from dim line: 1.5

c) Text Alignment

1. ISO Standard

then   **pick Fit tab and alter:**

a) Fit Options

1. Either the text or the arrows active (black dot)

b) Text Placement

1. Beside the dimension line active

c) Scale for Dimension Features

1. Use overall scale of: 1

d) Fine tuning: both inactive, i.e. blank

then **pick Primary Units tab and alter:**
    a) Linear Dimensions
        1. Unit Format: Decimal
        2. Precision: 0.00
        3. Decimal separator: '.' Period
        4. Round off: 0
    b) Measurement Scale
        1. Scale factor: 1
    c) Zero Suppression
        1. Trailing: active, i.e. tick
    d) Angular Dimensions
        1. Units Format: Decimal Degrees
        2. Precision: 0.0
        3. Zero Suppression: Trailing active

then **pick Alternate Units tab and:**
    a) Display alternate units: not active

then **pick Tolerance tab and:**
    a) Tolerance Format
        1. Method: None

then **pick OK from New Dimension Style dialogue box**
prompt Dimension Style Manager dialogue box
with 1. 3DSTD added to styles list
      2. preview of 3DSTD style displayed
      3. description of 3DSTD given
respond 1. pick 3DSTD and it becomes highlighted
      2. pick Set Current
      3. AutoCAD alert perhaps – just pick OK
      4. pick Close.

9 Make layer 0 current and menu bar with **Draw-Rectangle** and:
    prompt Specify first corner point and enter: **0,0 <R>**
    prompt Specify other corner point and enter: **420,290 <R>**
    This rectangle will save as a 'reference base' for our models.

10 Zoom-all and pan to suit.

11 Make layer MODEL current.

12 Menu bar with **File-Save As** and:
    prompt Save Drawing As dialogue box
    respond 1. Scroll and pick your named folder
        2. enter File name: **3DSTDA3**
        3. file type: **AutoCAD 2000 Drawing (*.dwg)**
        4. pick Save.

13 Menu bar with **File-Save As** and:
    prompt Save Drawing As dialogue box
    respond 1. scroll at Save as type
        2. pick **AutoCAD Drawing Template File (*.dwt)**
        3. enter File name as: **3DSTDA3**
        4. pick Save
    prompt Template Description dialogue box
    respond 1. enter: This is my 3D standard sheet
        2. pick OK.

14 The created standard sheet has been saved as a drawing file and a template file, both with the name 3DSTDA3. The drawing file has been saved to a named folder and the template file has been added to the existing list of AutoCAD templates in the Template folder.
Note.
a) we could have saved the template file to our named folder
b) you can re-save the standard sheet as a template to your folder if required
c) saving the standard sheet as a template will stop the user 'inadvertently' over-writing the basic 3DSTD standard sheet
d) all models will be created from the 3DSTDA3 template file
e) all completed models will be saved as drawings to your named folder
f) the standard sheet has been saved as a drawing for backup.

15 *Checking the standard sheet*
Menu bar with **File-Open** and:
prompt   Select File dialogue box
respond   1. scroll at Files of type
            2. pick **Drawing Template File(*.dwt)**
prompt   Template folder with list of template files
respond   1. note 3DSTDA3 listed
            2. pick Cancel

We are now ready to proceed with created 3D and solid models.

Chapter 2

Extruded 3D models

An extruded model is created by extruding a 'shape' upwards or downwards from a horizontal plane – called the ELEVATION plane. The actual extruded height (or depth) is called the THICKNESS and can be positive or negative relative to the set elevation plane. This extruded thickness is **always perpendicular** to the elevation plane. The extrusion is in the Z direction of the UCS icon – more on this later. The basic extruded terminology is displayed in Fig. 2.1.

Note. Extruded models were one of the first ever 3D displays with a CAD system. The term 3D model is not quite correct, a more accurate description being 2½D model.

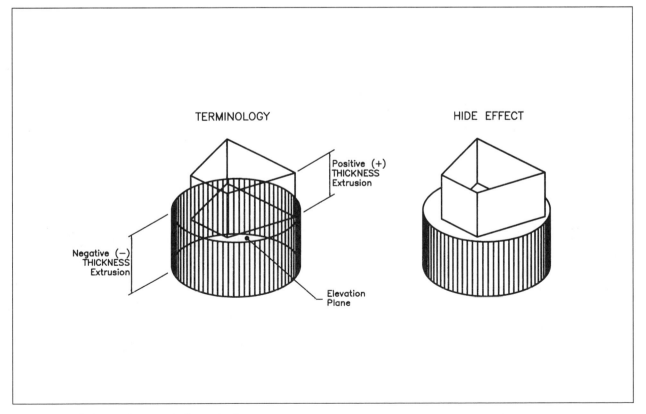

Figure 2.1 Basic extruded terminology.

Extruded example 1

The example is given as a series of user-entered steps, these steps also being displayed in Fig. 2.2. Open your 3DSTDA3 template file and display toolbars to suit, e.g. Draw, Modify and Object Snap. Layer MODEL should be current.

Step 1: the first elevation

1 At the command line enter **ELEV <R>** and:
   prompt   `Specify new default elevation<0.00>` and enter: **0 <R>**
   prompt   `Specify new default thickness<0.00>` and enter: **50 <R>**.

2 Nothing appears to have happened?

3 Select the LINE icon and draw:
   Start point   **40,40 <R>**
   Next point   **@100,0 <R>**
   Next point   **@100<90 <R>**
   Next point   **@-100,0 <R>**
   Next point   **C <R>** – the close option.

4 A red 'square' will be displayed.

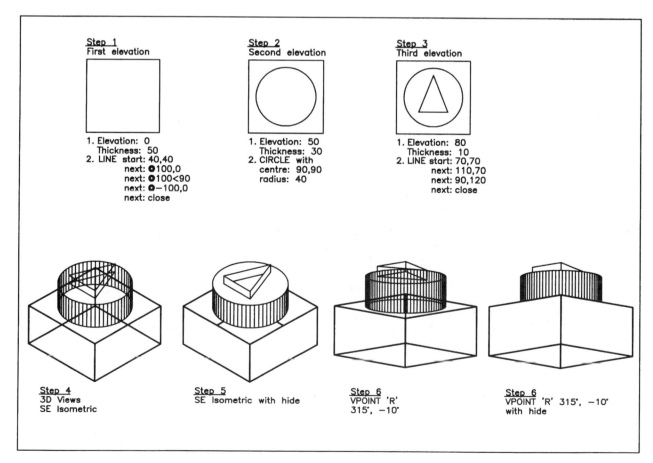

Figure 2.2 Extruded example 1.

Step 2: the second elevation

1 At the command line enter **ELEV <R>** and:
   prompt   Specify new default elevation<0.00> and enter: **50 <R>**
   prompt   Specify new default thickness<50.00> and enter: **30 <R>**.

2 Select the CIRCLE icon and:
   a) centre point: enter **90,90 <R>**
   b) radius: enter **40 <R>**.

3 At the command line enter **CHANGE <R>** and:
   prompt   Select objects
   respond **pick the circle then right-click**
   prompt   Specify change point or [Properties]
   enter   **P <R>** – the properties option
   prompt   Enter property to change [Color/Elev..
   enter   **C <R>** – the color option
   prompt   Enter new color
   enter   **green <R>**
   prompt   Enter property to change
   respond **right-click and pick Enter.**

4 The added circle will be displayed with a green colour.

Step 3: the third elevation

1 With the ELEV command:
   a) set the default elevation to 80
   b) set the default thickness to 10

2 With the LINE icon, draw:
   Start point   **70,70 <R>**
   Next point   **110,70 <R>**
   Next point   **90,120 <R>**
   Next point   **C <R>**.

3 With the CHANGE command, change the colour of the three lines to blue, using the same procedure as was used previously.

4 Now have a blue triangle inside a green circle inside a red square, and appear to have a traditional 2D plan type drawing. Each of the three shapes has been created on a different default elevation plane:
   a) square: elevation 0
   b) circle: elevation 50
   c) triangle: elevation 80.

Step 4: viewing the model in 3D

To 'see' the model in 3D the 3D Viewpoint command is required, so:

1 From the menu bar select **View-3D Views-SE Isometric.**

2 The model will be displayed in 3D. The black 'drawing border' is also displayed in 3D and acts as a 'base' for the model.

3 The orientation of the model is such that it is difficult to know if you are looking down on it, or looking up at it. This is common with 3D modelling and is called **AMBIGUITY**. Another command is required to 'remove' this ambiguity.

4 At this stage save your model with **File-Save As** and ensure:
   a) File type is: AutoCAD 2000 Drawing (*.dwg)
   b) Save in: MODR2000 – your named folder
   c) File name: **EXT-1** – the drawing name.

5 This saves the drawing as **MODR2000\EXT-1.dwg.**

Step 5: the hide command

1 From the menu bar select **View-Hide** and the model will be displayed with hidden line removal and is now easier to 'see'.

2 From the screen display it is obvious that the model is being viewed from above, but it is possible to view from different angles.

3 Menu bar with **View-Regen** to 'restore' the original model.

Step 6: another viewpoint

1 At the command line enter **VPOINT <R>** and:
   prompt   Specify a view point or [Rotate]
   enter   **R <R>** – the rotate option
   prompt   Enter angle in XY plane from X-axis and enter: **315 <R>**
   prompt   Enter angle in XY plane and enter: **–10 <R>**.

2 The model will be displayed from a different viewpoint without hidden line removal.

3 At the command line enter **HIDE <R>**.

4 The model will be displayed with hidden line removal and is being viewed from below.

5 At the command line enter **REGEN <R>** to restore the original.

Step 7: the shade command

1 Restore the original 3D view with the menu bar sequence **View-3D Views-SE Isometric.**

2 Menu bar with **View-Shade-Flat Shade** and the model will be displayed with a coloured effect, the result of changing the colours of the various objects as they were added. Note the icon!

3 Investigate the other SHADE options available, then restore the model to its original display with **View-Shade-2D Wireframe.**

Task

1 With the ERASE command pick any line of the 'base' and a complete 'side' is erased because it is an extrusion.

2 Undo the erase effect with **U <R>**.

3 Using the erase command pick any point on the top 'circle' and the complete 'cylinder' will be erased.

4 Undo this erase effect.

5 This completes our first extrusion exercise.

6 *Note.*
   Although Fig. 2.2 displays several different viewpoints of the model on 'one sheet' this concept will not be discussed until a later chapter. At present you will only display a single view of the model.

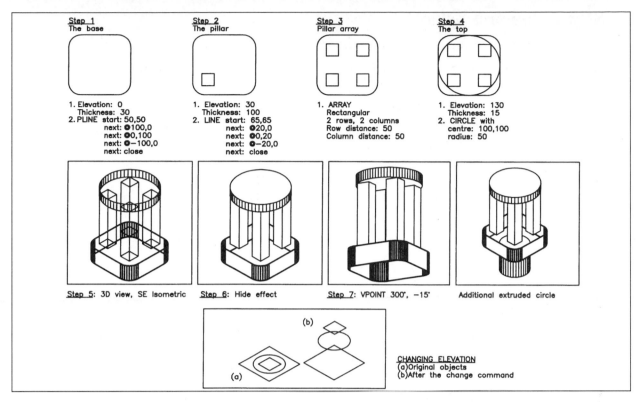

Figure 2.3 Extruded example 2.

Extrusion example 2

Open your 3DSTDA3 template file, layer MODEL current and refer to Fig. 2.3.

Step 1: the base

1   With ELEV at the command line, set the new default elevation to 0 and the new default thickness to 30.

2   With the polyline icon from the Draw toolbar, draw a 0 width polyline:
Start point   **50,50 <R>**
Next point   **@100,0 <R>**
Next point   **@0,100 <R>**
Next point   **@−100,0 <R>**
Next point   **C <R>**.

3   Menu bar with **Modify-Fillet** and:
prompt   Specify first object or [Polyline/Radius/Trim]
enter   **R <R>** – the radius option
prompt   Specify fillet radius
enter   **20 <R>**.

4   Select the FILLET icon from the Modify toolbar and:
prompt   Specify first object [Polyline/Radius/Trim]
enter: **P <R>** – polyline option
prompt   Select 2D polyline
respond   **pick any point on the polyline**.

5   The drawn polyline will be filleted at the four corners.

Step 2: the first pillar

1 Set the elevation to 30 and the thickness to 100.

2 With the LINE icon draw a 20 unit square the lower left corner being at the point 65,65.

Step 3: arraying the pillar

1 Select the ARRAY icon from the Modify toolbar and:
   prompt Select objects
   respond **window the square** then right-click
   prompt Enter the type of array and enter: **R <R>** – rectangular
   prompt Enter the number of rows and enter: **2 <R>**
   prompt Enter the number of columns and enter: **2 <R>**
   prompt Enter the distance between rows and enter: **50 <R>**
   prompt Specify the distance between columns and enter: **50 <R>**.

2 The square is arrayed in a 2 × 2 matrix pattern.

Step 4: the top

1 Set the elevation to 130 and the thickness to 15.

2 Draw a circle, centred on 100,100 with radius of 50.

Step 5: the 3D viewpoint

1 Menu bar with **View-3D Views-SE Isometric.**

2 The model is displayed in 3D but appears rather 'cluttered'.

Step 6: hiding the model

1 Menu bar with **View-Hide** model displayed with hidden line removal.

2 Menu bar with **View-Regen** to restore original.

3 At this stage save the model as **MODR2000\EXT-2.**

Step 7: setting another viewpoint

1 At the command line enter **VPOINT <R>** and:
   prompt Specify a new view point and enter: **R <R>** – the rotate option
   prompt Enter angle in XY plane from X axis and enter: **300 <R>**
   prompt Enter angle from XY plane and enter: **-15 <R>**.

2 Menu bar with **View-Hide** then **View-Regen.**

3 Restore the original 3D view with **View-3D Views-SE Isometric.**
   Before leaving this exercise, there are a few new concepts which I would like to introduce/discuss with the user.

Task 1

1 Still have the extruded model displayed?

2 Menu bar with **View-3D Views-Plan View-World UCS.**

3   The model is displayed 'as drawn'.

4   At the command line enter **PICKFIRST <R>** and:
   prompt   `Enter new value for PICKFIRST <?>`
   enter   **1 <R>**.

5   A small pick box will be 'added' to the cursor cross-hairs

6   Using the pickbox, pick the 16 lines of the 4 squares then pick the Properties icon from the Standard toolbar and:
   prompt   Properties dialogue box
   respond   1. pick the Color line – highlights
            2. scroll at the right
            3. pick Blue
            4. cancel the dialogue box – top right pick
            5. press the ESC key
   and   the four squares will be displayed in blue

7   With the command line PICKFIRST, enter a value of 0

8   At the command line enter **CHANGE <R>** and:
   prompt   `Select objects`
   respond   **pick the circle then right-click**
   prompt   `Specify change point or [Properties]`
   enter   **P <R>** – the properties option
   prompt   `Enter property to change..`
   enter   **C <R>** – the color option
   prompt   `Enter new color<BYLAYER>`
   enter   **GREEN <R>**
   prompt   `Enter property to change..`
   respond   **right-click and Enter** – no more properties to change.

9   We now have the following:
   a) the filleted square base: red
   b) the four pillars: blue
   c) the circular top: green.

10   Now display the model with the following menu bar selections:
   a) View-3D Views-SE Isometric
   b) View-Hide
   c) View-Shade-Flat Shade
   d) View-Shade-3D Wireframe
   e) View-Hide and note the green circle effect
   f) View-Shade-Flat Shade, Edges On
   g) View-Shade-2D Wireframe and note the green circle effect
   h) View-Regen to 'restore' the original model.

11   *Note.*
   Changing properties (e.g. colour) is obtained with the PICKFIRST variable and:
   a) PICKFIRST: 0 – CHANGE at command line, then select objects
   b) PICKFIRST: 1 – select objects, then Properties icon
   c) the method to use is at the user's discretion.

Task 2

1 Restore the original layout with the sequence View-3D Views-Plan View-World UCS.

2 With ELEV at the command line, set the elevation to 0 and the thickness to –60.

3 Draw a circle, centre 100,100 and radius 30, colour magenta.

4 View the model at a SE Isometric viewpoint.

5 Now have extruded the circle downwards.

6 Re-save the model with the added extruded circle.

7 View-3D Views-Plan View-World UCS to restore original layout.

Task 3

1 Set both the elevation and thickness to 0.

2 Draw the following objects to right of the model:
   a) a 100 sided square
   b) a 40 radius circle inside the square
   c) a 30 sided square inside the circle.

3 Menu bar with View-3D Views-SE Isometric and the three shapes will be displayed at elevation 0.

4 At the command line enter **CHANGE <R>** and:
   a) pick the circle then right-click
   b) enter P <R> for the property option
   c) enter E <R> for the Elev(ation) option
   d) enter 50 <R> as the new elevation
   e) right-click and Enter to end command.

5 Using the CHANGE command, alter the elevation of the four lines of the small square to 80.

   The extruded model exercise 2 is now complete and you can proceed to your first assignment, after reading the summary.

Summary

1 An extruded model is created from an elevation and thickness.

2 Extruded models created from straight lines have no top or bottom surfaces – only sides.

3 The elevation and thickness are usually set from the command line.

4 The elevation and thickness of objects can be altered with:
   a) command line CHANGE with PICKFIRST 0
   b) Properties icon with PICKFIRST 1.

5 Extruded models are viewed in 3D with the 3D Views command which will be discussed in detail in a later chapter.

7 3D models are displayed with AMBIGUITY, i.e. are you looking down from the top or up from the bottom?

8 The HIDE command is used to display 3D models with hidden line removal. This removes the AMBIGUITY effect.

9 The REGEN (regenerate) command restores a 3D model with all lines displayed.

10 The SHADE command gives useful displays with coloured objects.

Assignment

During the assignments you will frequently meet a character called MACFARAMUS. This august gentleman was a great architect in ancient times, but sadly most of his works have not been given the credit they deserve. Your first assignment is to create as a $2\frac{1}{2}$D model, the famous coloured rectangular pyramid of MACFARAMUS. This object has also been called (in modern times) 'the wedding cake pyramid'. (All the activity drawings are at the end of the book starting on page 302.)

Activity 1: Coloured rectangular pyramid of MACFARAMUS

Using the elevation and thickness method, create the $2\frac{1}{2}$D model of the rectangular pyramid. The relevant information is given for you. Setting the grid and snap to 10 will help. Use the LINE command and start at level 1 with the 90 square. Change the colour using the CHANGE command or the Properties icon – PICKFIRST value?

When the model is complete, view at different 3D viewpoints and then try hide and shade. At present you will not be able to obtain the two different views on the one screen (unless you have some prior AutoCAD 3D knowledge).

Remember to save the completed model.

Chapter 3

The UCS and 3D coordinates

AutoCAD uses two coordinate systems:

1 the world coordinate system (**WCS**) and
2 the user coordinate system (**UCS**).

The WCS

All readers should be familiar with the basic 2D coordinate concept of a point described as P1 (30,40) – Fig. 3.1. Such a point has 30 units in the positive X-direction and 40 units in the positive Y-direction. These ordinates are relative to an XY axes system with the origin at the point (0,0). This origin is normally positioned at the lower left corner of the screen and is perfectly satisfactory for 2D draughting but not for 3D modelling.

Drawing in 3D requires a third axis (the Z axis) to enable three-dimensional coordinates to be used. The screen monitor is a flat surface and it is difficult to display a three-axis coordinate system on it. AutoCAD overcomes this difficulty by using an **ICON** and this icon can be moved to different positions on the screen and can be orientated on existing objects.

Figure 3.2 shows the basic idea of how the icon has been constructed. The X and Y axes are displayed in their correct orientations while the Z axis is pointing outwards towards the user. The **W** on the icon indicates that the user is working with the world coordinate system. The origin is at the point (0,0,0) and is positioned at the lower left corner of the screen – as it is in 2D. The status bar displays the three coordinates of any point on the screen, but these figures can be misleading, especially when viewing in 3D. The origin point can be positioned to suit the model being created – more on this later.

The point P2 (30, 40, 50) is thus defined as 30 units in the positive X direction, 40 units in the positive Y direction and 50 units in the positive Z direction. Similarly the point P3 (–40, –50, –30) has 40 units in the negative X direction, 50 units in the negative Y direction and 30 units in the negative Z direction.

In the previous chapter, all the extruded models were created with the WCS.

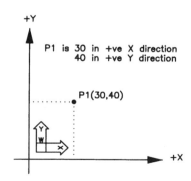

Figure 3.1 Coordination entry with the WCS at the (0,0) origin.

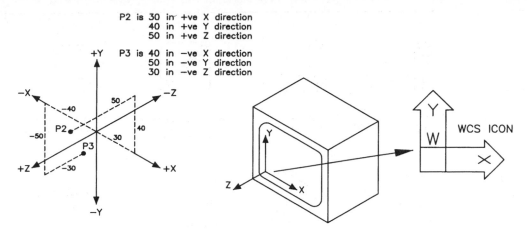

Figure 3.2 Coordination entry with the WCS at the (0,0) origin.

The UCS

The UCS is one of the most important concepts in 3D modelling and all users must be fully conversant with it. The user coordinate system allows the operator to:
a) set a new UCS origin point
b) move the origin to any point (or object) on the screen
c) align the UCS icon with existing objects
d) align the UCS icon to suit any 'plane' on a model
e) rotate the icon about the X, Y and Z axes
f) save UCS 'positions'
g) recall previously saved UCS settings.

The appearance of the UCS alters depending on:
a) its orientation, i.e. how it is 'attached' to objects
b) the viewpoint selected or entered.

UCS icon exercise

As an introduction to the UCS icon, the following exercise is given as a sequence of operations which the reader should complete. No drawing is involved and it should be noted that several of the commands will be new to some readers, all of which will be explained later. The object of the exercise is to make the reader aware of the 'versatility' of the UCS icon.

1 Open your 3DSTDA3 template file and refer to Fig. 3.3.

2 The icon displayed at the lower left corner of the screen has a W on it, indicating that it is the WCS icon – fig(a). This is the 'normal' default icon.

3 Menu bar with **View-Display-UCS Icon** and ensure both the On and Origin options are active, i.e. a tick at each name.

4 Select the PAN icon from the Standard toolbar or enter PAN <R> at the command line and:
   a) pan the screen upwards and to the right
   b) right-click and pick Exit.

5 The icon will be displayed as fig(b) with a + sign added at the 'box'. This indicates that the icon is positioned at the origin.

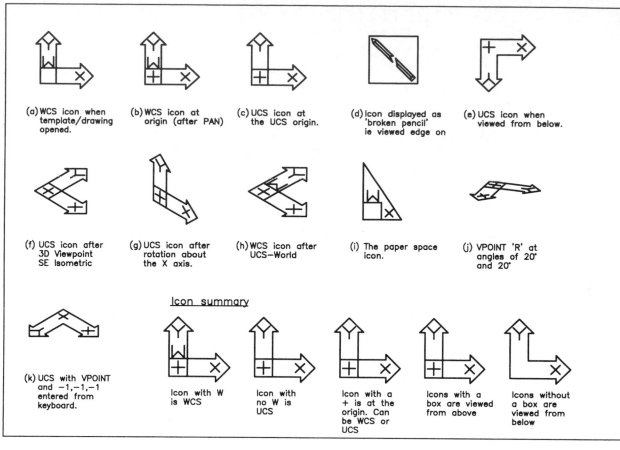

(a) WCS icon when template/drawing opened.

(b) WCS icon at origin (after PAN)

(c) UCS icon at the UCS origin.

(d) Icon displayed as 'broken pencil' ie viewed edge on

(e) UCS icon when viewed from below.

(f) UCS icon after 3D Viewpoint SE Isometric

(g) UCS icon after rotation about the X axis.

(h) WCS icon after UCS–World

(i) The paper space icon.

(j) VPOINT 'R' at angles of 20° and 20°

Icon summary

(k) UCS with VPOINT and −1,−1,−1 entered from keyboard.

Icon with W is WCS

Icon with no W is UCS

Icon with a + is at the origin. Can be WCS or UCS

Icons with a box are viewed from above

Icons without a box are viewed from below

Figure 3.3 WCS and UCS icon exercise.

6 With snap on, move the cursor onto the icon + and observe the status bar – the coordinates should be 0.00, 0.00, 0.00.

7 Pick the Undo icon from the Standard toolbar to restore the screen to its original display.

8 Menu bar with **Tools-New UCS-Origin** and:
prompt   Specify new origin point<0,0,0>
enter   **100,100 <R>**
and   the icon moves to the entered point and is as fig(c). It has no W indicating that it is a UCS icon and has a + indicating it is at the origin.

9 Move the cursor onto the + and observe the coordinates in the status bar. They should display 0.00, 0.00, 0.00.

10 Menu bar with **Tools-New UCS-X** and:
prompt   Specify rotation angle about X axis<0.0>
enter   **90 <R>**
and   icon displayed as fig(d). This is the AutoCAD 'broken pencil' icon indicating that we are looking at it 'edge-on'.

11 At the command line enter **UCS <R>** and:
 prompt Enter an option [New/Move/..
 enter   **N <R>** – the new option
 prompt Specify origin of new UCS or [ZAxis/3point/..
 enter   **X <R>** – the rotate about X axis option
 prompt Specify rotation angle about X axis
 enter   **90 <R>**
 and   icon displayed as fig(e) and is being viewed from below – there is no 'box'. The + is still displayed indicating the UCS icon is still at the origin.

12 Menu bar with **Tools-New UCS-X** and enter 180 as the rotation angle. The icon will again be displayed as fig(c).

13 Menu bar with **View-3D Views-SE Isometric** and the icon will be displayed in 3D as fig(f). It still has a + and is therefore still at the origin.

14 At the command line enter **UCS <R>** and:
 prompt Enter an option
 enter   **N <R>** then **X <R>** – new and X rotate options
 prompt Specify rotation angle about X axis
 enter   **90 <R>**
 and   icon displayed as fig(g).

15 Undo the UCS X rotation with U <R> or pick the Undo icon.

16 Menu bar with **Tools-New UCS-World** and the icon will be displayed as fig(h). This icon is at the original WCS origin at the lower left corner of the 'drawing sheet'. The icon is still in 3D.

17 Menu bar with **View-3D Views-Plan View-World UCS** and the icon should be as the original fig(a) – may need to pan?

18 Left click on the word MODEL in the status bar and:
 prompt Page Setup dialogue box
 respond **pick Cancel** – more on this later.

The icon will be displayed as fig(i). This is the paper space icon which will be discussed in more detail in a later chapter.

At present undo this paper space effect with U <R> to restore the icon as fig(a).

19 Enter/select the following sequences:
 a) Menu bar with Tools-New UCS-Origin and enter 100,100 – fig(c)
 b) enter VPOINT <R> then R <R> with angles of 20 and 20 – fig(j)
 c) enter VPOINT <R> then -1,-1,-1 to give the icon as fig(k)
 d) enter VPOINT <R> then R <R> with angles of 0 and 90 – fig(c)
 e) enter UCS <R> then W <R> – fig(a).

20 This completes the icon exercise. There is no need to save.

21 *Note*: we could have used the UCS toolbar with icons during this exercise, but at our level I think that the menu bar and command line selections give the user a 'better understanding' of that is actually happening. You can investigate the UCS toolbar for yourself.

22 *Icon summary*

Figure 3.3 displays a summary of the various icons which can be displayed on the screen. These are:

a) icon with a W is a WCS icon
b) icon with no W is a UCS icon
c) icon with a + is at the origin
d) icon with a 'box' is viewed from above
e) icon with no 'box' is viewed from below.

Orientation of the UCS

The completed exercise has demonstrated that the UCS icon can be moved to any point on the screen and rotated about the three axes (we only used the X axis rotation, but the procedure is the same for the Y and Z axes). It is thus important for the user to be able to determine the correct orientation of the icon, i.e. how the X, Y and Z axes are configured in relation to each other.

The axes orientation is determined by the **right-hand rule** and is demonstrated in Fig. 3.4. The knuckle of the right hand is at the origin and the position of the thumb, index finger and second finger determine the direction of the positive X, Y and Z axes, respectively.

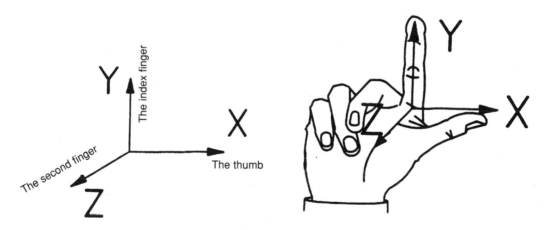

Figure 3.4 The right-hand rule.

Three-dimensional coordinate input

Coordinate input is generally required at some time during the creation of a 3D model. With 3D draughting there are three types of coordinates available, each having both absolute and relative entry modes. The three coordinate types are:

Type	Format	Absolute	Relative
Cartesian	x dist,y dist,z dist	100,150,120	@300, −100, −50
Cylindrical	dist<angle,Z dist	150<55,120	@75< −15, −120
Spherical	dist<angle 1<angle 2	80<30<50	@120< −10<75

To investigate the different types of coordinate input we will draw some objects on the screen. We will also investigate the effect of the icon position on the coordinate entries.

1 Open your 3DSTDA3 template file and refer to Fig. 3.5.

2 Menu bar with **View-Display-UCS Icon** and:
   a) On – tick
   b) Origin – tick.
   These selections ensure that the icon is displayed on the screen and is always 'set' to the origin point.

3 Menu bar with **View-3D Views-SE Isometric** to display the screen in 3D.

4 Menu bar with **View-Zoom-Scale** and:
   prompt   Enter a scale factor and enter: **0.75 <R>**.

5 The WCS icon should be positioned at the left vertex of the black border – point A.

6 Make three new layers – L1, L2, L3 with continuous linetype and colour numbers 30, 72, 240, respectively.

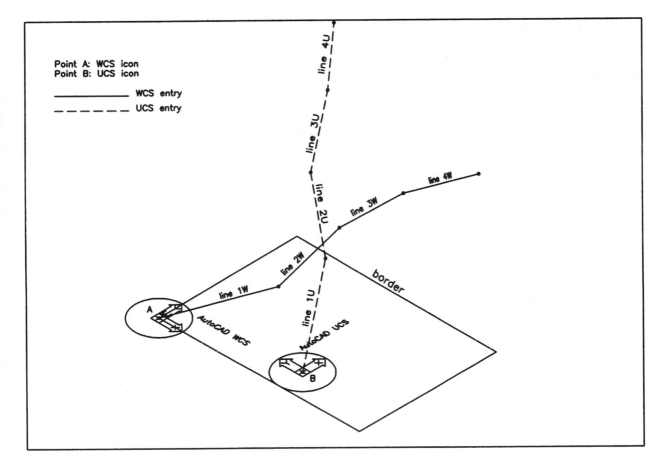

Figure 3.5   Coordinate entry exercise.

WCS entry

1 With layer L1 current, use the LINE icon and draw:

Start point	**0,0,0 <R>**		
Next point	**150,100,80 <R>**	absolute	line 1W
Next point	**@50,80,90 <R>**	relative absolute	line 2W
Next point	**@100<30,80 <R>**	relative cylindrical	line 3W
Next point	**@120<40<20 <R>**	relative spherical	line 4W
Next point	**right-click and pick Enter**.		

2 Menu bar with **View-Zoom-All** to 'see' the lines.

3 Draw a circle, centre: 0,0,0 with radius: 50.

4 Add the following item of text:
   a) start point: 40,40,0
   b) height: 10 with 0 rotation
   c) item: AutoCAD WCS.

UCS entry

1 Menu bar with **Tools-New UCS-Origin** and:
   prompt Specify new origin point
   enter   **250,50,0 <R>**.

2 Menu bar with **Tools-New UCS-Z** and:
   prompt Specify rotation angle about Z axis
   enter   **90 <R>**.

3 The icon should be positioned and orientated at point B.

4 With layer L2 current, use the LINE icon and draw:

Start point	**0,0,0 <R>**		
Next point	**150,100,80 <R>**	absolute	line 1U
Next point	**@50,80,90 <R>**	relative absolute	line 2U
Next point	**@100<30,80 <R>**	relative cylindrical	line 3U
Next point	**@120<40<20 <R>**	relative spherical	line 4U
Next point	**right-click and Enter**.		

5 Draw a circle, centred on 0,0,0 with a 50 radius.

6 Add the text item:
   a) start point: 40,40,0
   b) height: 10 with 0 rotation
   c) item: AutoCAD UCS.

WCS entry with UCS icon

1 Make layer L3 current.

2 With LINE icon draw:
   From point   ***0,0,0 <R>**
   To point   ***150,100,80 <R>**
   To point   **@*50,80,90 <R>**
   To point   **@*100<30,80 <R>**
   To point   **@*120<40<20 <R> then right-click and Enter**.

3 These lines will be identical to those entered with the WCS coordinates.

Task

1 Save the coordinate exercise if required, but we will not refer to it again.

2 With **File-Open** recall your 3DSTDA3 template file.

3 Menu bar with **View-Display-UCS icon** and ensure:
   a) On – tick
   b) Origin – tick.

4 Menu bar with **View-3D Views-SE Isometric**.

5 Menu bar with **View-Zoom-Scale** and enter a factor of **0.75**.

6 The WCS icon should be positioned at left vertex of the border.

7 Save this layout as:
   a) the **3DSTDA3.dwt** template file and replace the existing template file. Enter a suitable template description
   b) the **3DSTDA3.dwg** drawing file, overwriting the existing file.

8 This will allow the template file to opened in 3D with the icon always 'set' to the origin position.

Summary

1 There are two coordinate systems:
   a) the world coordinate system, WCS
   b) the user coordinate system, UCS.

2 Each system has its own icon.

3 The WCS is a fixed system, the origin being at 0,0,0.

4 The WCS icon is 'standard' and does not alter in appearance. The WCS icon is denoted with the letter W.

5 The UCS system allows the user to define the origin, either as a point on the screen or referenced to an existing object.

6 The UCS icon alters in appearance dependent on the viewpoint.

7 The UCS icon can be rotated about the three axes.

8 The UCS current position can be saved and recalled.

9 3D coordinate input can be:
   a) Cartesian, e.g. 10,20,30
   b) Cylindrical, e.g. 10<20,30
   c) Spherical, e.g. 10<20<30.

10 Both absolute and relative modes of input are possible with the three 'types' of coordinates, e.g.
   a) absolute cylindrical: 100<200,50
   b) relative cylindrical: @100<200,50.

11 3D coordinate input can be relative to the current UCS position or to the WCS, e.g.
   a) 100,200,150 for UCS entry
   b) *100,200,150 for WCS entry.

12 It is recommended that **3D coordinate input is relative to the current UCS position.**

Chapter 4

Creating a 3D wire-frame model

In this chapter we will create a 3D wire-frame model and use it to:
a) investigate how the UCS can be set and saved
b) add 'objects' and text to the model 'planes'
c) modify the model.

Getting started

1 Open your 3DSTDA3 template file to display:
 a) a 3D viewpoint with the black border
 b) the WCS icon at the left vertex of the border.

2 Ensure layer MODEL is current and refer to Fig. 4.1.

3 Display the Draw, Modify and Objects Snap toolbars.

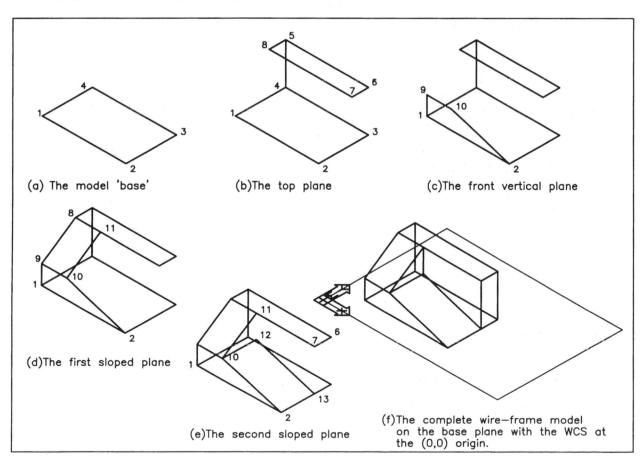

Figure 4.1 Construction of the wire-frame model 3DWFM.

Creating the wire-frame model
The base

1 With the LINE icon draw:

Start point	**50,50 <R>**	pt1
Next point	**@200,0 <R>**	pt2
Next point	**@0,120 <R>**	pt3
Next point	**@-200,0 <R>**	pt4
Next point	**close** – fig(a).	

The top plane

2 With the LINE icon draw:

Start point	**Intersection icon of pt4**	
Next point	**@0,0,100 <R>**	pt5
Next point	**@200,0,0 <R>**	pt6
Next point	**@0,-40,0 <R>**	pt7
Next point	**@-200,0,0 <R>**	pt8
Next point	**@0,40,0 <R>**	pt5
Next point	right-click and pick Enter.	

3 Menu bar with **View-Zoom-Scale** and enter a scale factor of **0.9** to 'see' the complete construction – fig(b).

The front vertical plane

4 LINE icon and draw:

Start point	**Intersection icon of pt1**	
Next point	**@0,0,45 <R>**	pt9
Next point	**@60,0,0 <R>**	pt10
Next point	**Intersection icon of pt2**	
Next point	right-click and Enter – fig(c).	

The first sloped plane

5 With the LINE icon draw:

Start point	**Intersection of pt9**
Next point	**Intersection of pt8** then right-click/enter.

6 LINE icon again:

Start point	**Intersection of pt10**	
Next point	**Perpendicular to line 78**	pt11
Next point	right-click and Enter – fig(d).	

The second sloped plane

7 Select the LINE icon and draw:

Start point	**Intersection of pt10**	
Next point	**@0,80,0 <R>**	pt12
Next point	**Perpendicular to line 23**	pt13
Next point	right-click and Enter – fig(e).	

Completing the model

8 The model requires three lines to be added, so with the LINE
icon draw:
   a) from pt3 to pt6
   b) from pt7 to pt13
   c) from pt11 to pt12.

9 The completed model is displayed in fig(f) on 'its base', i.e. the black border.

10 At this stage save the model as a drawing file with the name **MODR2000\3DWFM.dwg**.

11 *Note*.
   The model has been created using 3D coordinate input with the WCS, i.e. no attempt
   has been made to use the UCS. This is a perfectly valid method of creating wire-frame
   models, but difficulty can be experienced if objects and text have to be added to the
   various 'surfaces' of the model when the coordinates need to be calculated. Using the
   UCS usually overcomes this type of problem.

Moving around with the UCS

To obtain a better understanding of the UCS and how it is used with 3D models, we will
use the created wire-frame model to add some objects and text. The sequence is quite
long but it is important that you persevere and complete the exercise. Both menu bar
and keyboard entry methods will be used to activate the UCS command.

1 Open the wire-frame model **MODR2000\3DWFM** or continue from the previous
exercise. This model has the WCS icon at the black border origin point – the left vertex

2 Refer to Fig. 4.2.

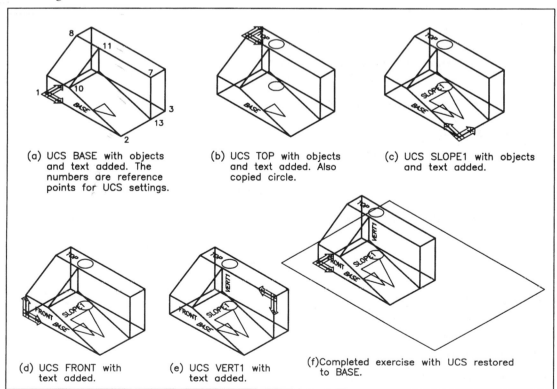

(a) UCS BASE with objects and text added. The numbers are reference points for UCS settings.

(b) UCS TOP with objects and text added. Also copied circle.

(c) UCS SLOPE1 with objects and text added.

(d) UCS FRONT with text added.

(e) UCS VERT1 with text added.

(f) Completed exercise with UCS restored to BASE.

Figure 4.2 Investigating the UCS and adding objects and text.

3 Menu bar with **View-Zoom-Scale** and enter a scale factor of 0.75. This will allow us to 'see' any UCS movements.

4 Menu bar with **Tools-New UCS-Origin** and:
prompt Specify new origin point<0,0,0>
respond **Intersection icon and pick pt1**
and *a*) icon 'moves' to selected point – fig(a)
  b) it is a UCS icon – no W
  c) it is at the origin – the +
Note. if the icon does not move to the selected point, menu bar with **View-Display-UCS Icon** and pick Origin (i.e. tick).

5 Now that the icon has been repositioned at point 1, we want to save this 'position' for future recall, so at the command line
enter **UCS <R>** and:
prompt Enter an option
enter **S <R>** – the save option
prompt Enter name to save current UCS
enter **BASE <R>**.

6 Make layer OBJECTS current and use the LINE icon to draw:
Start point 100,25,0
Next point @0,30,0
Next point 145,40,0
Next point close.

7 Make layer TEXT current and menu bar with **Draw-Text-Single Line Text** and:
a) start point: 60,10,0
b) height: 10 and 0 rotation
c) text item: BASE – fig(a).

8 Menu bar with **Tools-New UCS-Origin** and:
prompt Specify new origin point<0,0,0>
respond **Intersection icon and pick pt8**
and icon 'jumps' to the selected point – fig(b).

9 At the command line enter **UCS <R>** and:
prompt Enter an option
enter **S <R>** – the save option
prompt Enter name to save current UCS
enter **TOP <R>**.

10 With layer OBJECTS current draw a circle with centre: 60,20 and radius: 15.

11 With layer TEXT current, add single line text using:
a) start point: 10,15
b) height: 10 with 0 rotation
c) text item: TOP.

12 Using the COPY icon:
a) select objects: pick the circle then right-click
b) base point: Center icon and pick the circle
c) second point: enter @0,0,–100 <R> – fig(b)
d) why these coordinates?

13 Menu bar with **Tools-UCS-3Point** and:
prompt Specify new origin point<0,0,0>
respond **Intersection icon and pick pt2**

prompt   Specify point on positive portion of the X-axis
respond   **Intersection icon and pick pt3**
prompt   Specify point on positive-Y portion of the UCS XY plane
respond   **Intersection icon and pick pt10**.

14   The UCS icon will move to point 2 and be 'aligned' on the sloped surface – fig(c).

Note. The 3 point option of the UCS command is 'asking the user' for three points to define the UCS icon orientation, these being:

first prompt   the origin point
second prompt   the direction of the X axis
third prompt   the direction of the Y axis.

15   Save this UCS position by entering at the command line **UCS <R>**
then   **S <R>** and:
prompt   Enter name to save current UCS
enter   **SLOPE1 <R>**.

16   With layer OBJECTS current use the LINE icon to draw:
From   15,100,0
To   @50,0,0
To   40,30,0
To   close.

17   With layer TEXT current, add a single text item using:
a) start point: centred on 10,110
b) height: 10 with 0 rotation
c) item: SLOPE1 – fig(c).

18   At command line enter **UCS <R>** and:
prompt   Enter an option
enter   **R <R>** – the restore option
prompt   Enter name of UCS to restore
enter   **BASE <R>**
and   icon restored to the base point as fig(a).
Note. The restore option is used extensively.

19   Menu bar with **Tools-New UCS-X** and:
prompt   Specify rotation angle about X axis
enter   **90 <R>**
and   icon displayed as fig(d).

20   At command line enter **UCS <R>** then **S <R>** for the save option and **FRONT <R>** as the UCS name to save.

21   With layer TEXT current add an item of text with:
a) start point: 25,20
b) height: 10 with 0 rotation
c) text: FRONT – fig(d).

22   Menu bar with **Tools-New UCS-3 Point** and:
prompt   Specify new origin point
respond   **Intersection icon and pick pt7**
prompt   Specify point on positive portion of the X-axis
respond   **Intersection and pick pt11**
prompt   Specify point on positive-Y portion of the UCS XY plane
respond   **Intersection icon and pick pt13**.

23 The UCS icon will be aligned as fig(e).

24 Save this UCS position as VERT1 – easy? (UCS-S-VERT1).

25 With layer TEXT current add a text item with:
   a) start point: 120,50
   b) height: 10
   c) rotation: –90
   d) text: VERT1 – fig(e).

26 Restore UCS BASE and the model will be displayed as fig(f).

27 Make layer MODEL current and save the drawing at this stage as **MODR2000\3DWFM**
updating the original wire-frame model.

Modifying the wire-frame model

To further investigate the UCS we will modify the wire-frame model, so refer to Fig. 4.3 and:

1 3DWFM still on the screen? – if not open the drawing file.

2 Layer MODEL current with UCS BASE – fig(a).

3 Select the CHAMFER icon from the Modify toolbar and:
   a) set both chamfer distances to 30
   b) chamfer lines 7-11 and 7-13
   c) chamfer lines 5-6 and 6-3.

4 Now add two lines to complete the 'chamfered corner' and erase the unwanted original
corner line – fig(b).

5 Restore UCS VERT1 and note its position – fig(c).

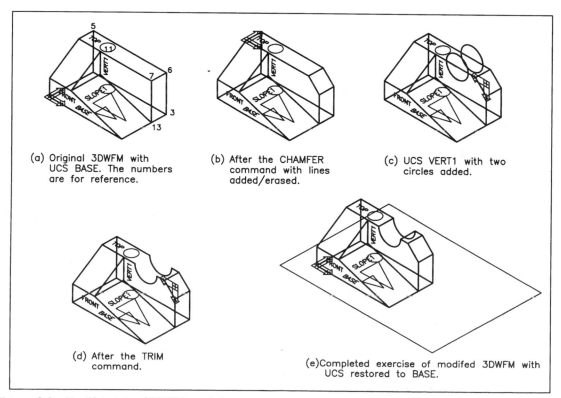

(a) Original 3DWFM with UCS BASE. The numbers are for reference.

(b) After the CHAMFER command with lines added/erased.

(c) UCS VERT1 with two circles added.

(d) After the TRIM command.

(e) Completed exercise of modifed 3DWFM with UCS restored to BASE.

Figure 4.3   Modifying the 3DWFM model.

6 Draw two circles:
  a) centre at 80,0,0 with radius 30
  b) centre at 80,0,–40 with radius 30 – fig(c).

7 Using the TRIM icon from the Modify toolbar:
  a) trim the two circles 'above' the model
  b) trim the two lines 'between' the circles – fig(d).

8 Draw in the two lines on the top plane and restore UCS BASE.

9 The modified model is now complete – fig(e).

10 Save the model as **MODR2000\3DWFM** updating the existing drawing.

11 *Note*.
The user should realize that the UCS is an important concept with 3D modelling. Indeed 3D modelling would be very difficult (if not impossible) without it.

Task

The wire-frame model has eleven flat planes and one 'curved surface'. We have set and saved UCS positions for five of these planes – BASE, TOP, SLOPE1, FRONT and VERT1. You now have to set and save the other six flat UCS positions, i.e. one for each surface and add an appropriate text item to that surface.

My suggestions for the UCS name and text item are LEFT, RIGHT, REAR, SLOPE2, SLOPE3 and VERT2 but you can use any names that you consider suitable.

Figure 4.4 displays the complete wire-frame model with text added to every plane (with the exception of the curved surface). When complete, remember to save as **MODR2000\3DWFM** as it will be used in other chapters.

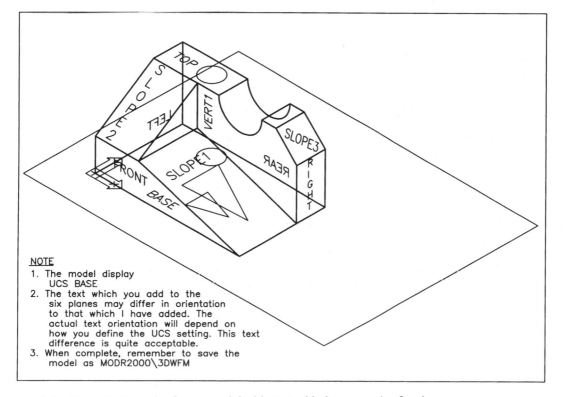

Figure 4.4 The complete wire-frame model with text added to every 'surface'.

Summary

1 Wire-frame models are created by coordinate input and by referencing existing objects.

2 Both the WCS and UCS entry modes can be used, but I would recommend:
  a) use the WCS to create the basic model outline
  b) use the UCS to modify and add items to the model.

3 It is strongly recommended that a UCS be set and saved for every surface on a wire-frame model.

Assignments

Creating wire-frame models is important as it allows the user to:
a) use 3D coordinate entry with the WCS and/or the UCS
b) set and save different UCS positions
c) become familiar with the concept of 3D modelling.

I have included two 3D wire-frame models which have to be created. The suggested approach is:

1 Open your 3DSTDA3 template file.

2 Complete the model with layer MODEL current, starting at some convenient point, e.g. 50,50,0 Use WCS entry and add one 'plane' at a time.

3 Save each completed model as a drawing file in your named folder with a suitable name, e.g. **MODR2000\ACT2,** etc.

4 *Note.*
  a) **do not attempt to add dimensions**
  b) do not attempt to display the two models on 'one screen' – you will soon be able to achieve this for yourself
  c) these models will be used for later assignments.

The activities concern our master builder MACFARAMUS, and you have to create 3D wire-frame models of two of his famous shaped blocks.

Activity 2: MACFARAMUS's shaped block 1

A relatively simple wire-frame model to create. I suggest that you construct it in a similar manner to the worked example, i.e. create the base, then the front vertical plane. The 'back' vertical plane can be drawn or copied from the front plane. The top and slopes are then easy to complete. When finished, save as **MODR2000\ACT2.**

Activity 3: MACFARAMUS's shaped block 2

This shaped block is slightly more difficult due to the curves. Create the basic shape as two rectangular blocks, then add four circles, using an obvious 'corner point' as the circle centre. The circles and lines can then be trimmed 'to each other'.

Chapter 5

The UCS

The UCS is one of the basic 3D draughting 'tools' and it has several commands associated with it. In this chapter we will investigate:

a) setting a new UCS position
b) moving the UCS
c) the UCS and UCS II toolbars
d) the UCS dialogue box
e) Orthographic UCSs
f) UCS specific commands.

Getting started

1   Open your MODR2000\3DWFM model from the previous chapter. This model has several blue objects with several saved UCS positions and is 'positioned' on the black 'sheet border'.

2   Restore the UCS BASE – probably is current?

3   Layer MODEL current and freeze layer TEXT. Refer to Fig. 5.1 which does not display the black sheet border. This is for clarity only.

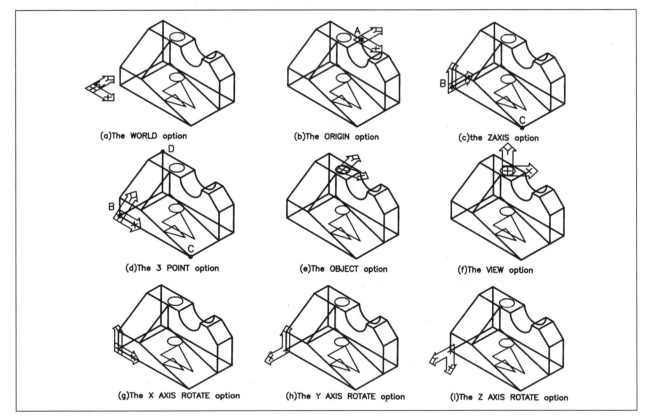

(a)The WORLD option   (b)The ORIGIN option   (c)the ZAXIS option

(d)The 3 POINT option   (e)The OBJECT option   (f)The VIEW option

(g)The X AXIS ROTATE option   (h)The Y AXIS ROTATE option   (i)The Z AXIS ROTATE option

Figure 5.1   The UCS option exercise.

Setting a new UCS position

The user can set a new UCS position from the menu bar with **Tools-New UCS** or by entering **UCS <R>** then **N <R>** at the command line. Both methods give the user access to the same options, these being:

Object/Face/View/Origin/ZAxis vector/3 Point/X/Y/Z/World

World: this option restores the WCS setting irrespective of the UCS position. It is the default AutoCAD setting. At the command line enter UCS <R> then W <R> to display the WCS icon on the sheet border at the left vertex – fig(a).

Origin: used to set a new origin point. The user specifies this new origin point:
a) by picking any point on the screen
b) by coordinate entry
c) by referencing existing objects. When used, the UCS icon is positioned at the selected point if the UCS Icon is set to Origin. This option has been used in previous exercises.
Menu bar with **Tools-New UCS-Origin** and:
prompt   `Specify new origin point<0,0,0>`
respond   **Intersection icon and pick ptA**
and   icon positioned as fig(b).

Z-Axis: defines the UCS position relative to the Z axis, the user specifying:
a) the origin point
b) any point on the Z axis
Menu bar with **Tools-New UCS-Z Axis Vector** and:
prompt   `Specify new origin point`
respond   **Intersection icon and pick ptB**
prompt   `Specify point on positive portion of Z-axis`
respond   **Intersection icon and pick ptC** – fig(c).
The icon will be aligned with:
a) the X axis along the shorter base left edge
b) the Y axis along the front left vertical edge
c) the Z axis along the line BC.

3point: defines the UCS orientation by specifying three points:
a) the actual origin point
b) a point on the positive X axis
c) a point on the positive Y axis
At the command line enter **UCS <R>** and:
prompt   `Enter an option [New/Move/..`
enter   **N <R>** – the new option
prompt   `Specify origin of new UCS or [ZAxis/3 Point/..`
enter   **3<R>**
prompt   `Specify new origin point`
respond   **Intersection of ptB**
prompt   `Specify point on positive portion of the X-axis`
respond   **Intersection of ptC**
prompt   `Specify point on positive-Y portion of the UCS`
             `XY plane`
respond   **Intersection of ptD** – icon as fig(d)
This is a very useful option especially if the icon is to be aligned on sloped surfaces. It is probably my preferred method of setting the UCS.

Object: aligns the icon to an object, e.g. a line, circle, polyline, item of text, dimension, block, etc.
Menu bar with **Tools-New UCS-Object** and:
prompt   Select object to align UCS
respond   **pick any point on circle on top surface**
The icon is aligned as fig(e) with:
a) the origin at the circle centre point
b) the positive X axis pointing towards the circumference of the circle at the selected point.

View: aligns the UCS so that the XY plane is always perpendicular to the view plane.
At the command line enter **UCS <R>** then **N <R>** and **V <R>**
The UCS icon will be displayed as fig(f) and is similar to the traditional 2D icon?
This is a useful UCS option as it allows 2D text to be added to a 3D drawing – try it for yourself.

X/Y/Z: allows the UCS to be rotated about the entered axis by an amount specified by the user
1. Restore UCS BASE
2. At the command line enter **UCS <R>**, **N <R>** then **X <R>** and:
prompt   Specify rotation angle about the X axis
enter   **90 <R>** – fig(g)
3. Menu bar with **Tools-New UCS-Y** and:
prompt   Specify rotation angle about the Y axis
enter   **–90 <R>** – fig(h)
4. Menu bar with **Tools-New UCS-Z** and:
prompt   Specify rotation angle about the Z axis
enter   **–90 <R>** – fig(i).

Face: Aligns the UCS with a selected solid model face. This option cannot be used with 3D wire-frame models.
1. Restore UCS BASE
2. Menu bar with **Tools-New UCS-Face** and:
prompt   Select face of solid object
respond   **pick any line of the top plane**
prompt   A 3D solid must be selected
         No solids detected.

Moving a UCS

This option allows the user to move the UCS to a new origin position, the UCS icon retaining both its orientation and name. Refer to Fig. 5.1 and:

1   UCS restored to BASE.

2   Menu bar with **Tools-Move UCS** and:
prompt   Specify new origin point or [Zdepth]
respond   **Intersection icon and pick ptA**
and   icon moved to point A and retains the name BASE.

3   Restore UCS TOP.

4 At the command line enter **UCS <R>** and:
prompt Enter an option [New/Move/..
enter **M <R>** – the move option
prompt Specify new origin point or [Zdepth]
respond **Intersection icon and pick ptC**
and icon moves to point A and retains the name TOP.

5 Restore UCS FRONT.

6 Menu bar with **Tools-Move UCS** and:
prompt Specify new origin point or [Zdepth]
enter **Z <R>** – the Z depth option
prompt Specify Z depth<0>
enter **−120 <R>**
and icon moved to 'back of model' and retains name FRONT.

7 This UCS option should be used with caution as the user may not want a named UCS to be 'repositioned'.

8 *TASK*: reset the three moved UCS's, i.e. BASE, TOP and FRONT to their original positions, or re-open the 3DWFM drawing.

Other UCS options

There are six other UCS options available to the user from the command line entry, these being:

Prev: restores the previously 'set' UCS position and can be used to restore the last 10 UCS positions.
At the command line enter **UCS <R>** then **P <R>** continually until the command line displays '*no previous coordinate system saved*'.

Restore: allows the user to restore a previously saved UCS position but the names of the saved UCS's must be remembered (This will be rectified shortly). This option has been extensively used.
At the command line enter **UCS <R>** then **R <R>** and:
prompt Enter name of UCS to restore or [?]
enter **TOP <R>**
then restore UCS BASE.

Save: allows the user to save a UCS position for future recall. It should be used every time a new UCS has been defined. The option is activated from the command line with **UCS <R>** then **S <R>** and the user can enter any name for the UCS position.

Del: Entering **UCS <R>** then **D <R>** prompts for the UCS name to be deleted. The default is none. Use with care!

Apply: An option which allows the user to apply the current UCS setting to a specific viewport. We will use this option in later chapters, but not yet.

?: the query option which will list all saved UCS positions
At the command line enter **UCS <R>** then **? <R>** and:
prompt Enter UCS name(s) to list<*>
respond **press the RETURN key**
prompt AutoCAD Text Window with:
Current UCS Name: BASE
Saved Coordinate systems
BASE Origin, and X, Y, Z axes numbers etc
respond **cancel the window.**

The UCS toolbar

All the UCS options have so far been activated by keyboard entry with **UCS <R>** or from the menu bar with **Tools**. The only reason for this is that I think it easier for the user to understand what option is being used. The UCS options can also be activated in icon form from the UCS and UCS II toolbars – Figs 5.2 and 5.3. The toolbars have no icon selection for the orthographic options or for Restore, Save, Delete or (?), although these can easily be activated by selecting the UCS icon which displays the keyboard options. An additional icon in both the UCS and UCS II toolbars is Display UCS Dialog, while the UCS II toolbar allows saved UCS's to be made current, in a similar manner that layers and dimension styles can be made current.

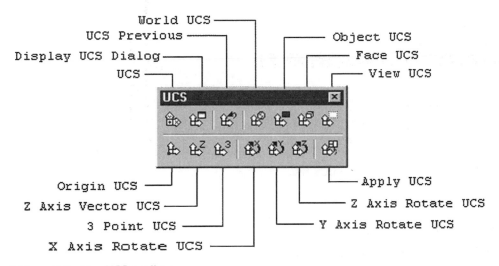

Figure 5.2 The UCS toolbar.

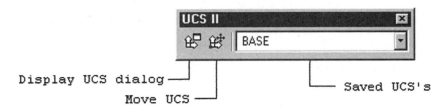

Figure 5.3 The UCS II toolbar.

The UCS dialogue box

The UCS dialogue box in R2000 is slightly different from previous releases, and allows the user more flexible management of the UCS. The dialogue box can be activated by three different methods:
a) from the menu bar with Tools-Named UCS
b) by selecting the Display UCS dialog icon from either UCS toolbars
c) by entering **UCSMAN <R>** at the command line.

When activated, the dialogue box allows the user three tab selections, these being:
1. Named UCSs – the default
2. Orthographic UCSs
3. Settings.

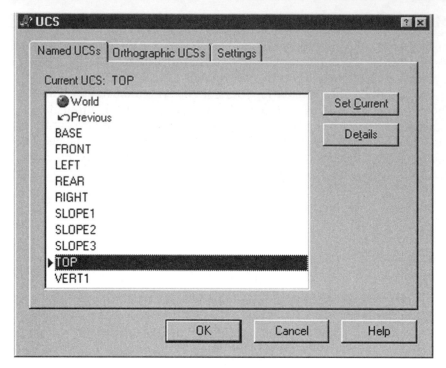

Figure 5.4 The UCS dialogue box – named UCS tab.

To demonstrate using the UCS dialogue box:

1 Ensure the 3DWFM is displayed with UCS BASE.

2 Menu bar with **Tools-Named UCS** and:
   prompt   UCS dialogue box with three tab selections – Named UCSs active
   with   a list of saved UCS names for the model as well as World and Previous
                 'names'
   respond   1. pick Top
                 2. pick Set Current – Fig. 5.4
                 3. pick OK.

3 The model will be displayed with the UCS TOP setting.

4 Use the Named UCS tab of the UCS dialogue box to set current some other saved UCS
   positions, then set UCS BASE current.

5 Activate the UCS dialogue box and:
   prompt   UCS dialogue box – Named UCS
   respond   1. pick TOP and it becomes highlighted
                 2. right-click the mouse
   prompt   shortcut menu with selections for: Set Current, Rename,
                 Delete, Details
   respond   1. pick Rename
                 2. enter new name: ABOVE <R>
                 3. pick Set Current
                 4. pick OK.

6 The UCS will be displayed in the 'old top position'.

7 Now rename the ABOVE UCS to TOP again using the UCS dialogue box.

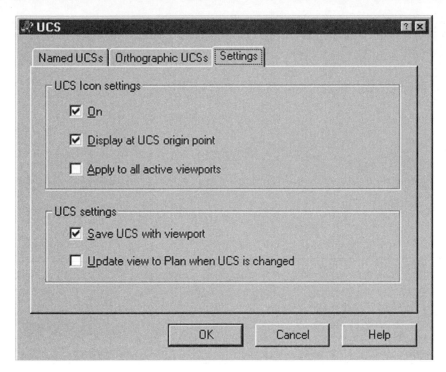

Figure 5.5 The UCS dialogue box – settings tab.

8 Activate the UCS dialogue box and pick the Settings tab and:
   prompt   Settings tab – Fig. 5.5
   with   1. UCS icon settings for ON and ORIGIN
              2. UCS settings for viewports and plan
   respond   **note the settings then pick Cancel.**

   Note.
   a) The UCS icon settings from the dialogue box are the same as the menu bar selection of View-Display-UCS Icon-On/Origin.
   b) The other Settings options will be discussed in later chapters.

Setting an orthographic UCS

This option allows the user to restore six preset UCS positions, the orientation being set relative to a saved UCS. Refer to Fig. 5.6 and:

1 Ensure the 3DWFM is displayed with the original UCS settings from the previous exercise with UCS SLOPE1 current – fig(a). If in doubt, re-open 3DWFM.

2 Activate the UCS dialogue box and pick the Orthographic UCS tab and:
   prompt   Orthographic tab display
   respond   1. scroll at Relative to
              2. pick BASE – Fig. 5.7
              3. pick Top, Set Current then OK
   and   icon displayed as fig(b).

3 With the Orthographic tab of the UCS dialogue box, set Bottom current relative to BASE – fig(c).

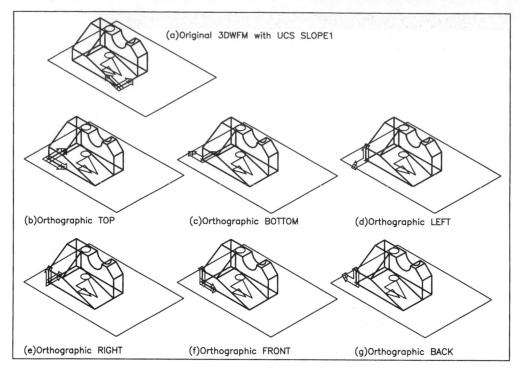

Figure 5.6 The orthographic UCS options exercise relative to BASE with UCS SLOPE1 current.

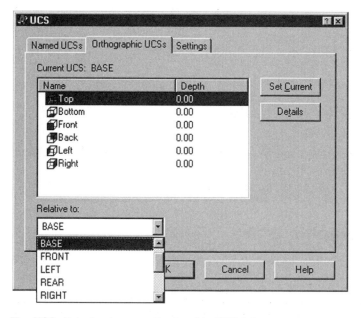

Figure 5.7 The UCS dialogue box – orthographic UCS tab.

4 Menu bar with **Tools-Orthographic UCS-Left** to display the icon as fig(d).

5 At the command line enter **UCS <R>** and:

    prompt   `Enter an option [New/Move/orthoGraphic/..`
    enter   **G <R>** – the orthographic option
    prompt   `Enter an option [Top/Bottom/Front/..`
    enter   **R <R>** – the right orthographic UCS option
    and   the icon will be displayed as fig(e).

6 With the menu bar **Tools-Orthographic UCS** sequence, select the other options and the icon will be displayed as: fig(f) FRONT; fig(g) BACK.

7 Activate the Orthographic tab of the UCS dialogue box and:
   a) set relative to SLOPE1
   b) activate the six orthographic UCS positions
   c) note the orientation of the UCS with each orthographic name
   d) restore UCS BASE.

8 The exercise with the UCS dialogue box is now complete.

9 *Note:* The menu bar sequence **Tools-Orthographic UCS-Presets** will display the Orthographic UCSs tab of the UCS dialogue box.

UCS specific commands

The UCS has several specific commands associated with it. At this stage, we will investigate the PLAN command and the UCSFOLLOW system variable.

Plan

Plan is a command which displays any model perpendicular to the XY plane of the current UCS position.

1 Ensure the 3DWFM is displayed with UCS BASE. Refer to Fig. 5.8.

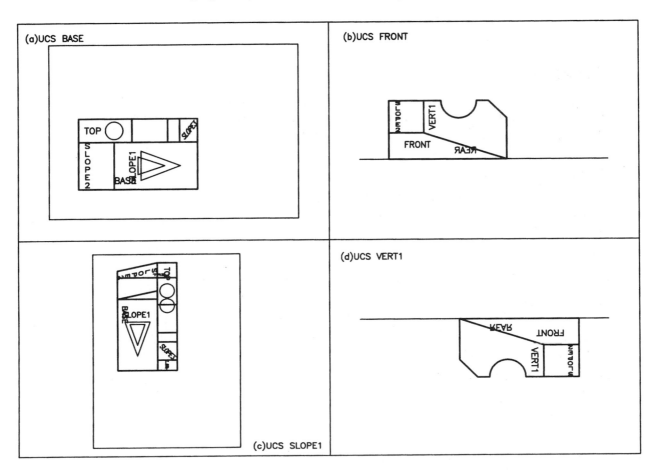

Figure 5.8

2   At the command line enter **PLAN <R>** and:

prompt   Enter an option [Current ucs/Ucs/World] <Current>
enter   **<R>**, i.e. accept the Current UCS default.

3   The screen will display the model as a plan view – fig(a). This view is perpendicular to the current UCS setting (BASE) and is really a 'top' view in orthogonal terms.

4   Restore UCS FRONT.

5   Menu bar with **View-3D Views-Plan View-Current UCS** and the model will be displayed as fig(b). This is a plan view to the current UCS FRONT and is a 'front' view in orthogonal terms.

6   Menu bar with View-3D Views-Plan View-Named UCS and:

prompt   Enter name of UCS
enter   **SLOPE1 <R>.**

7   The model will be displayed as a plan to the UCS SLOPE1 setting as fig(c).

8   At the command line enter **PLAN <R>** and:

prompt   Enter an option [Current ucs/Ucs/World]<Current>
enter   **U <R>** – the Ucs option
prompt   Enter name of UCS
enter   **VERT1 <R>.**

9   The model display is as fig(d), i.e. a plan view to the UCS setting VERT1. This display should be upside-down – why?

10 Finally restore UCS BASE and menu bar with View-3D Views-SE Isometric to return the original model display.

UCSFOLLOW

UCS FOLLOW is a system variable which controls the screen display of a model when the UCS position is altered. The variable can only have the values of 0 (default) or 1 and:
a) UCSFOLLOW 0: no effect on the display with UCS changes
b) UCSFOLLOW 1: generates a plan view when the UCS is altered.

1   Original 3D display with UCS BASE on the screen?

2   At the command line enter **UCSFOLLOW <R>** and:

prompt   Enter new value for UCSFOLLOW <0>
enter   **1 <R>.**

3   Nothing has changed?

4   Restore UCS FRONT – plan view as Fig. 5.5(b).

5   Restore UCS SLOPE1 – plan view as fig(c).

6   Restore UCS VERT1 – plan view as fig(d).

7   Restore UCS BASE – plan view as fig(a).

8   Set UCSFOLLOW to 0 and restore the original screen display with View-3D Views-SE Isometric.

9   This completes the exercises with the UCS.

Summary

1 The UCS is an essential 3D modelling aid.

2 The UCS command has several options including:
   a) New: origin, 3 point, X,Y,Z rotate
   b) Move: which should be used with caution
   c) Orthographic: six preset UCS settings.

3 The orientation of the UCS icon is dependent on the option used.

4 The UCS toolbars offer fast option selection.

5 It is **STRONGLY RECOMMENDED** that the UCS icon and the UCS icon origin are ON when working in 3D. These can be activated with:
   a) the menu bar sequence View-Display-UCS Icon
   b) the Settings tab of the UCS dialogue box.

6 The UCS dialogue box allows flexible management of the UCS with three tab selections:
   a) Named UCSs – set current, rename, delete
   b) Orthographic UCSs (Presets)
   c) Settings.

7 PLAN is a command which displays the model perpendicular to the XY plane of the current UCS.

8 UCSFOLLOW is a system variable which can be set to give automatic plan views when the UCS is re-positioned. It is recommended that this variable be set to 0, i.e. off.

Chapter 6

The modify commands with 3D models

All the modify commands are available for use with 3D models, but the results are dependent on the UCS position. We will investigate how the COPY, ARRAY, ROTATE and MIRROR commands can be used with our 3D wire-frame model so:

1 Open MODR2000\3DWFM with UCS BASE.

2 Display the Modify, Object snap and UCS toolbars.

3 Erase all text but the FRONT text item.

The COPY command

1 Select the COPY icon from the Modify toolbar and:
   prompt   Select objects
   respond **pick the 4 red lines and the green FRONT text item on the 'front vertical' surface then right-click**
   prompt   Specify base point
   respond **Intersection icon and pick ptA**
   prompt   Specify second point of displacement
   enter   **@0,0,260 <R>** – Fig. 6.1.A(a).

2 Restore UCS FRONT.

3 Select the COPY icon and:
   prompt   Select objects
   enter: **P <R><R>** – previous selection set option
   prompt   Specify base point and: **pick Intersection of ptA**
   prompt   Specify second point and enter: **@0,0,260 <R>** – Fig. 6.1.A(b).

4 May need a Zoom-All?

5 Undo (or erase) the copied effects to leave the original model.

The ARRAY command

1 Restore UCS BASE.

2 Select the ARRAY icon from the Modify toolbar and:
   prompt   Select objects
   respond **pick the FRONT text item then right-click**
   prompt   Enter the type of array and enter: **R <R>**
   prompt   Enter the number of rows and enter: **2 <R>**
   prompt   Enter the number of columns and enter: **6 <R>**
   prompt   Enter the row distance and enter: **40 <R>**
   prompt   Specify the distance between columns and enter: **60 <R>.**

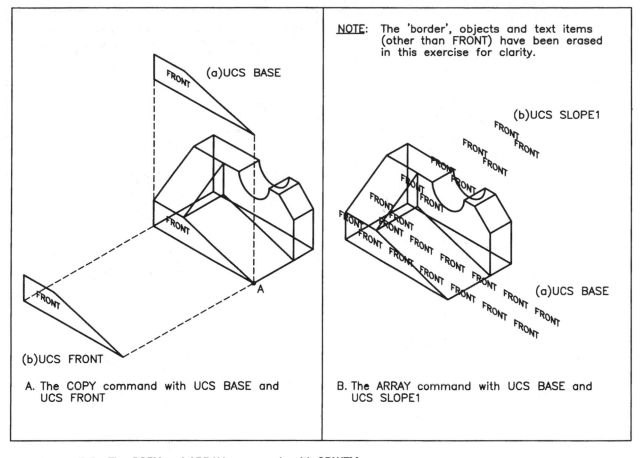

Figure 6.1 The COPY and ARRAY commands with 3DWFM.

3 The text item is arrayed in a 2 × 6 rectangular matrix as Fig. 6.1.B(a).

4 Restore UCS SLOPE1.

5 Rectangular array the original FRONT text item using the same entries as step 2 – Fig. 6.1.B(b).

6 Undo (or erase) the arrayed effects.

The ROTATE command

1 Restore UCS BASE.

2 Select the ROTATE icon from the Modify toolbar and:
> *prompt*   Select objects
> *respond*   **pick the 4 red lines and the FRONT text item as before then right-click**
> *prompt*   Specify base point
> *respond*   **Intersection icon and pick ptA**
> *prompt*   Specify rotation angle
> *enter*   **90 <R>.**

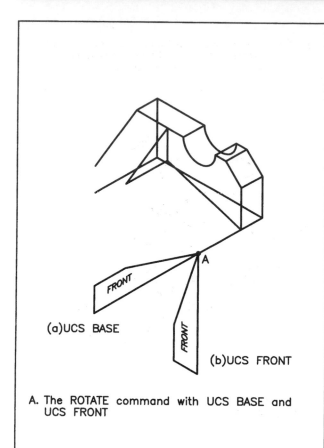

NOTE: The 'border', objects and text items (other than FRONT) have been erased in this exercise for clarity.

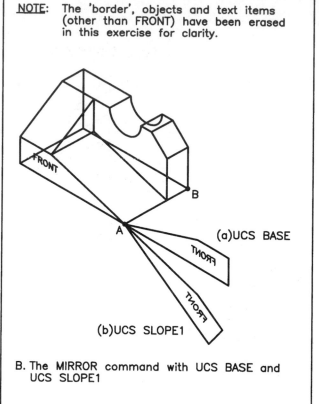

Figure 6.2

3 The selected objects will be rotated as Fig. 6.2.A(a).

4 Undo this rotated effect.

5 Restore UCS FRONT and rotate the same objects with the same entries as step 2. This will give Fig. 6.2.A(b).

6 Undo this effect.

The MIRROR command

1 Restore UCS BASE, activate the Mirror icon and:
   prompt   Select objects
   respond   **pick the four lines and text item as before and right-click**
   prompt   Specify first point of mirror line
   respond   **Intersection icon and pick ptA**
   prompt   Specify second point of mirror line
   respond   **Intersection icon and pick ptB**
   prompt   Delete source objects
   enter   **N <R>.**

2 The selected objects will be mirrored about the line AB as Fig. 6.2.B(a).

3 Restore UCS SLOPE1 and repeat the mirror command with the same objects and same entries as step 1. This will give Fig. 6.2.B(b).

Other modify commands

All of the modify commands are available for use with 3D models, but the final result is dependent on the UCS position. The only requirement for the user is to ensure that the icon is positioned on the 'plane' for the modification. Certain commands (e.g. Trim, Extend) may give the following message prompts:

View is not plan to UCS. Command results may not be obvious.

Summary

The AutoCAD modify commands with 3D models have to be used with care. The result is UCS dependent.

Chapter 7

Dimensioning in 3D

There are no special commands to add dimensions in 3D. Dimensioning is a 2D concept, the user adding the dimensions to the XY plane of the current UCS setting. This means that the orientation of the complete 'dimension object' will depend on the UCS position. The user should be aware of:

a) AutoCAD's automatic dimensioning facility

b) linear dimensioning will be horizontal or vertical, depending on where the dimension line is located in relation to the object being dimensioned.

We will demonstrate how dimensions can be added to 3D models with two examples. The first will be the 3D wire-frame model 3DWFM, and the second will use AutoCAD's stored 3D objects.

Example 1

1 Open MODR2000\3DWFM and display the Dimension, Object Snap and other toolbars to suit.

2 Freeze layer TEXT and make layer DIM current.

3 *Note*: the standard sheet created for the template file had a created dimension style – 3DSTD. You may want to 'alter' the Overall Scale (Fit tab) to a higher value than the 1 default.

4 Ensure UCS BASE is current and refer to Fig. 7.1.

5 *a*) select the LINEAR dimension icon and:
   prompt Specify first extension line origin
   respond **Intersection icon and pick pt1**
   prompt Specify second extension line origin
   respond **Intersection icon and pick pt2**
   prompt Specify dimension line location
   respond **pick to suit**
   b) repeat the LINEAR dimension selection and dimension line 23, positioning the dimension line to suit
   c) Select the DIAMETER icon and:
   prompt Select circle or arc
   respond **pick the circle on the TOP 'plane'**
   prompt Specify dimension line location
   respond **pick to suit** – interesting result?
   d) the three added dimensions will be displayed as fig(a).

6 Erase the added dimensions and restore UCS FRONT.

7 Using the dimension icons:
   a) linear dimension lines 12 and 14
   b) align dimension line 56
   c) try and add a diameter dimension to the top circle
   d) dimensions displayed as fig(b).

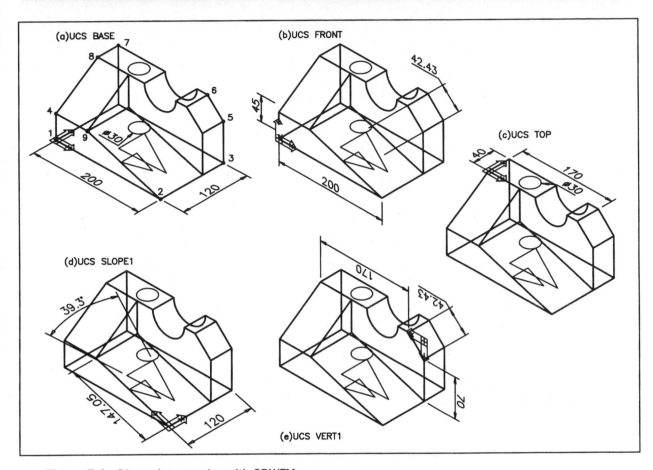

Figure 7.1 Dimension exercise with 3DWFM.

8 Erase these added dimensions and restore UCS TOP and:
   a) linear dimension line 67 and line 78
   b) diameter dimension the circle on the top
   c) result as fig(c).

9 Restore UCS SLOPE1, erase the previous dimensions and:
   a) linear dimension line 23 and line 29
   b) angular dimension a vertex of the blue triangle 'on the slope'
   c) the three dimensions will be displayed as fig(d).

10 With UCS VERT1 current, erase the dimensions from SLOPE1 and:
   a) linear dimension line 67 and line 35
   b) align dimension line 56
   c) interesting result as fig(e) – why?

11 *Note.*
   This exercise should demonstrate to the user that:
   a) adding dimensions to a 3D model is **VERY UCS DEPENDENT**
   b) there are no special 3D dimension commands
   c) the actual orientation of added dimensions depends on the UCS
   d) dimensions are added to the XY plane of the current UCS.

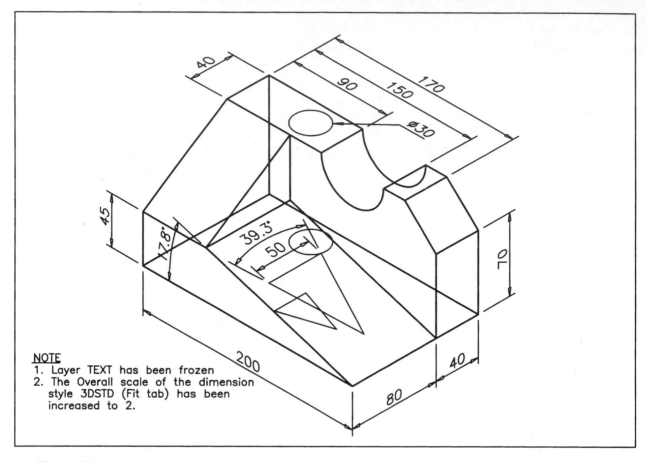

Figure 7.2 Required dimensions to be added to 3DWFM.

12 *Task.*
   a) erase any dimensions still displayed
   b) with layer DIM current refer to Fig. 7.2 and add the dimensions shown to the model
   c) some of the existing saved UCS positions will be used
   d) you may have to set a new UCS position for the continuous 80,40 and the 70 dimensions
   e) when complete save if required, but not as 3DWFM.

Example 2

1 Menu bar with **File-New** and:
   a) pick Use a Template
   b) pick **3DSTDA3.dwt** – your 3D template file
   c) pick OK.

2 The screen will display a black border:
   a) in SE Isometric viewpoint
   b) layer MODEL current
   c) WCS icon at left vertex of border.

3 Display the Surfaces toolbar.

4 Menu bar with **Draw-Surfaces-3D Surfaces** and:
   prompt 3D Objects dialogue box
   respond **pick Box3D** then OK
   prompt Specify corner of box and enter: **50,50,0 <R>**
   prompt Specify length of box and enter: **120 <R>**
   prompt Specify width of box and enter: **80 <R>**
   prompt Specify height of box and enter: **60 <R>**
   prompt Specify rotation of box about Z axis and enter: **0 <R>**.

5 Select the WEDGE icon from the surface toolbar and:
   prompt Specify corner of wedge and enter: **200,150,0 <R>**
   prompt Specify length of box and enter: **100 <R>**
   prompt Specify width of box and enter: **75 <R>**
   prompt Specify height of box and enter: **65 <R>**
   prompt Specify rotation of wedge about Z axis and enter: **0 <R>**.

6 Using the 3 point UCS option:
   a) origin at point 1
   b) x axis along line 12
   c) y axis along line 13
   d) save UCS position as POS1
   e) add two linear dimensions with this UCS.

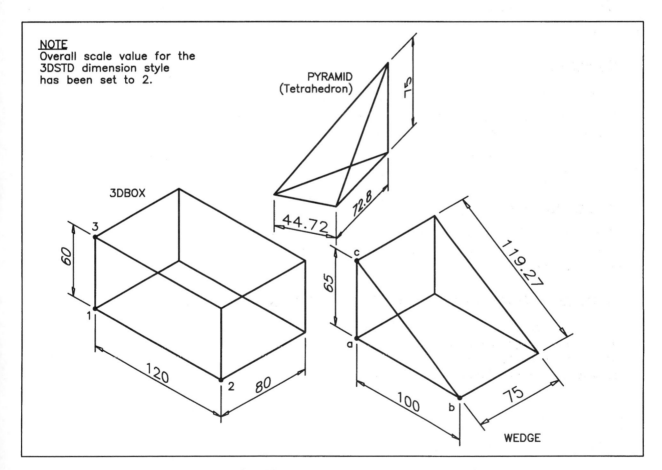

Figure 7.3 Adding dimensions to 3D objects.

7   Use the 3 point UCS option again with:
    a) origin at point a
    b) x axis along line ab
    c) y axis along line ac
    d) save as POS2
    e) add two linear dimensions with this UCS.

8   Now add the three other dimensions, i.e. one to the box and two to the wedge. Some UCS manipulation is required but you should manage this without any problems.

9   *Task*.
    Another 3D object has to be created and dimensioned so select the pyramid icon from the Surfaces toolbar and:

    prompt   Specify first corner point for base of pyramid and enter:
               40,220 <R>
    prompt   Specify second corner point for base of pyramid and enter:
               80,250 <R>
    prompt   Specify third corner point for base of pyramid and enter:
               60,320 <R>
    prompt   Specify fourth corner point for base of pyramid or
               [Tetrahedron]
    enter   **T <R>** – the tetrahedron option
    prompt   Specify apex point of tetrahedron
    enter   **60,320,75 <R>**

    Now set appropriate UCS positions and add the three linear dimensions given.

10 Save if required, but the drawing will not be used again.

Summary

1   There are no special 3D dimension commands.

2   Dimensioning is a 2D concept and dimensioning a 3D model involves adding the dimensions to the XY plane of the required UCS setting.

3   If the UCS is not positioned correctly, dimensions can have the 'wrong orientation' in relation to the object being dimensioned.

Assignment

Two dimensioning assignments for you to complete, one being an existing wire-frame model, the other being a new wire-frame model. Both involve the work of our great architect MACFARAMUS.

Activity 4: Shaped block of MACFARAMUS

Recall the shaped block from activity 2 and:
a) set and save appropriate UCS positions
b) add the given dimensions
c) save the completed model for later recall.

Activity 5: The famous rectangular topped pyramid of MACFARAMUS

The rectangular topped pyramid designed by Macfaramus was never built but his design is still considered unique. You have to:

a) create a wire-frame model of the pyramid using the sizes given
b) set and save several UCS positions, these being on the following surfaces:
    1. the base and top – obvious
    2. four sloped surfaces – names and orientation given
    3. two vertical surfaces – should give you no problems. Use your own names, e.g. V_1 and V_2
c) add the given dimensions
d) save the completed model.

MACFARAMUS required to know the following dimensions:
1. the angle of the two sloped 'planes' in relation to the base
2. the length of the three sloped 'edges'.

Can you help him?

Chapter 8

Hatching in 3D

There are no special 3D hatch commands. Hatching (like dimensioning) is a 2D concept, the hatch pattern being added to the XY plane of the current UCS. Two examples will be used to demonstrate adding hatching to 3D models.

Example 1

1 Open your 3DSTDA3.dwt template file.

2 Display the Draw, Modify and Object Snap toolbars.

3 With layer MODEL current, refer to Fig. 8.1 and draw the four 'mutually perpendicular planes' using the LINE icon with:

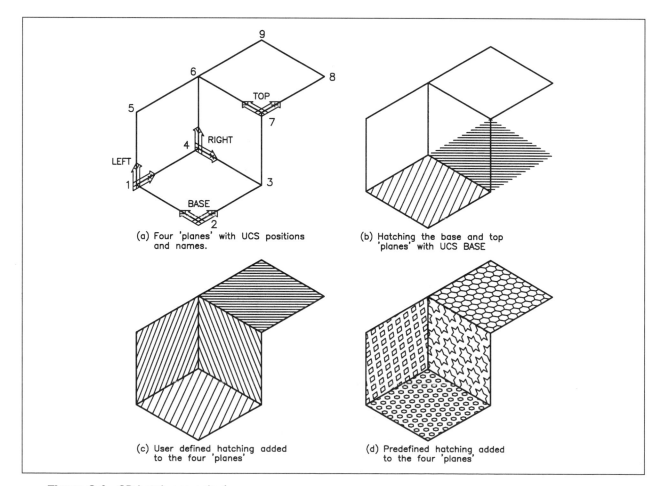

(a) Four 'planes' with UCS positions and names.

(b) Hatching the base and top 'planes' with UCS BASE

(c) User defined hatching added to the four 'planes'

(d) Predefined hatching added to the four 'planes'

Figure 8.1   3D hatch example 1.

	Plane 1234	*Plane 1564*	*Plane 3764*	*Plane 7896*
Start	30,30,0	30,30,0	130,130,0	130,130,100
Next	@100,0,0	@0,0,100	@0,0,100	@0,100,0
Next	@0,100,0	@0,100,0	@−100,0,0	@−100,0,0
Next	@−100,0,0	@0,0,−100	<RETURN>	@0,−100,0
Next	close	<RETURN>		<RETURN>

4 Erase the black border and pan the drawing to suit.

5 Set and save the four UCS positions as fig(a).

6 Restore UCS BASE and make SECT the current layer.

7 Select the HATCH icon from the Draw toolbar and using the Boundary Hatch dialogue box:
   a) pick User defined pattern type
   b) set angle to 30 and spacing to 8
   c) use the **Pick Points <** option and:
       i) select a point within the 1234 plane then right-click/enter
       ii) Preview-right click-OK.

8 Repeat the HATCH icon selection and:
   a) using the Pick Points option pick a point within the 6789 plane
       prompt   Boundary Definition Error dialogue box – Fig. 8.2
       respond   **pick OK** then <RETURN>
   b) using the Select Objects option pick the four lines of the 6789 plane then right-click/ enter and:
       i) set angle to −45 and spacing to 5
       ii) Preview-right click-OK.

9 The result of the two hatch operations is displayed in fig(b). Plane 1234 has the correct hatching, but plane 6789 has none, the hatching having been added to the plane of UCS BASE.

10 Use the HATCH icon and try and add hatching to the vertical planes 1564 and 3467. Not possible? Unable to hatch the boundary message at the command line. Why is this?

11 Erase the 'wrong' hatching and restore UCS TOP

12 Hatch the top plane (6789) using the HATCH icon with:
   a) pick points option
   b) angle −45 and spacing 5.

13 Add hatching to the two vertical planes remembering to restore UCS LEFT and UCS RIGHT – fig(c). Use your own angle and spacing values.

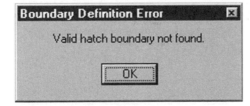

Figure 8.2 Boundary Definition Error dialogue box.

14 *Task*.
   a) Erase the added hatching then add the following predefined hatch patterns using the information given:

UCS	Pattern	Scale	Angle
BASE	HEX	1	−10
TOP	HONEY	2	0
LEFT	SQUARE	2	10
RIGHT	STARS	2	0

   c) the result is fig(d)
   d) this completes example 1, which does not have to be saved.

Example 2

1 Open the drawing MODR2000\3DWFM and refer to Fig. 8.3.

2 Make layer SECT current and freeze layers TEXT and DIM.

3 Restore UCS TOP.

4 Select the HATCH icon and:
   a) Predefined pattern type: STARS
   b) scale: 1 and angle: 0
   c) pick points: pick points in the **TWO** top planes then right-click/enter
   d) preview-right click-OK.

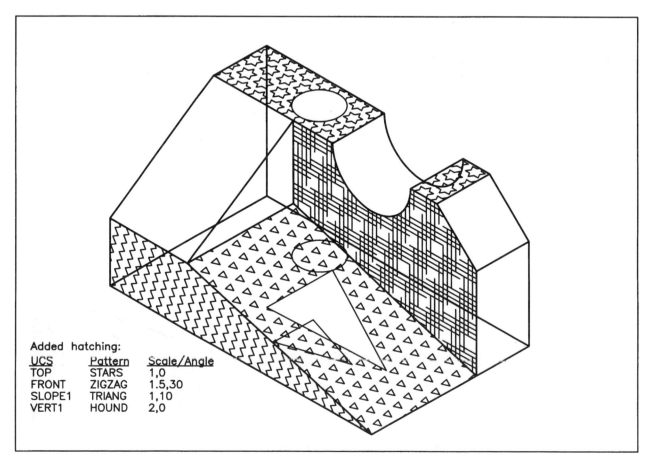

Added hatching:

UCS	Pattern	Scale/Angle
TOP	STARS	1,0
FRONT	ZIGZAG	1.5,30
SLOPE1	TRIANG	1,10
VERT1	HOUND	2,0

Figure 8.3 Hatch exercise with 3DWFM.

5 Restore UCS FRONT and with the HATCH icon:
   a) pattern type: ZIGZAG
   b) scale: 1.5 and angle: 30
   c) select objects: pick the four lines of front vertical plane then right-click/enter
   d) preview-right click-OK.

6 Repeat the HATCH icon selection and add the following hatch patterns:

UCS	Pattern	Scale, angle	Type
SLOPE1	TRIANG	1,10	pick points
VERT1	HOUND	2,0	pick points

7 Menu bar with **View-Hide** and the model is as before. Hatching a wire-frame model does not produce a hide effect.

8 Save your completed hatched model as MODR2000/3DWFM.

9 *Note.*
   In the two hatch exercises we used the one layer (SECT) for all hatching. It is sometimes desirable to have a different layer for each current UCS that is to be used for hatching. This is a procedure which is recommended.

Summary

1 Hatching is a 2D concept.

2 Hatching a 3D model requires the UCS to be set to the 'plane' which is to be hatched.

3 *a*) both user-defined and predefined hatch patterns can be used
   b) both the select objects and pick points methods are permitted.

4 It is recommended that a hatch layer is made for each 'plane' which is to be hatched.

Assignments

Two hatch activities have been included, both using previously created wire-frame models these being MACFARAMUS's shaped block and rectangular topped pyramid. In both activities:

1 Open the saved drawing.

2 Freeze layer DIM, or erase the dimensions if necessary.

3 Add appropriate hatching, making new hatch layers for each UCS position if required – your decision!

4 Use the pick points method where possible.

5 Save the completed model.

Activity 6: The shaped block of MACFARAMUS

Restore the appropriate UCS and add the following user defined hatching:

UCS	Angle, Spacing
FRONT	45,8
RIGHT	−45,8
TOP	−45,8
SLOPE1	45,8
SLOPE2	−45,8

When complete save the model as **MODR2000\SHBLOCK** for recall.

Activity 7: The rectangular topped pyramid of MACFARAMUS

Using the correct UCS, add the following predefined hatch patterns:

UCS	Pattern	Scale, Angle
four 'base' surfaces	BRICK	2,0
four vert 'top' surfaces	BRSTONE	1,0
the horiz top surface	EARTH	1.5,0

Save the complete hatched model as **MODR2000\PYRAMID.**

Chapter 9

Tiled viewports

The graphics screen can be divided into a number of separate viewing areas called **viewports** and each viewport can display any part of a drawing. Viewports are **interactive**, i.e. what is drawn in one viewport is automatically drawn in the others and the user can switch between viewports when creating a model. Viewport layouts (**configurations**) can be saved thus allowing different displays of the same model to be stored for future recall. Viewports are essential with 3D modelling as they allow different views of the model to be displayed on the screen simultaneously. When used with the VIEWPOINT command (next chapter) the user has a very powerful 3D draughting tool.

There are two types of viewport, displayed in Fig. 9.1, these being:
1. tiled or fixed
2. untiled or floating.

The type of viewport which is displayed is controlled by the **TILEMODE** system variable and:
a) Tilemode 1: tiled viewports – cannot be moved (default setting)
b) Tilemode 0: untiled viewports – can be moved.

In this chapter we will only investigate TILED viewports and leave the untiled viewport discussion to a later chapter when we will investigate model and paper space.

Making viewports can be activated by keyboard entry or from the menu bar.

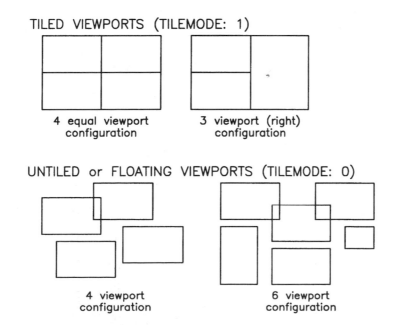

Figure 9.1 Tiled and untiled viewports.

Example 1

This exercise is rather long, but persevere with it.

1 Open your 3DWFM drawing of the wire-frame model on the black border with layer MODEL current and UCS BASE.

2 Deactivate all floating toolbars and display the model without any text, dimensions or hatching. Erase or freeze layers?

3 At the command line enter **TILEMODE <R>** and:
prompt   `Enter new value for TILEMODE<1>`
and   observe the 1 default then press **ESC.**

4 The TILEMODE value of 1 indicates that only TILED viewports can be used. The same condition is also evident with:
a) Status bar: word MODEL is displayed
b) Menu bar: View-Viewports indicate that Polygonal Viewport and Object are not available for selection.

5 Menu bar with **View-Viewports-3 Viewports** and:
prompt   `Enter a configuration [Horizontal/Vertical/Above..`
enter   **R <R>** – the right configuration option.

6 The drawing screen will:
a) be divided into three separate 'areas' – one large at the right and two smaller to the left. The three viewports will 'fill the screen' – Fig. 9.2(a)
b) display the same view of the model in the three viewports.

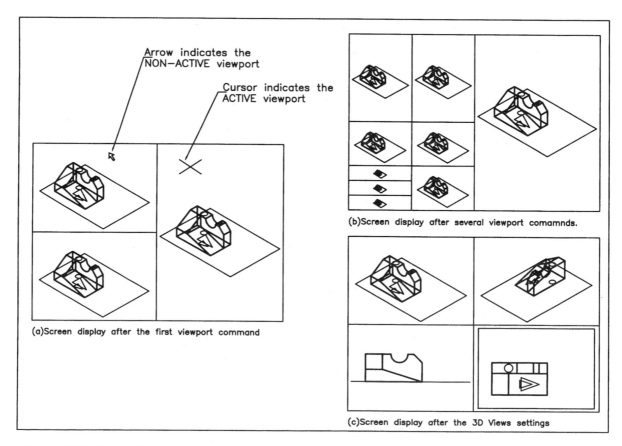

Figure 9.2   Viewport example 1.

7 Move the mouse about the screen and:
   a) the large viewport will display the cursor cross-hairs and is the ACTIVE viewport, i.e. it is 'current'
   b) the other viewports will display an arrow and these viewports are NON-ACTIVE.

8 Any viewport can be made active by:
   a) moving the mouse into the viewport area
   b) left-click
   c) try this for yourself a few times.

9 At the command line enter **-VPORTS <R>** and:
   prompt   `Enter an option [Save/Restore/Delete/..`
   enter   **S <R>** – the save option
   prompt   `Enter name for new viewport configuration`
   enter   **CONF1 <R>**.

10 Make the upper left viewport active and select the menu bar sequence **View-Viewports-2 Viewports** and:
   prompt   `Enter a configuration option [Horizontal/Vertical..`
   enter   **V <R>** – the vertical option
   and   the top left viewport will be further divided into two equal vertical viewports, each displaying the model.

11 Make the lower left viewport active and menu bar with **View-Viewports-4 Viewports** to display an additional four viewports of the model.

12 At the command line enter **-VPORTS <R>** and:
   prompt   `Enter an option [Save/Restore/..`
   enter   **S <R>** – the save option
   prompt   `Enter name for new viewport configuration`
   enter   **CONF2 <R>**.

13 With the lower left viewport active, enter **-VPORTS <R>** at the command line and:
   prompt   `Enter an option [Save/Restore..`
   enter   **3 <R>** – the 3 viewport option
   prompt   `Enter a configuration option [Horizontal/Vertical/Above..`
   enter   **H <R>** – the horizontal option.

14 The lower left viewport will be further divided into another three viewports and at this stage your screen should resemble Fig. 9.2(b).

15 Make the lower left viewport active and enter **-VPORTS <R>**
   then   **4 <R>** and the following message will be displayed at the prompt line:
   The current viewport is too small to divide.

16 Save the screen viewport configuration as CONF3 – easy?

17 *a*) Make the large right viewport active
   b) menu bar with View-Viewports-1 Viewport
   c) original screen displayed?
   d) zoom-all needed?

18 Menu bar with **View-Viewports-4 Viewports** to 'fill the screen' with four viewports of the model.

19 Using the menu bar **View-3D Views** selection make each viewport current and set
different viewpoints using the following:

Viewport   *3D View*
top left   SE Isometric
top right   NE Isometric
lower right   Plan-Current UCS
lower left   Front.

20 The screen display should resemble Fig. 9.2(c).

21 Save the screen configuration as CONF4.

22 *Task.*
Return the screen to a single viewport configuration to display the original model.

23 At the command line enter **-VPORTS <R>** and:
prompt   Enter an option [Save/Restore..
enter   **R <R>** – the restore option
prompt   Enter name of viewport configuration to restore
enter   **CONF1 <R>**
and   screen displays the first saved configuration.

24 Restore the other three saved viewport configurations then return the display to a single
viewport.

25 *Notes.*
a) The command line entry **-VPORTS** gives the user the viewport options at the
command line. This was deliberate for this first example.
b) Generally the viewports command is activated from the menu bar in dialogue box form.

26 Menu bar with **View-Viewports-Named Viewports** and:
prompt   Viewports dialogue box
with   Named Viewports tab active
and   four saved viewport configurations
respond   **pick CONF2 then OK** – Fig. 9.3.

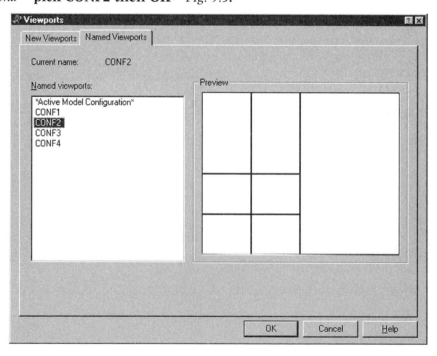

Figure 9.3   Named Viewports dialogue box.

27 The screen will display the named viewport configuration.

28 Using the Named viewport dialogue box, display the other named named viewports.

29 This completes the first viewport exercise. If you want to save the exercise (with the viewport configurations). **DO NOT USE THE NAME 3DWFM.**

Example 2

The first exercise used an already created 3D model to investigate the viewport command and configurations. This exercise will create a new 3D wire-frame model interactively using a four viewport configuration with preset 3D viewpoints. This will allow the user to 'see' the model being created in all four viewports at the one time.

1 Open your **3DSTDA3.dwt** template file to display the black border at a 3D viewpoint with layer MODEL current. Refer to Fig. 9.4.

2 Menu bar with **Tools-New UCS-Origin** and:
    prompt   Specify new origin point
    enter   **50,50,0 <R>.**

3 Save the UCS position as BASE.

4 At the command line enter **UCSICON <R>** and:
    prompt   Enter an option [ON/OFF?All/..
    enter   **A <R>** – the all viewports option
    prompt   Enter an option [ON/OFF/All/..
    enter   **OR <R>** – set UCS to origin in all viewports.

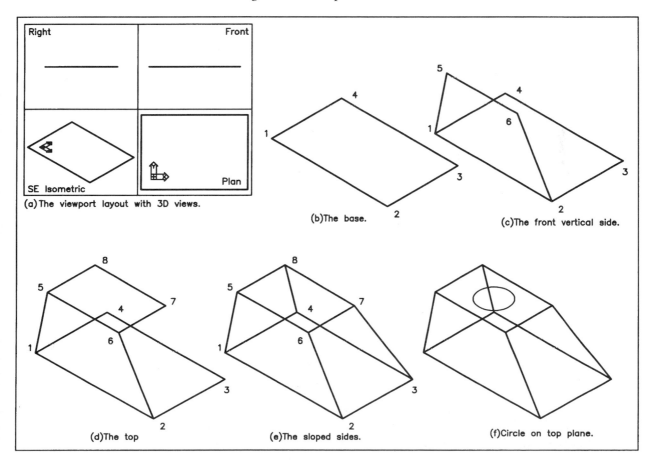

Figure 9.4 Construction of viewport example 2.

5   Set a four viewport configuration with the menu bar sequence **View-Viewports-4 Viewports.**

6   Making the appropriate viewport active, use the menu bar sequence **View-3D Views** to set the following viewpoints:
Viewport   *3D View*
lower right   Plan View-Current UCS
lower left   SE Isometric
upper left   Right
upper right   Front.

7   In the upper left and upper right viewports, enter **ZOOM <R>** and:
prompt   Specify corner of window or enter a scale factor
enter   1 <R>.

8   Making each viewport active in turn, enter **UCSVP <R>** at the command line and:
prompt   Enter new value for UCSVP
enter   0 <R> – more on this later.

9   The screen display should resemble fig(a).

10 With the lower left viewport active, construct the model base using the LINE icon with:
Start point   **0,0,0 <R>**   pt1
Next point   **@200,0,0 <R>**   pt2
Next point   **@0,120,0 <R>**   pt3
Next point   **@200<180,0 <R>**   pt4
Next point   **close** – fig(b).

11 Using the LINE command construct the front vertical side with:
Start point   **Intersection icon of pt1**
Next point . **@20,0,100 <R>**   pt5
Next point   **@120,0,0 <R>**   pt6
Next point   **Intersection icon of pt2**
Next point   **right-click/enter** – fig(c).

12 The top surface is created with the LINE command and:
Start point   **Intersection icon of pt6**
Next point   **@0,80,0 <R>**   pt7
Next point   **@-120,0,0 <R>**   pt8
Next point   **Intersection icon of pt5**
Next point   **right-click/enter** – fig(d).

13 Add the sloped sides with lines joining points 3–7 and 4–8 as fig(e).

14 Make layer OBJECTS (blue) current and draw a circle with:
centre: 80,40,100 and radius: 25 – fig(f).

15 Menu bar with **Draw-Surfaces-3D Surfaces-Box3d** and:
prompt   Specify corner of box and enter: **80,30,0**
prompt   Specify length of box and enter: **50**
prompt   Specify width of box and enter: **40**
prompt   Specify height of box and enter: **30**
prompt   Specify rotation angle of box about Z axis and enter: **20.**

16 *Task.*
a) Make layer TEXT current
b) Rotate UCS about X axis by 90 and save as FRONT
c) Add the text item AutoCAD, centred on 80,50 with height 10 and rotation 0.

d) Set a 3 point UCS on the right sloped surface with:
    1. origin: midpoint of line 23 – Fig. 9.4(e)
    2. x axis: intersection of pt 3
    3. y axis: perpendicular to line 67
    4. save UCS as SLOPE
e) Add the text item R2000, centred on 0,50 with a height of 10 and a rotation of 0.

17   The complete four viewport configuration display should be similar to Fig. 9.5.

18   Save the drawing as **MODR2000\TEST3D**.

19   This completes the two exercises on viewports.

20   *Note.* Two new system variables were used during this exercise, these being:
    a) UCSICON: allows the user to decide whether the UCS icon should be displayed and positioned at the origin an any (or all) viewports. It is recommended that the user sets **A** and **OR**. This will always position the UCS icon at the origin point in all viewports.
    b) UCSVP: determines whether the UCS in an active viewport will 'reflect' the UCS of that active viewport and:
        1. UCSVP 0: unlocked, i.e. the UCS will reflect the UCS of the active viewport
        2. UCSVP 1: locked, i.e. UCS is independent of the UCS in the active viewport
        3. It is recommended that UCSVP be set to 0, i.e. reflects the UCS position in any active viewport
        4. The UCSVP must be set in every created viewport.

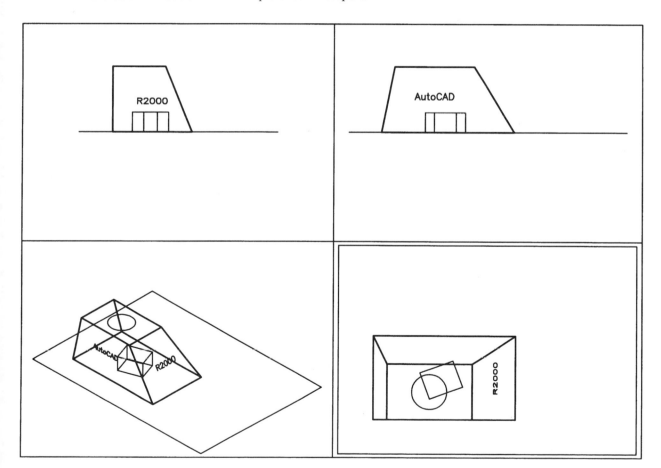

Figure 9.5 Completed viewport example 2 – TEST3D.

Summary

1 Viewports allow multi-screen configurations.

2 There are two types of viewport – TILED and UNTILED.

3 The viewport type is controlled by the system variable TILEMODE and:
TILEMODE 1: tiled viewports (fixed)
TILEMODE 0: untiled viewports (movable) – more later.

4 Tiled viewports can have between 1 and 4 'divisions' and 'fill the screen drawing area'.

5 Multi-screen viewports are generally used with the viewpoint command.

6 Multiple viewport layouts are extremely useful with 3D modelling.

Assignments

No specific activities for this chapter. Viewports activities will be assigned after the chapters on viewpoints and centring models.

Chapter 10

3D views (viewpoints)

3D views (or viewpoints) determine how the user 'looks' at a model and has been used in previous chapters without any discussion about how it is used. In this chapter we will investigate the command in detail using previously created models. When combined with viewports, the user has a very powerful draughting aid – multiple viewports displaying different views of a model.

The viewpoint command has the following selections:

1 Isometric views: SW, SE, NE, NW.

2 Orthographic views: Top, Bottom, Left, Right, Front, Back.

3 Plan view: to current UCS, WCS, named UCS.

4 VPOINT: with rotate, compass and tripod, vector options.

5 Viewpoint Presets: dialogue box selection.

6 Real-time 3D rotation.

7 New Viewports dialogue box.

In this chapter we will investigate all of the above selections.

The VPOINT ROTATE option

This option requires two angles:
a) the angle in XY plane from the X-axis – the **view** direction
b) the angle from XY plane – the **inclination** (**tilt**).

1 Open your MODR2000\3DWFM drawing and erase any dimensions and hatching. Leave the text items – they will act as a 'reference' as the model is viewed from different angles.

2 Layer MODEL current, UCS BASE and SE Isometric viewpoint.

3 Refer to Fig. 10.1 section A.

4 At the command line enter **VPOINT <R>** and:
prompt	***Switching to WCS***
and	Current view direction
then	Specify a view point or [Rotate]
enter	**R <R>** – the rotate option
prompt	Enter angle in XY plane from X-axis
enter	**40 <R>**
prompt	Enter angle from XY plane
enter	**0 <R>**
prompt	***Returning to UCS***
then	Regenerating drawing
and	model displayed as fig(a1), i.e. looking towards the right-rear side from a horizontal 'stand-point' – the view direction.

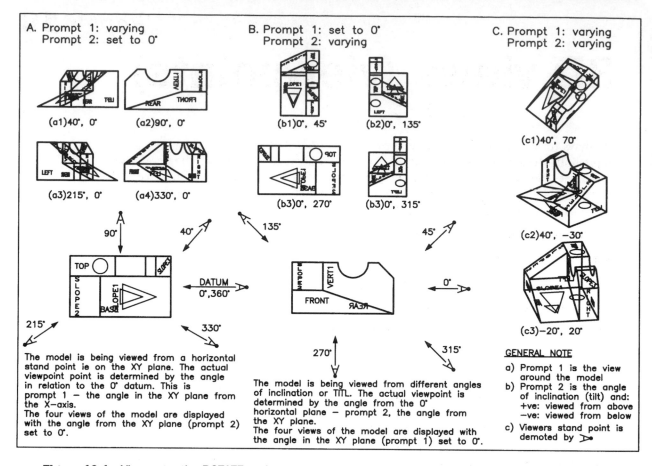

Figure 10.1 Viewport – the ROTATE option.

5 At the command line enter **VPOINT <R>** and:

prompt   Specify a view point or [Rotate]

enter   **R <R>** – the rotate option

prompt   Enter angle in XY plane from X-axis and enter: **90 <R>**

prompt   Enter angle from XY plane and enter: **0 <R>**

and   model displayed as fig(a2).

6 Repeat the VPOINT-Rotate command from the command line and enter the following angle values at the prompts:

prompt 1	prompt 2	fig
215	0	a3
330	0	a4.

7 Restore the original SE Isometric viewpoint and refer to Fig. 10.1 section B.

8 Use the VPOINT-Rotate command and enter the following angles at the prompts:

prompt 1	prompt 2	fig
0	45	b1
0	135	b2
0	270 (−90)	b3
0	−45 (315)	b4.

9 Restore the SE Isometric viewpoint and refer to Fig. 10.1 section C. Activate the VPOINT-Rotate command and enter the following angles:

prompt 1	prompt 2	fig
40	70	c1
40	−30	c2
−20	20	c3

10 Restore the original viewpoint.

11 *Task*.
Restore some other UCS settings, e.g. SLOPE1, VERT1, etc. and repeat the viewpoint rotate command using some of the above angle entries. The model display should be unaffected by the UCS. Think about the prompt: ***Switching to the WCS***.

12 Explanation of option.
a) Prompt 1: angle in XY plane from the X-axis. This is the viewer's standpoint **on the XY horizontal plane** looking towards the model, i.e. it is your view direction. If this angle is 0° you are looking at the model from the right side. If the angle is 270° you are looking onto the front of the model. The value of this angle can vary between 0° and 360°. It can also be positive or negative and remember that 270° is the same as −90°.
b) Prompt 2: angle from the XY plane This is the viewer's 'head inclination' looking at the model, i.e. it is the **angle of tilt**. A 0° value means that you are looking at the model horizontally and a 90° value is looking vertically down. The angle of tilt can vary between 0° and 360° and be positive or negative and:
positive tilt: looking down on the model
negative tilt: looking up at the model.

13 *Note*.
The reader must realize that the displays in Fig. 10.1 have been 'scaled' to fit the one sheet, and that your model displays will be larger than those illustrated.

VPOINT ROTATE using the presets dialogue box

1 3DWFM displayed at SE Isometric setting with UCS BASE?

2 Menu bar with **View-3D Views-Viewpoint Presets** and:
prompt   Viewpoint Presets dialogue box – Fig. 10.2
with   1. viewing angle: absolute to WCS
           2. angle from X-axis: 315 – left-hand 'clock'
           3. angle from XY plane: 35.3 – right-hand 'arc'.

3 This dialogue box allows:
a) viewing angle to be absolute to WCS or relative to UCS
b) angles to be set by selecting circle/arc position
c) angles to be set by altering values at From: line
d) plan views to be set.

4 Respond to the dialogue box with:
a) do not change to absolute to WCS
b) change the X-axis angle from 315 to 150
c) change the XY plane angle from 35.3 to 10
d) pick OK
e) the model will be displayed at the entered viewpoint angles.

5 Make UCS SLOPE1 current.

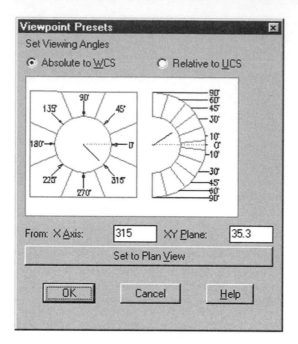

Figure 10.2 The Viewpoint Presets dialogue box.

6 Menu bar with View-3D Views-Viewpoint Presets and:
   a) make Absolute to UCS active – black dot
   b) leave the two angle values as 150 and 10
   c) pick OK
   d) the model is displayed at the entered viewpoint angles but differs from the step 4 display due to the UCS setting.

7 *Task.*
   a) Try some other entries from the Viewpoint Presets dialogue box using both selection methods, i.e. the clock/arc and altering the angles.
   b) Investigate the difference in the display with the Absolute to WCS and Relative to UCS selections.
   c) Restore UCS BASE and the SE Isometric viewpoint.

8 This completes the viewpoint rotate exercise. Do not save any changes to the 3DWFM model.

The VPOINT COMPASS and TRIPOD option

This option allows the user to set 'infinite viewpoints' and has been called the bulls-eye and target method – for obvious reasons. We will demonstrate the command with a different model so:

1 Open the MODR2000\TEST3D model created during the viewport exercise and refer to Fig. 10.3.

2 Ensure UCS BASE is current and make the lower left viewport active, i.e. the 3D viewport.

3 Menu bar with **View-Viewports-1 Viewport** to display a single viewport of the model at a 3D viewpoint. This model 'fills the screen'.

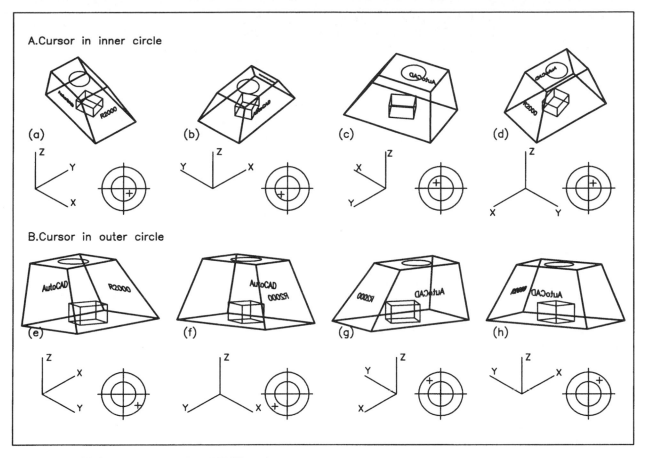

A.Cursor in inner circle

(a) (b) (c) (d)

B.Cursor in outer circle

(e) (f) (g) (h)

Figure 10.3 Viewpoint – the TRIPOD option.

4 Menu bar with **View-3D Views-VPOINT** and:
    prompt   1. model 'disappears'
              2. screen displays the XYZ tripod and the compass, which was previously termed the bulls-eye target
    and   axes and cross (+) move as mouse is moved
    respond move the cross (+) into the circle quadrant indicated in Fig. 10.3(a) and left-click
    and   model displayed at this viewpoint, and is viewed from above.

5 At the command line enter **VPOINT <R>** and:
    prompt   ***Switching to WCS***
    then   Specify a viewpoint or [Rotate]<display compass and tripod>
    respond **press <RETURN>**
    prompt   tripod and compass displayed
    respond move the cross (+) into the circle quadrant indicated in Fig. 10.3(b) and left-click
    and   model displayed at this new viewpoint.

6 Repeat the tripod viewpoint option (menu bar or command line) and position the cross (+) in the quadrants indicated in Fig. 10.3, i.e. (c)–(d): within the inner circle (e)–(h): within the outer circle.

7 *Task.*

When you are capable of using the compass and tripod, try the following:

a) position the + at different points on the two axes and observe the resultant displays

b) position the + at different points on the circle circumferences and note the displays.

8 *Explanation of option*

a) The 'bulls-eye' is in reality a representation of a glass globe and the model is located at the centre of the globe. The XY plane is positioned at the equator. The north pole of the globe is at the circle centres and the two concentric circles represent the surface of the world, stretched out onto a flat plane with:

circle centre: the north pole

inner circle: the equator

outer circle: the south pole.

b) As the cross(+) is moved about the circles, the user is moving around the surfaces of the globe and:

Cross (+) position	*View result*
in inner circle	above equator, looking down on model
in outer circle	below equator, looking up at model
on inner circle	looking horizontally at model
below horizontal	viewing from the front
above horizontal	viewing from the rear

9 This completes the tripod option exercise. Do not save changes.

The VPOINT VECTOR option

1 Open MODR2000\3DWFM with UCS BASE and SE Isometric viewpoint. Erase any dimensions and hatching, but leave the text items as they will act as a 'reference' as the model viewpoint is altered.

2 Refer to Fig. 10.4.

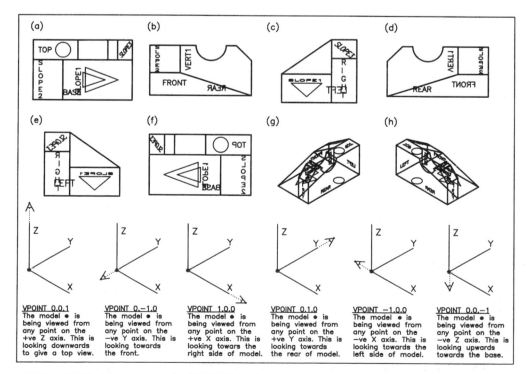

Figure 10.4 Viewpoint – the VECTOR option.

3 Menu bar with **View-3D Views-VPOINT** and:
   prompt   ```***Switching to WCS***```
   then   ```Current view direction```
   and   ```Specify a view point or [Rotate]```
   enter   **0,0,1 <R>.**

4 The model will be displayed at this viewpoint. It is a top view as fig(a) and 'fills the screen'.

5 At the command line enter **VPOINT <R>** and:
   prompt   ```Specify a view point or [Rotate]```
   enter   **0,–1,0 <R>**
   and   model displayed as fig(b) – a front view.

6 Repeat the viewpoint vector option (menu bar or command line) and enter the following coordinates at the prompt:

co-ords	view	fig
1,0,0	from right	c
0,1,0	from rear	d
–1,0,0	from left	c
0,0,–1	from below	f
1,1,1	3D from above	g
–1,–1,–1	3D from below	h.

7 Restore the original SE Isometric viewpoint.

8 *Task*.
   Try some vector entries for yourself then restore the original SE Isometric viewpoint

9 *Explanation of option*.
   a) The vector option allows the user to enter x,y,z coordinates. These are the coordinates of the viewers 'stand point' looking at the model which is considered to be at the origin. Thus if you enter 0,0,1 you are 'standing' at the point 0,0,1 looking towards the origin. As this point is on the positive Z axis you are looking down on the model, i.e. a top view.
   b) The actual numerical value of the vector entered does not matter, i.e. 0,0,1; 0,0,12; 0,0,99.99; 0,0,3456 are all the same viewpoint entries. I prefer to use the number 1, hence 0,0,1; –1,0,0, etc.
   c) Certain vector entries give the same display as rotate options and the following lists some of these similarities:

vector	rotate	view
0,0,1	90,90	top
0,–1,0	270,0	front
1,0,0	0,0	right
0,1,0	90,0	rear
–1,0,0	180,0	left
0,0,–1	90,-90	bottom
1,1,1	45,35	3D from above
–1,–1,–1	–135,–35	3D from below.

10 This completes the vector option. Do not save any changes.

The Isometric viewpoints

The isometric 3D views allow the user to view a model from four 'preset' viewpoints, these being SW, SE, NE and NW. These four viewpoints are used extensively as they allow easy access to viewing a model in 3D.

1 Open model TEST3D to display the four viewport configuration saved from the previous chapter.

2 Restore UCS BASE with layer MODEL current.

3 Making the appropriate viewport active, menu bar with **Views-3D Views** and set the following viewpoints:

viewport	*viewpoint*
top left	SW Isometric
top right	SE Isometric
lower right	NE Isometric
lower left	NW Isometric.

4 When the viewpoints have been entered, zoom-all in each viewport and the result should be Fig. 10.5. This does not need to be saved.

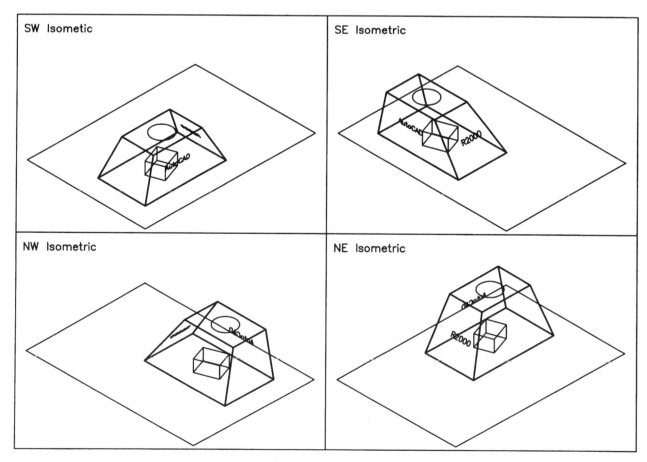

Figure 10.5

5 *Notes*.

   a) The four preset isometric viewpoints only allow viewing from above. If a model is to be viewed from below, another option is required. My choice for this is VPOINT-Rotate with a negative second angle value.

   b) The equivalent VPOINT-Rotate angles for the four isometric presets are:

3D View	*angle in XY plane*	*angle from XY plane*
SW Isometric	225	35.3
SE Isometric	315	35.3
NE Isometric	45	35.3
NW Isometric	135	35.3.

The orthographic viewpoints

There are six 'preset' orthographic viewpoints these being Top, Bottom, Left, Right, Front and Back. The options are independent of the UCS position.

1 Open model 3DWFM and erase any dimensions and hatching.

2 Restore UCS BASE with layer MODEL current. Refer to Fig. 10.6.

3 Menu bar with **View-Viewports-2 Viewports** and:

   prompt   Enter a configuration option and enter: **H <R>**.

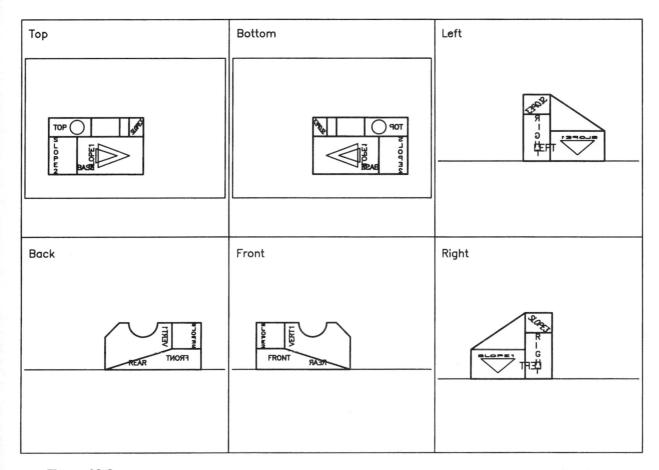

Figure 10.6

4 With the top viewport active, menu bar with **View-Viewports-3 Viewports** and:
   prompt   Enter a configuration option and enter: **V <R>.**

5 With the bottom viewport active, repeat step 4.

6 Making each viewport active, menu bar with **View-3D Views** and set the following orthographic viewpoints:

viewport	*viewpoint*
top left	top
top middle	bottom
top right	left
lower right	right
lower middle	front
lower right	back.

7 This layout does not need to be saved.

Viewpoint PLAN

This viewpoint selection was discussed during the chapter on the UCS and gives a view perpendicular to a UCS position.

1 Open the four viewport configuration TEST3D and:
   a) create a single viewport configuration of the 3D view
   b) set any 3 viewport configuration
   c) UCS FRONT current and refer to Fig. 10.7.

2 Make any viewport active and menu bar with **View-3D Views-Plan View-Current UCS** and the model will be displayed as fig(a). It is a plan view perpendicular to the UCS FRONT XY plane.

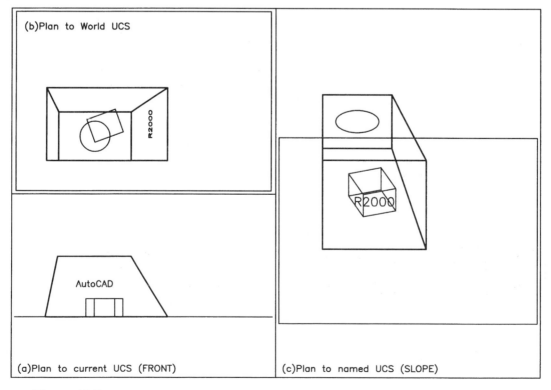

Figure 10.7

3 With another viewport active, menu bar with **View-3D Views-Plan View-World UCS** and the model will be displayed as fig(b).

4 Make the third viewport active and select the menu bar sequence **View-3D Views-Plan View-Named UCS** and:
prompt   Enter name of UCS and enter: **SLOPE <R>.**

5 The model will be displayed as a view perpendicular to the XY plane of UCS SLOPE.

6 This layout does not need to be saved.

The VIEW command

Different views of a model can be saved within the current drawing, thus allowing the operator to create a series of 'pictures'. These could be of the model being constructed, of a completed model at differing viewpoints, etc. These views (pictures) can be recalled at any time.

1 Open the 3DWFM model and erase any dimensions and hatching (or freeze the appropriate layers).

2 Model displayed at SE Isometric viewpoint with UCS BASE and layer MODEL current.

3 At the command line enter **-VIEW <R>** and:
prompt   Enter an option [?/Orthographic/Delete/Restore/Save..
enter   **S <R>** – the save option
prompt   Enter view name to save
enter   **V1 <R>.**

3 Menu bar with View-3D Views and set to NW Isometric.

4 Menu bar with **View-Named Views** and:
prompt   View dialogue box
respond **pick New View**
prompt   New View dialogue box
respond 1. enter View name: V2
          2. ensure Current display active, i.e. black dot
          3. UCS name: BASE – Fig. 10.8
          4. pick OK
prompt   View dialogue box with V2 added to list
respond **pick OK.**

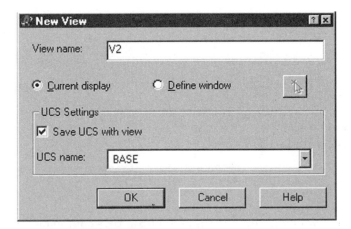

Figure 10.8 The New View dialogue box.

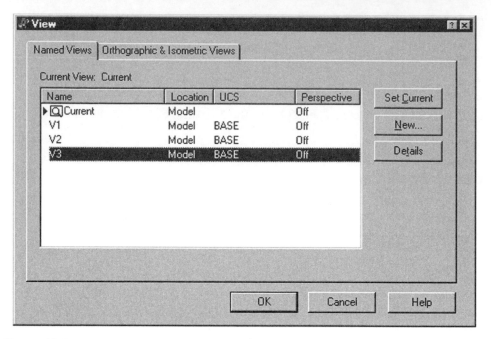

Figure 10.9 View dialogue box (Named View tab).

5 Menu bar with View-3D Views and set to SW Isometric.

6 Activate the View dialogue box with View-Named Views from the menu bar and:
   a) pick New
   b) View name: V3 with current display, UCS BASE then OK
   c) View dialogue box as Fig. 10.9
   d) pick OK.

6 At the command line enter **-VIEW <R>** and:
   prompt   Enter an option and enter: **R <R>** – the restore option
   prompt   Enter view name to restore and enter: **V1 <R>**.

7 Menu bar with **View-Named Views** and:
   prompt   View dialogue box
   respond   1. pick V3
                2. pick Set Current
                3. pick OK
   and   screen displays the saved V3 view.

8 *Task.*
   a) create, save and display some other views
   b) investigate the Details option from the Named Views tab
   c) investigate the Orthographic & Isometric Views tab
   d) investigate altering the UCS with saved views.

9 When complete, restore the SE Isometric viewpoint. Save if required but not as 3DWFM.

10 *Note.*
   Do not confuse the VIEW command with the View option of the UCS command. They are two entirely different concepts.

Real-tine 3D rotation

AutoCAD R20000 has real-time 3D rotation with the introduction of the 3D orbit command. The command allows interactive 3D rotation in the active viewport, the user controlling the rotation with the mouse. To introduce the reader to this topic, we will use one of our extruded models from Chapter 2, so:

1　Open extruded model 2 from Chapter 2, saved as EXT-2?

2　*a*) erase the black border
　　b) menu bar with **View-Shade-Flat Shaded**.

3　Menu bar with **View-3D Orbit** and:
　　prompt　　*a*) screen displays the shaded model
　　　　　　　b) the 3D orbit *ARCBALL* is displayed
　　　　　　　c) a new screen cursor is displayed and alters in appearance dependent on whether the cursor is inside or outside the arcball
　　respond　1. hold down the left mouse button
　　　　　　　2. move the mouse with the screen cursor outside the arcball and note the rotation of the shaded model
　　　　　　　3. move the mouse with the screen cursor inside the arcball and note the model display
　　　　　　　4. when you want to end the command, right-click the mouse button and pick Exit
　　　　　　　5. return the screen to the original layout by selecting the Undo icon from the Standard toolbar.

4　The introduction of this type of interactive rotation to AutoCAD is long overdue. AutoCAD 3D users now have a real-time 3D rotation command which can compete with 'larger CAD software packages'. The command is very easy to use, and our example used a shadcd model. The full benefit of 3D orbit will become apparent when we have created some surface and solid models.

5　*Task*: Investigate using the 3D orbit command with the two created wire-frame models (3DWFM and TEST3D) and the other saved extruded model (EXT-1).

6　We will investigate the 3D orbit command in more detail in a later chapter.

Using the Named Viewports to set viewpoints

Until now viewpoints have been set by the user using one of the 3D view options. It is possible however to 'preset' 3D views when creating multiple viewports. To demonstrate this effect:

1　Open the 3DWFM model – no dimensions or hatching.

2　UCS BASE and layer MODEL both current.

3　Menu bar with **View-Viewports-Named Viewports** and:
　　prompt　　Viewport dialogue box
　　respond　1. pick the New Viewport tab
　　　　　　　2. enter View name: **LAY1**
　　　　　　　3. pick Standard viewports: **Four Equal**
　　　　　　　4. Apply to: Display
　　　　　　　5. Setup: 3D
　　　　　　　6. dialogue box as Fig. 10.10
　　　　　　　7. pick OK.

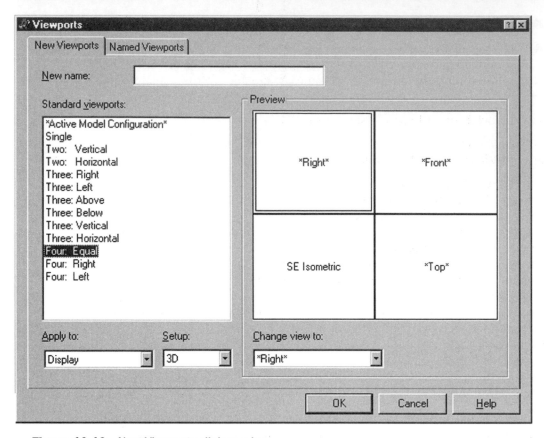

Figure 10.10 New Viewports dialogue box.

4 The screen will display a four viewport configuration with Right, Front, Top and SE Isometric views of the model. This is easier than creating a viewport layout then setting the viewpoint?

5 Repeat the menu bar sequence View-Viewports-Named Viewports and:
    a) pick the New Viewport tab
    b) enter View name as LAY2
    c) pick a Four Left standard viewport
    d) apply to display with 3D setup
    e) pick OK
    f) screen displays the same four views of the model as before, but in a different viewport configuration.

6 Now restore the original single SE isometric layout.

7 This completes all the viewpoint exercises.

The View toolbar

All commands have been activated from the command line or the menu bar. The view toolbar has several icons which can be used to obtain several viewpoints of a model. The toolbar is displayed in Fig. 10.11.

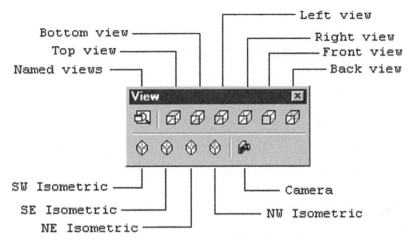

Figure 10.11 The View toolbar.

Summary

1 The viewpoint command allows models to be viewed from different 'stand points'.

2 The command has several selections including:
   a) four preset isometric views – SW, SE, NE and NW
   b) six orthographic preset views – top bottom, left, right, front and back
   c) three plan views – current UCS, world UCS, named UCS
   d) VPOINT with three options – rotate, compass and tripod, vector
   e) real-time 3D rotation with the 3D orbit command.

3 The VPOINT rotate option requires two angles:
   a) the angle 'around' the model – the direction
   b) the angle of inclination – the tilt.

4 The VPOINT rotate option can be set from a dialogue box.

5 The VPOINT compass/tripod option allows unlimited viewpoints.

6 The VPOINT vector option requires an x,y,z coordinate entry.

7 Viewpoints are generally set **absolute to the WCS** and the relative to the UCS option is **not recommended**.

9 All wire-frame models exhibit **ambiguity** when the viewpoint command is used, i.e. viewed from above or from below?

10 The VIEW command allows different views of a model to be saved in the current drawing for future recall. This is useful when the model is being displayed at various viewpoints.

Assignments

No specific activities for the viewpoint command.

Chapter 11

Centring viewports

When 3D models are displayed in multiple viewport configurations, three 'problems' can initially occur:

a) the model may 'fill the viewport'
b) the model may be displayed at different sizes in the viewports
c) the model views may not 'line up' between viewports.

These 'problems' are easily overcome by zooming each viewport by a scale factor or about a specified centre point determined by the user, who then decides on the 'scale effect' in the viewports. We will demonstrate the concept with two previously created models.

Example 1 – centring by scale

1   Open MODR2000\3DWFM of the wire-frame model and:
   a) erase any dimensions
   b) freeze layer TEXT
   c) leave the hatching displayed
   d) erase the black border
   e) Zoom-all and the model 'fills the screen'
   f) ensure UCS BASE is current
   g) command line with **UCSICON** and:
      prompt   Enter an option and enter: **A <R>**
      prompt   Enter an option and enter: **OR <R>**
   h) command line with **UCSVP <R>** and:
      prompt   Enter new value for UCSVP and enter: **0 <R>**.

2   Menu bar with **View-Viewports-4 Viewports** and the model is displayed in 3D in each viewport.

3   Entering **VPOINT <R>** at the command line, set the following vector viewpoints in the named active viewports:

viewport	*viewpoint*
top left	1,0,0
top right	0,–1,0
lower right	0,0,1
lower left	1,–1,1.

4   The model will be displayed at the viewpoints entered and will be of differing sizes in each viewport. The model needs to be centred about a specific point.

5   With the top left viewport active, menu bar with **View-Zoom-Scale** and:
   prompt Enter a scale factor and enter: **2 <R>**.

6   Repeat the zoom-scale selection in the other three viewports, and enter a scale factor of 2 in the top right and lower right viewports, but 1.25 in the lower left viewport.

7   When the zoom-scale command has been completed, the model will be 'neatly centred' in all viewports as Fig. 11.1.

8   Save as MODR2000\MV3DWFM.

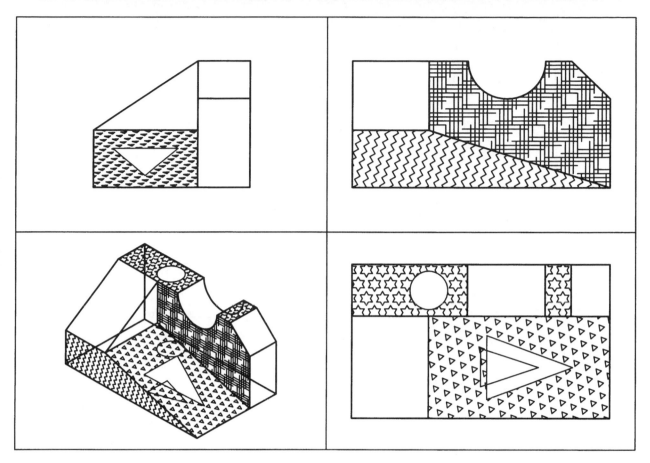

Figure 11.1 Centre viewport example – 3DWFM.

Example 2 – centring about a centre point

1 Open drawing TEST3D to display the four viewport configuration of the created model with text on two 'planes'.

2 Erase the black border and zoom-all in each viewport and the model will be displayed at different 'sizes' in the viewports.

3 Ensure UCS BASE is current.

4 *a*) Command line with UCSICON and enter A <R> then OR <R>
   b) in each viewport use the command line UCSVP and enter a value of 0.

5 The model has overall sizes of $200 \times 120 \times 100$ and its 'centre' ***relative to UCS BASE*** is the point 100,60,50.

6 With the top left viewport active, menu bar with **View-Zoom-Center** and:
   prompt   Specify centre point and enter: **100,60,50 <R>**
   prompt   Enter magnification or height and enter: **175 <R>**.

7 Repeat the zoom-center command in the other three viewports and enter the centre point as 100,60,50 and the magnification as 175 but 225 in the 3D viewport.

8 The model will be centred in each viewport as Fig. 11.2.

9 Save this display as MODR2000\MVTEST3D.

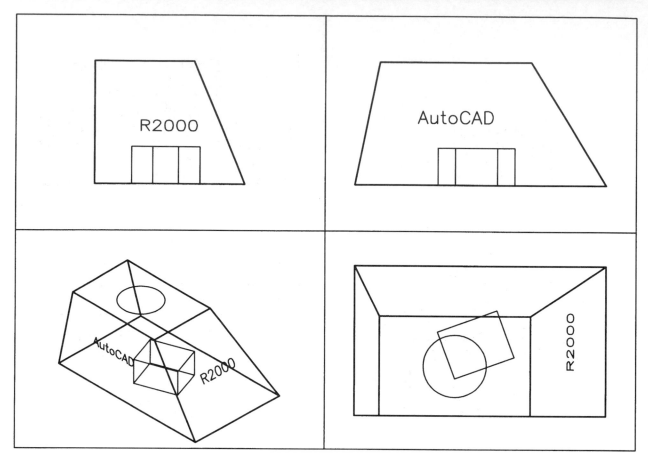

Figure 11.2 Centre viewport example 2 – 3DWFM.

Summary

1 Models can be centred in multiple *tiled* viewports using:
   a) Zoom-scale, the user entering the scale factor
   b) Zoom-center, the user entering the centre point and the magnification.

2 The centre point entered with zoom-center is **dependent on the UCS position**.

3 I like to zoom-centre relative to UCS BASE which is usually 'set' at a convenient base vertex. It is then easy for me to work out the model centre point in relation to the overall size of the model.

4 The magnification value entered is a 'scale' effect and is relative to the given default, e.g. if the default is <180> then:
   a) a value less than 180 will increase the model size
   b) a value greater than 180 will decrease the model size.

Assignments

Two activities have been included at this stage, both of which involve creating multiple tiled viewports, setting viewpoints and scaling/centring the models. The models have already been created (hopefully) during the hatching activities.

Activity 8: The hatched shaped block of Macfaramus

1 Open the drawing of the hatched block from activity 6 and erase the border.

2 Create a four viewport configuration to display top, front, right and a 3D view. Zoom-all in each viewport.

3 With UCS BASE current, zoom centre about the point 100,60,55 at 150 magnification in the three orthographic viewports, but 225 in the 3D viewport.

4 When complete, save as MODR2000\MVBLOCK.

Activity 9: The hatched pyramid of Macfaramus

1 Open hatched pyramid model from activity 7 and erase the border.

2 Create a four viewport configuration to display top, front, right and a NW Isometric view.

3 *a*) Zoom-scale in each viewport with a scale factor of 1, but with a different scale factor in the 3D viewport
 b) with UCS BASE current, zoom centre about the point 100,100,125 at 300 magnification in the three orthogonal viewports and your own entered magnification in the 3D viewport.

4 When complete, save as MODR2000\MVPYR.

Chapter 12

Model space and paper space – untiled viewports

AutoCAD R2000 has new multi-view capabilities which allow the user to layout, organize and plot multiple views of any 3D model. The multiple viewport concept has already been used with our wire-frame models, these viewports being TILED, i.e. fixed.

In this chapter we will investigate how to create UNTILED or FLOATING viewports which are used in the same way that the tiled viewports were used. The creation of untiled viewports requires an understanding of the two drawing environments – model space and paper space.

Model space

This is the drawing environment that exists in any viewport and is the default. All models which have been created have been completed in model space. Model space is used for all draughting and design work and for setting 3D viewpoints. Multiple viewports are possible in model space but are TILED, i.e. they cannot be moved or altered in size as Fig. 12.1(a). While model space multi-views are useful, they have one major disadvantage – only the active viewport can be plotted, i.e. model space multiple viewports cannot be plotted on one sheet of paper.

Paper space

This is a drawing environment which is independent of model space. In paper space the user creates the drawing sheet, i.e. border, title box, etc. as well as arranging the multiple viewport layout. The viewports created in paper space are UNTILED, i.e. they can be positioned to suit, altered in size and additional viewports can be added to the layout – Fig. 12.1(b). In paper space the 3D viewpoint command is not valid although objects (particularly text) can be added to the sheet layout. The real advantage of working with paper space multiple viewports is that any viewport configuration can be plotted on the one sheet of paper.

Tilemode

The system variable which controls the 'type' of viewport to be created is **TILEMODE** and:
a) TILEMODE 1: model space (FIXED) viewports paper space is not available
b) TILEMODE 0: paper space (FLOATING) viewports model space is available.

Tiled (model space) viewports are always displayed as edge-to-edge and fill the screen like a tiled wall. Untiled (paper space) viewports can be positioned anywhere within the screen area with spaces between them if required. They can also be copied, moved, stretched, etc.

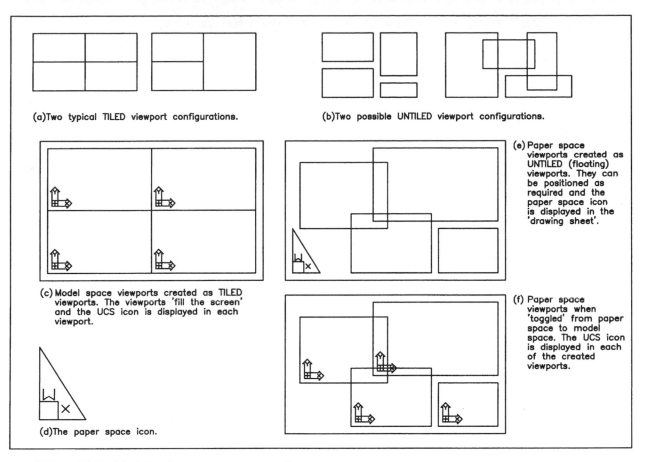

Figure 12.1 Model and paper space concepts.

Icons

When working in model space the normal WCS/UCS icon will be displayed in all viewports, orientated to the viewport viewpoint as Fig. 12.1(c). In paper space, the paper space icon – Fig. 12.1(d) is displayed.

When viewports are created in paper space, the paper space icon is displayed in the lower left corner of the screen as Fig. 12.1(e), but when model space 'is entered' the UCS icon is again displayed in all created viewports as Fig. 12.1(f).

Toggling between model and paper space

All AutoCAD users will be familiar with the toggle concept, e.g. toggling the grid on/off with the F7 key or from the Status bar with a left-click on the word GRID. It is possible to toggle between model space and paper space but only if the TILEMODE system variable is set to 0. The toggle effect can be activated by:

1 *Command line*
   a) if in paper space, toggle to model space with **MS <R>**
   b) if in model space, toggle to paper space with **PS <R>**.

2 *Status bar*
   a) left-click on PAPER to toggle to model space
   b) left-click on MODEL to toggle to paper space.

Model/paper space example – untiled viewports

This example will use a model created in model space to demonstrate the paper space multiple viewport concept. The example is quite long but if you are unsure of paper space, persevere with it – it is important that you understand how to create and use paper space viewports.

Note

a) Pre-R2000 users who are familiar with model/paper space should complete this exercise. The method of creating paper space multiple viewports is different from previous releases.

b) R2000 assumes that the user has access to a printer/plotter, this being connected to the computer. As all printer/plotters differ in their configurations, paper size, etc., I have **assumed** that no printer is configured. This does not exclude the user from obtaining a hard copy of completed drawings, it is simply a matter of convenience for me when detailing the various steps in the exercises.

c) There are different methods of creating paper space untiled viewports from a model space drawing. This example demonstrates one of these methods.

1 Open drawing MODR2000\3DWFM and:
  a) erase the black border, hatching and any dimensions
  b) leave the text items – they will 'act as a reference'
  c) layer MODEL and UCS BASE current
  d) zoom-all and model 'fills the screen'
  e) refer to Fig. 12.2.

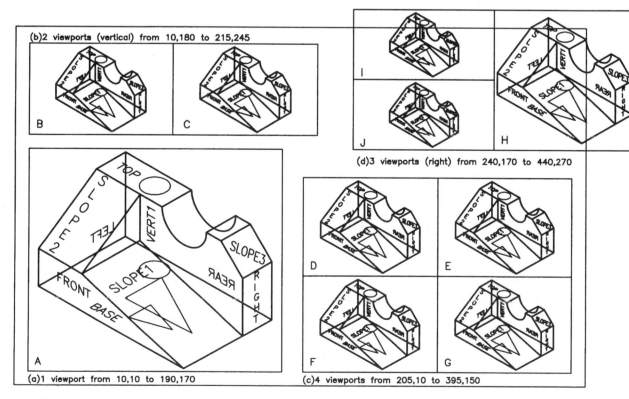

Figure 12.2 Creating the paper space viewports with 3DWFM.

2 Make a new layer called VP, linetype continuous, colour to suit.

3 At the command line enter **PS <R>** and prompt:
  ** *Command not allowed in Model tab* ******.

4 Menu bar with **Tools-Wizards-Create Layout** and:
  prompt Create Layout - Begin dialogue box
  respond enter layout name: **MYFIRST** then pick Next
  prompt Create Layout - Printer dialogue box
  respond pick **None** then pick Next
  prompt Create Layout - Paper Size dialogue box
  respond 1. scroll and pick **ISOA3 (420.00 × 297.00MM)**
       2. Drawing units: Millimeters
       3. pick Next
  prompt Create Layout – Orientation dialogue box
  respond ensure **Landscape** active then pick Next
  prompt Create Layout – Title Block dialogue box
  respond pick **None** then pick Next
  prompt Create Layout – Define Viewports dialogue box
  respond pick **None** then pick Next
  prompt Create Layout -Finish dialogue box
  respond pick **Finish**
  and   1. screen returned in paper space – note the icon
       2. the white area is the A3 paper
       3. the dotted area is the permitted drawing area within the white A3 paper –
         for plot purposes
       4. a new layout name MYFIRST is added to the tab bar.

5 Make layer 0 current and menu bar with **Draw-Rectangle** and:
  prompt Specify first corner point and enter: **0,0 <R>**
  prompt Specify other corner point and enter: **405,257 <R>**.

6 This rectangle is our drawing area outline.

7 Make layer VP current.

8 Menu bar with **View-Viewports-1 Viewport** and:
  prompt Specify corner of viewport and enter: **10,10 <R>**
  prompt Specify opposite corner and enter: **190,170 <R>**
  and   a viewport (A) is created with the model 3DWFM displayed as fig(a).

9 Menu bar with **View-Viewports-2 Viewports** and:
  prompt Enter viewport arrangement and enter: **V <R>**
  prompt Specify first corner and enter: **10,180 <R>**
  prompt Specify opposite and enter: **215,245 <R>**
  and   two additional viewports (B and C) are created, each displaying the model in
       3D – fig(b).

10 Menu bar again with **View-Viewports-4 Viewports** and:
  prompt Specify first corner and enter: **205,10 <R>**
  prompt Specify opposite corner and enter: **395,150 <R>**
  and   four new viewports (D,E,F,G) are created with the model displayed in
       each – fig(c).

11 Final menu bar selection with **View-Viewports-3 Viewports** (Right option) and:
 prompt Specify first corner and enter: **225,155 <R>**
 prompt Specify opposite corner and enter: **375,235 <R>**
 and three viewports (H,I,J) are created each with the model displayed as fig(d). These viewports extend 'outwith' the drawing paper.

12 What has been achieved?
 a) ten different sized viewports have been created
 b) the viewports have been created in paper space
 c) each viewport displays the original 3DWFM model.

13 At the command line enter **MS <R>** and:
 a) toggled to model space
 b) the last viewport (top right) is active?
 c) each viewport displays the UCS icon at BASE?
 d) any viewport can be made active as before, i.e. move to required viewport and left-click.

14 Investigate the paper/model space toggle:
 a) from the command line with PS and MS
 b) status bar with left-click on MODEL/PAPER
 c) decide on which toggle method you prefer.

15 Investigate the model tab line:
 a) pick Model – the original 3DWFM model is displayed
 b) pick MYFIRST – our multiple viewport layout is displayed.

16. At this stage the layout is as Fig. 12.2.

Setting the viewpoints

1 Enter model space and set the following viewpoints in the named viewports:

viewport	*viewpoint*
A	SW Isometric
B	NE Isometric
C	NW Isometric
D	Right
E	Front
F	SE Isometric
G	Top
H	Bottom
I	Left
J	Back.

2 The model is now displayed at a different viewpoint in each viewport. Using the Zoom-Scale command, enter the following scale factors in the appropriate viewport:
 a) scale factor of 1.75 in orthogonal view viewports
 b) scale factor of 1.25 in 3D view viewports.

Adding text

1 In model space, make layer TEXT current and viewport (A) active

2 Add an item of text using the following:
 a) start point: 0,–30
 b) height: 15 and rotation: 0
 c) text item: AutoCAD R2000 (MS).

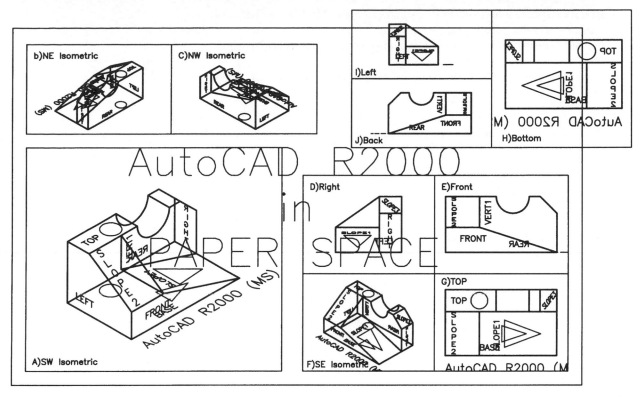

Figure 12.3 Working with the created paper space viewports.

3 This item of text will be displayed in the ten viewports at different orientations due to the viewpoints. In some viewports (D,E,I,J) the text is viewed 'end-on'.

4 Enter paper space with PS <R>.

5 Add an item of text using:
   a) start point: centred on 200,150
   b) height: 20 and rotation: 0
   c) text: AutoCAD R2000<R>
      text: in <R>
      text: PAPER SPACE <R><R> – two returns.

6 At this stage your screen layout should resemble Fig. 12.3.

Modifying the layout

1 In paper space try and erase the model – you cannot.

2 In model space try and erase the paper space text – not possible.

3 In paper space, activate the ZOOM command and window viewport A. The viewport will nearly fill the screen and by entering model space, it is easier to work on the model.

4 In paper space, zoom previous.

5 In paper space, select the SCALE icon from the Modify toolbar and:

prompt   Select objects

respond   **completely window viewports H,I,J then right-click**

prompt   Specify base point

respond   **Intersection of lower left corner of viewport J**

prompt   Specify scale factor

enter   **0.75 <R>**.

6 In model space, zoom-all in viewports H, I and J, then zoom-scale with the same 1.75 scale factor as before.

7 Enter paper space and freeze the layer VP.

8 The ten views of the model will be displayed with text but without the viewport borders – Fig. 12.4.

9 If you have access to a printer/plotter:
   a) print from any viewport in model space
   b) print from paper space.

10 This completes the exercise.

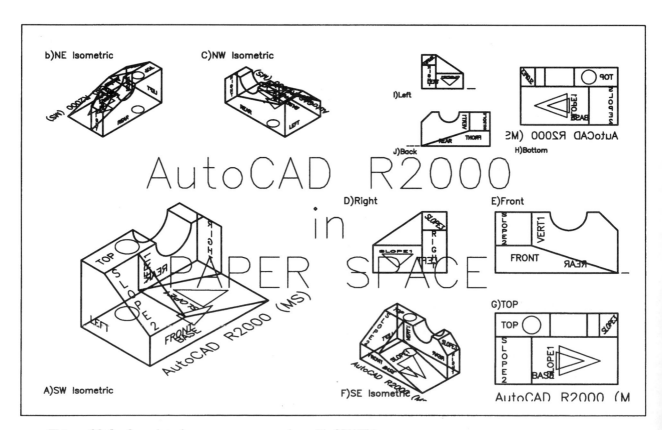

Figure 12.4 Completed paper space exercise with 3DWFM.

Comparison between model space and paper space

The following table gives a comparison between the model and paper space drawing environments:

Model space	Paper space
used to create the model	used to create the paper layout
model can be modified	model cannot be modified
tiled (fixed) viewports	untiled (floating) viewports
tilemode: 1	tilemode: 0
viewports restricted in size	viewports to any size
viewports 'fill screen'	viewports positioned to suit
viewports cannot be altered	viewports can be moved, copied etc
cannot add viewports	additional viewports can be created
plot only active viewport	all viewports can be plotted
3D views active	cannot use 3D viewpoint
WCS or UCS icon	paper space icon
zoom in active viewport	zoom complete viewports

A new 3D multiple viewport template file

Now that the model/paper space concept has been discussed, a new template and drawing file will be created which will allow all future models (surface and solid) to be displayed in multiple viewports. We will modify our existing 3DSTDA3 template file as it:
a) already has layers, e.g. MODEL, OBJECTS, TEXT, etc.
b) has a created dimension style – 3DSTD
c) other variables set.

Getting ready

1 Menu bar with **File-New** and:
   prompt   Create New Drawing dialogue box
   respond 1. pick Use a Template
              2. scroll and pick **3DSTDA3.dwt**
              3. pick OK.

2 The screen will display a black border at a SE Isometric viewpoint with the WCS at the left vertex of the border.

3 Erase the black border – we will not use it again.

4 Menu bar with **View-3D Views-Plan View-World UCS**.

5 Menu bar with **Format-Layer** and create two new layers:
name	*colour*	*linetype*
VP	number 14	continuous
SHEET	number 212	continuous.

6 Menu bar with **Tools-Wizards-Create Layout** and use the Create Layout dialogue box as step 4 in the previous exercise:
   a) Begin: enter **MV3DSTD** then Next
   b) Printer: None then Next
   c) Paper Size: Millimeters, ISO A3 (420 × 297) then Next
   d) Orientation: Landscape then Next
   e) Title Block: None then Next
   f) Define viewports: None then Next
   g) Finish: pick Finish.

7 A white paper area will be returned with a dotted drawing area within, this being in paper space.

Creating the drawing paper layout and viewports

1 Make layer SHEET current.

2 Menu bar with **Draw-Rectangle** and:
   prompt Specify first corner point and enter: **0,0 <R>**
   prompt Specify other corner point and enter: **405,257 <R>**.

3 Zoom-all and PAN to suit.

4 Draw a line from: 0,15 to: @405,0.

5 The area at the bottom of the 'paper' is for you to 'customize' as required.

6 Make layer VP current.

7 Menu bar with **View-Viewports-4 Viewports** and:
   prompt Specify first corner and enter: **10,20 <R>**
   prompt Specify opposite corner and enter: **395,247 <R>**.

8 Screen displays four paper space viewports within the sheet border.

9 Enter model space with **MS <R>**.

Setting the UCS and viewpoints

1 In model space enter **UCSICON <R>** and:
   prompt Enter an option and enter: **A <R>**
   prompt Enter an option and enter: **OR <R>**.

2 This will ensure the UCS icon is positioned at the origin point in each viewport.

3 Making each viewport active, enter **UCSVP <R>** and:
   prompt Enter new value for UCSVP and enter: **0 <R>**.

4 Menu bar with **Tools-New UCS-Origin** and:
   prompt Specify new origin point and enter: **10,10,0 <R>**.

5 At command line enter **UCS <R>** then **S <R>** and:
   prompt Enter name to save current UCS and enter: **BASE <R>**.

6 Set the following viewpoints making the appropriate viewport active with the menu bar sequence **View-3D Views** and:

viewport	*viewpoint*
lower right	Top
upper right	Front
upper left	Right
lower left	SE Isometric.

7 At command line enter **UCS <R>** then **R <R>** and:
   prompt Enter name of UCS to restore and enter: **BASE <R>**.

8 Menu bar with **Tools-New UCS-X** and:
   prompt Specify rotation angle about X axis and enter: **90 <R>**.

9 Command line with **UCS <R>** then **S <R>** and enter: **FRONT <R>**.

10 Menu bar with **Tools-New UCS-Y** and:
   prompt Specify rotation angle about Y axis and enter: **90 <R>**.

11 Command line with **UCS <R>** then **S <R>** and enter: **RIGHT <R>**.

12 *Note.* This section has set the UCS to the origin in each viewport and saved three UCS positions – BASE, FRONT and RIGHT. These three UCS positions will assist with future model creation.

Finally

1   Restore UCS BASE, make layer MODEL current and make the lower left viewport (3D) active.

2   Menu bar with **File-Save As** and:
   prompt   Save Drawing As dialogue box
   respond   1. scroll at Save as Type
             2. pick **AutoCAD Drawing Template File (*.dwt)**
   prompt   list of existing template files
   respond   1. enter File name as: **MV3DSTD**
             2. pick Save
   prompt   Template Description dialogue box
   respond   1. enter: **My multi-view 3D prototype layout drawing created on XX/YY/ZZ**
             2. pick Save.

3   Menu bar with **File-Save As** and:
   prompt   Save Drawing As dialogue box
   respond   1. scroll and pick **AutoCAD 2000 Drawing (*.dwg)**
             2. scroll and pick your named folder (MODR2000)
             3. enter file name: **MV3DSTD**
             4. pick Save.

4   The template/drawing file will be used continuously when starting new exercises.

Checking the new MV3DSTD layout

Now that the MV3DSTD template file has been created we will add some 3D objects to 'check' the layout. Try and reason out the coordinate entries.

1   Close any existing drawings on which are displayed.

2   Menu bar with **File-New** and:
   prompt   Create New Drawing dialogue box
   respond   1. pick Use a Template
             2. scroll and lick **MV3DSTD.dwt**
             3. pick OK.

3   The created multiple viewport drawing should be displayed with layer MODEL current, UCS BASE and lower left viewport active.

4   Display the Object Snap and Surfaces toolbars.

5   Menu bar with **Draw-Surfaces-3D Surfaces** and:
   prompt   3D Objects dialogue box
   respond   **pick Box3d then OK**
   prompt   Specify corner of box and enter: **0,0,0 <R>**
   prompt   Specify length of box and enter: **200 <R>**
   prompt   Specify width of box and enter: **100 <R>**
   prompt   Specify height and enter: **80 <R>**
   prompt   Specify rotation angle about Z axis and enter: **0 <R>**.

6   Menu bar with **Draw-Surfaces-3D Surfaces** and:
   prompt   3D Objects dialogue box
   respond   **pick Wedge then OK**
   prompt   Specify corner point of wedge and enter: **0,0,0 <R>**
   prompt   Specify length of wedge and enter: **100 <R>**
   prompt   Specify width of wedge and enter: **100 <R>**
   prompt   Specify height of wedge and enter: **100 <R>**
   prompt   Specify rotation angle of wedge about Z axis and enter: **–90 <R>**.

7 At the command line enter **CHANGE <R>** and:

prompt   Select objects
respond   **pick the wedge then right-click**
prompt   Specify change point or [Properties] and enter: **P <R>**
prompt   Enter property to change and enter: **C <R>**
prompt   enter new color and enter: **BLUE <R><R>** – two returns.

8 Select the CONE icon from the Surfaces toolbar and:

prompt   Specify center point for base of cone and enter: **70,50,80 <R>**
prompt   Specify radius for base of cone of base and enter: **50 <R>**
prompt   Specify radius for top of cone and enter: **0 <R>**
prompt   Specify height of cone and enter: **100 <R>**
prompt   Enter number of segments for surface of cone and enter: **16 <R>**.

9 Change the colour of the cone to green.

10 Select the DISH icon from the Surface toolbar and:

prompt   Specify center point of dish and enter: **150,50,0 <R>**
prompt   Specify radius of dish and enter: **50 <R>**
prompt   Enter number of longitudinal segments for surface of dish and enter: **16<R>**
prompt   Enter number of latitudinal segments for surface of dish and enter: **8 <R>**.

11 Change the colour of the dish to magenta.

12 In each viewport, zoom-centre about the point **100,0,80** at **300** magnification – why these coordinates?

13 With UCS BASE make layer TEXT current and menu bar with **Draw-Text-Single Line Text** and:

prompt   Specify start point of text and enter: **130,80,80 <R>**
prompt   Specify height and enter: **10 <R>**
prompt   Specify rotation angle of text and enter: **0 <R>**
prompt   Text and enter: **AutoCAD <R><R>**.

14 Add two other text items using the following information:

	first item	*second item*
Named UCS	FRONT	RIGHT
start point	110,40,0	15,15,200
height	15	20
rotation	0	0
item	Release	2000.

15 Restore UCS BASE.

16 Enter paper space with **PS <R>**.

17 At the command line enter **DTEXT <R>** and add the following text using the information given:

a) start point: centred on 202.5,133.5
b) height: 10 and rotation: 0
c) enter text: AutoCAD <R>
     enter text: R2000 <R>
     enter text: Paper space <R><R>.

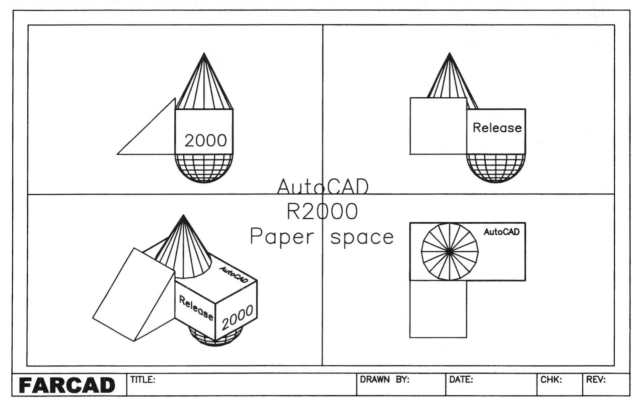

Figure 12.5 The MV3DSTD prototype A3 drawing sheet layout.

18 Save if required, but take care with the name.

19 Return to model space with **MS <R>**.

20 Menu bar with **View-Hide** in each viewport and your screen layout should resemble Fig. 12.5.

22 In each viewport, menu bar with **View-Shade-Flat Shaded** to display the model in colour. Note the effect of the shading on the model space and paper space text.

23 If you are adventurous, try the 3D Orbit command with the shaded model in the 3D viewport – it is quite impressive. When you have rotated the model, select the undo icon to restore the original 3D view of the model.

24 In each viewport, menu bar with **View-Shade-2D Wireframe** to restore the original views of the model. This will also restore the paper space text – interesting? Pre-R2000 users should note that REGEN and REGENALL do not remove the shade effect.

25 This (long) chapter is now complete and we can concentrate on surface and solid modelling.

Note

One of the major benefits of paper space is the ability to zoom a complete viewport. This allows the zoomed viewport to be enlarged, thus allowing the user to 'see more clearly' the model being created/worked on when in model space. This is a concept with which the user should become familiar, i.e.

1. Enter paper space with PS <R>.
2. Zoom-window a specific viewport, e.g. the 3D viewport.
3. Return to model space with MS <R>.
4. Complete (or modify) the model.
5. Enter paper space with PS <R>.
6. Zoom-previous (or All) to restore the complete layout.
7. Return to model space with MS <R>.

This zoom a viewport in paper space is a very useful concept.

Chapter 13

Surface modelling

The best way of describing a surface model is to think of a wire-frame model with 'skins' covering all the wires from which the model is constructed. The 'skins' convert a wire-frame model into a surface model with several advantages:

1 The model can be displayed with hidden line removal.

2 There is no ambiguity.

3 The model can be shaded and rendered.

AutoCAD R2000 adds **FACETED** surfaces using a polygon mesh technique, but this mesh only approximates to curved surfaces. The mesh density (the number of facets) is controlled by certain system variables which will be discussed in the chapters which follow.

The different types of surface models available with R2000 are:
- 3D faces
- 3D meshes
- polyface meshes
- ruled surfaces
- tabulated surfaces
- revolved surfaces
- edge surfaces
- 3D objects
- elevation/thickness surfaces.

Each surface type will be considered in a chapter on its own, with the exception of the elevation/thickness surfaces. This has already been discussed in Chapter 2 with 2½D extrusions – did you realize that you were creating surface models at this early stage?

The surface commands can be activated:

1 From the menu bar with **Draw-Surfaces**.

2 In icon form from the Surfaces toolbar.

3 By direct keyboard entry, e.g. **3DFACE <R>**.

The various exercises will use all methods mentioned.

Chapter 14

3DFACE and PFACE

These two commands appear similar in operation, both adding faces (skins) to wire-frame models. If these added faces are in colour, the final model display can be quite impressive.

3D face example

A 3D face is a three- or four-sided surface added irrespective of the UCS position.

1 Menu bar with **File-New** and 'open' your **MV3DSTD** template file layer MODEL and UCS BASE. Display toolbars to suit.

2 Before creating the model, zoom-centre about 60,35,50 at 175 magnification in the 3D viewport and 150 in the other three.

3 With the lower left (3D) viewport active, create a wire-frame model using the LINE command and the reference sizes in Fig. 14(a). The point 1 should be at (0,0,0).

4 The created model has five 'planes' so make five new layers: F1 red, F2 blue, F3 green, F4 magenta and F5 colour 14.

5 Make layer F1 current.

6 Still with the 3D viewport active, menu bar with **Draw-Surfaces-3Dface** and:
prompt   Specify first point and **Intersection icon and pick pt1**
prompt   Specify second point and **Intersection icon and pick pt2**
prompt   Specify third point and **Intersection icon and pick pt3**
prompt   Specify fourth point and **Intersection icon and pt4**
prompt   Specify third point and right-click/enter.

7 Make layer F2 current and select the 3DFACE icon from the Surfaces toolbar and:
prompt   Specify first point and pick Intersection pt2
prompt   Specify second point and pick Intersection pt3
prompt   Specify third point and pick Intersection pt5
prompt   Specify fourth point and pick Intersection pt2 then <R>.

8 Make layer F3 current, enter **3DFACE <R>** at the command line and:
prompt   First point and pick Intersection pt3
prompt   Second point and pick Intersection pt4
prompt   Third point and pick Intersection pt6
prompt   Fourth point and pick Intersection pt2 then <R>.

9 Use the 3DFACE command and add faces to:
a) face: 1256 with layer F4 current
b) face: 146 with layer F5 current.

10 Menu bar with **View-Hide** in each viewport – Fig. 14.1.

11 Remove the hide effect with the menu bar sequence **View-Regenall**.

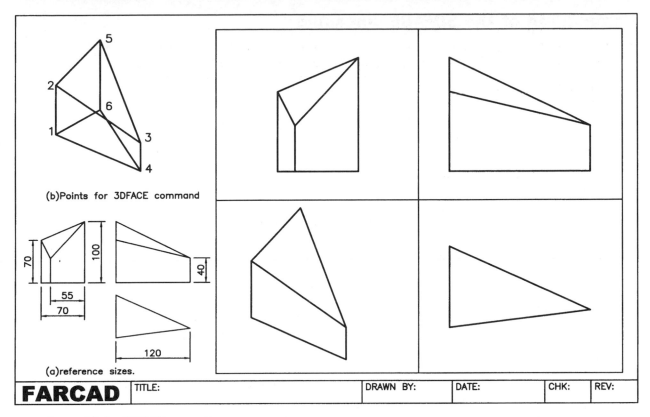

Figure 14.1 3DFACE example.

12 In each viewport **View-Shade-Flat Shaded** and:

viewport	colours displayed
top left	red, blue, green
top right	blue, red
lower right	blue
lower left	red, blue.

13 In each viewport **View-Shade-2D Wireframe** to remove the shade effect then save the model as **MODR2000\CHEESE**.

14 *Task*.
   a) Shade the 3D viewport.
   b) Select the 3D Orbit icon from the Standard toolbar.
   c) Interactively rotate the 3D shade model to 'see' the surfaces not displayed in the four viewports.
   d) Select the Undo icon to restore the 3D view.

15 This first 3D FACE exercise is now complete.

Explanation of the 3DFACE command

The 3DFACE command can be used to face any three or four sided 'plane'. The command allows 'continuous' faces to be created and will be demonstrated with a 2D example so:

1 With the screen display from the first example:
   a) erase the model – saved?
   b) make the lower right viewport active
   c) snap and grid on – set to 5 or 10
   d) refer to Fig. 14.2.

2 Activate the 3DFACE command and:

prompt	Specify first point and pick a pt1
prompt	Specify second point and pick a pt2
prompt	Specify third point and pick a pt3 – 1st pt of next face
prompt	Specify fourth point and pick a pt4 – 2nd pt of next face
and	Face 1-2-3-4 displayed
prompt	Specify third point and pick pt5 – 3rd pt of face,1st of next
prompt	Specify fourth point and pick a pt6 – 4th pt of face,2nd of next
and	Face 3-4-5-6 displayed
prompt	Specify third point and pick a pt7 – 3rd pt of face,1st of next
prompt	Specify fourth point and pick a pt8 – 4th of face,2nd of next
and	Face 5-6-7-8 displayed
prompt	Specify third point.
respond	pick points 9 and 10; 11 and 12; 13 and 14 in response to the third and fourth prompts then right-click/enter
and	Faces 7-8-9-10; 9-10-11-12; 11-12-13-14 will be displayed as fig(a).

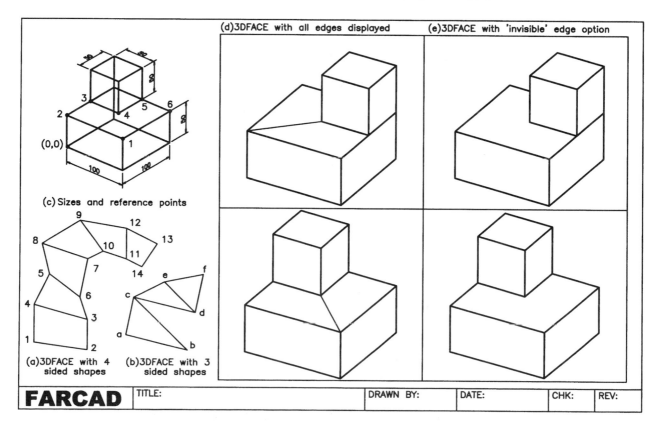

Figure 14.2 3DFACE example 2 – the INVISIBLE edge option.

3 Activate the 3DFACE command again and:
prompt   Specify first point and pick a pta
prompt   Specify second point and pick a ptb
prompt   Specify third point and pick a ptc – 1st of next face
prompt   Specify fourth point and press <RETURN> – note the prompt
and   Face a-b-c displayed
prompt   Specify third point and pick a ptd – 2nd pt of face
prompt   Specify fourth point and pick a pte – 3rd pt of face
and   Face c-d-e displayed
prompt   Specify third point and pick a ptf
prompt   Specify fourth point and <R><R> – two returns
and   Face d-e-f displayed as fig(b).

4 Now erase the two continuous 3D faces.

The invisible edge 3D FACE example

When the 3DFACE command is used with continuous three/four-sided 'shapes', all three/four sides of the face are displayed. It is possible to create a 3DFACE with an 'invisible edge'.

1 Refer to Fig. 14.2(c) and use the existing blank four viewport configuration to:
   a) with layer MODEL and UCS BASE current and the lower left viewport active, create a wire-frame model using the sizes given. This should be easy for you?
   b) change the viewpoint in the viewports as follows:
      lower left: VPOINT 'Rotate' at 300° and 30°
      upper left: VPOINT 'Rotate' at 30° and 30°
      upper right and lower right: your own VPOINT 'Rotate' values.

2 Set the running object snap to INTERSECTION.

3 With layer F1 current, 3DFACE the four vertical sides of the lower part of the model.

4 With layer F3 current, 3DFACE the four vertical sides of the upper part of the model.

5 With layer F4 current, 3DFACE the top of the model.

6 With layer F2 current:
   a) activate the 3DFACE command and:
      prompt   Specify first point and pick pt1
      prompt   Specify second point and pick pt2
      prompt   Specify third point and pick pt3
      prompt   Specify fourth point and pick pt4 the right-click/enter
   b) activate the 3DFACE command and:
      prompt   Specify first point and pick pt1
      prompt   Specify second point and pick pt6
      prompt   Specify third point and pick pt5
      prompt   Specify fourth point and pick pt4 then right-click/enter.

7 Menu bar with **View-Hide** and the model will be displayed with hidden line removal. The edge between point 1 and 4 is visible – fig(d).

8 Menu bar with **View-Shade-Flat Shaded** and the model is displayed with coloured 3D faces. No edge is visible between points 1 and 4 due to the two added faces having the same colour.

9 Restore the original wire-frame model with the menu bar sequence of **View-Shade-2D Wireframe**.

10 Erase the two blue 3D face surfaces by picking the edges between points 1 and 4.

11 Still with layer F2 current and OSNAP INT set:
    a) activate the 3DFACE command and:
prompt	`Specify first point` and pick pt1	
prompt	`Specify second point` and pick pt2	
prompt	`Specify third point` and pick pt3	
prompt	`Specify fourth point`	
enter	**I <R>** – the invisible edge option	
prompt	`Specify fourth point` and pick pt4	
prompt	`Specify third point` and right-click/enter	
and	the 3D face is displayed without edge 1-4.	

    b) 3DFACE again and:
prompt	`Specify first point` and pick pt1
prompt	`Specify second point` and pick pt6
prompt	`Specify third point` and pick pt5
prompt	`Specify fourth point` and enter: **I <R>**
prompt	`Specify fourth point` pick pt4
prompt	`Specify third point` and right-click/enter
and	the 3D face is displayed without edge 1-4.

12 Display the model with hidden line removal – fig(e).

13 Try some different shade effects then restore the original wire-frame model.

14 Cancel the object snap intersection mode.

15 Save if required, but it will not be used again.

PFACE

A PFACE is a polygon mesh and is similar to a 3DFACE. It allows the user to define a number of vertices for the surface to be faced, not the 3 or 4 allowed with the 3DFACE command. The following example has a rather long set of prompts:

1 Open your MV3DSTD template file and:
    a) make four new layers: F1 blue, F2 green, F3 magenta, F4 cyan
    b) layer MODEL current, restore UCS FRONT, set OSNAP Intersection
    c) lower left viewport (3D) active.

2 Set the elevation to 0 and the thickness to –200.

3 Select the POLYGON icon from the Draw toolbar and:
    a) number of sides: 5
    b) centre of polygon: 0,0
    c) circumscribed circle radius: 50.

4 Zoom centre about the point 0,0,-100 at 225 magnification.

5 Refer to Fig. 14.3 which only considers the 3D viewport.

6 Menu bar with **View-Hide** to display the pentagonal prism without a 'top surface' – fig(a).

7 Make layer F1 current and:
    a) select the 3DFACE icon and:
First point	pick pt2
Second point	pick pt3
Third point	pick pt4
Fourth point	<R><R> – two returns.

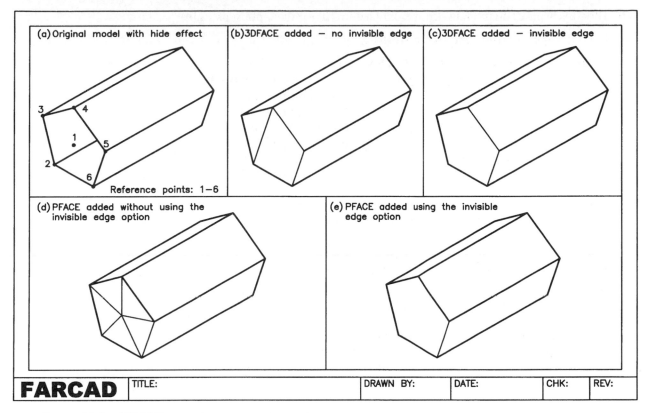

Figure 14.3 3DFACE example.

b) select the 3DFACE icon and:

First point	pick pt2
Second point	pick pt6
Third point	pick pt5
Fourth point	pick pt4
Third point	right-click/enter.

8 Hide the model to display the 'top surface' as fig(b), i.e. with hidden line removal. Restore the original wire-model from the menu bar with View-Regen.

9 Make layer F2 current and freeze layer F1 then:

a) activate the 3DFACE command and:

First point	pick pt2
Second point	pick pt3
Third point	enter **I <R>** then pick pt4
Fourth point	<R><R> – two returns

b) 3DFCAE again and:

First point	pick pt2
Second point	pick pt6
Third point	pick pt5
Fourth point	enter **I <R>** then pick pt4
Third point	right-click/enter.

10 Hide to display the model with the 3D face invisible edge option as fig(c).

11 Make layer F3 current and freeze layer F2.

12 At the command line enter **PFACE <R>** and:

prompt	`Specify location for vertex 1` and enter: **0,0 <R>**, i.e. pt1
prompt	`Specify location for vertex 2` and pick pt2
prompt	`Specify location for vertex 3` and pick pt3
prompt	`Specify location for vertex 4` and pick pt4
prompt	`Specify location for vertex 5` and pick pt5
prompt	`Specify location for vertex 6` and pick pt6
prompt	`Specify location for vertex 7` and right-click: no more vertices
prompt	`Face 1,vertex 1`
then	`Enter a vertex number` and enter **1 <R>**
and	`Enter the following in response to the vertex number prompts:`
prompt	`Face 1,vertex 2` and enter: **2 <R>**
prompt	`Face 1,vertex 3` and enter: **3 <R>**
prompt	`Face 1,vertex 4` and <RETURN>, i.e. end of face 1
prompt	`Face 2, vertex 1` and enter: **1**
prompt	`Face 2, vertex 2` and enter: **3**
prompt	`Face 2, vertex 3` and enter: **4**
prompt	`Face 2, vertex 4` and <RETURN>, i.e. end of face 2
prompt	`Face 3, vertex 1` and enter: **1**
prompt	`Face 3, vertex 2` and enter: **4**
prompt	`Face 3, vertex 3` and enter: **5**
prompt	`Face 3, vertex 4` and <RETURN>, i.e. end of face 3
prompt	`Face 4, vertex 1` and enter: **1**
prompt	`Face 4, vertex 2` and enter: **5**
prompt	`Face 4, vertex 3` and enter: **6**
prompt	`Face 4, vertex 4` and <RETURN>, i.e. end of face 4
prompt	`Face 5, vertex 1` and enter: **1**
prompt	`Face 5, vertex 2` and enter: **6**
prompt	`Face 5, vertex 3` and enter: **2**
prompt	`Face 5, vertex 4` and <RETURN>, i.e. end of face 5
prompt	`Face 6, vertex 1` and <RETURN> to end command.

13 Menu bar with View-Hide to display the end of the prism with a PFACE surface – fig(d).

14 Make layer F4 current and freeze layer F3.

15 Repeat the PFACE command line entry and:

prompt	`Specify location for vertex 1` and enter: **0,0 <R>**
prompt	`Specify location for vertex 2` and pick pt2
prompt	`Specify location for vertex 3` and pick pt3
prompt	`Specify location for vertex 4` and pick pt4
prompt	`Specify location for vertex 5` and pick pt5
prompt	`Specify location for vertex 6` and pick pt6
prompt	`Specify location for vertex 7` and <RETURN>
prompt	`Face 1, vertex 1, Enter a vertex number` and enter: **–1 <R>**
prompt	`Face 1, vertex 2` and enter: **2 <R>**
prompt	`Face 1, vertex 3` and enter: **–3 <R>**
prompt	`Face 1, vertex 4` and <RETURN>
prompt	`Face 2, vertex 1` and enter: **–1**
prompt	`Face 2, vertex 2` and enter: **3**

prompt	Face 2, vertex 3 and enter: **−4**
prompt	Face 2, vertex 4 and <RETURN>
prompt	Face 3, vertex 1 and enter: **−1**
prompt	Face 3, vertex 2 and enter: **4**
prompt	Face 3, vertex 3 and enter: **−5**
prompt	Face 3, vertex 4 and <RETURN>
prompt	Face 4, vertex 1 and enter: **−1**
prompt	Face 4, vertex 2 and enter: **5**
prompt	Face 4, vertex 3 and enter: **−6**
prompt	Face 4, vertex 4 and <RETURN>
prompt	Face 5, vertex 1 and enter: **−1**
prompt	Face 5, vertex 2 and enter: **6**
prompt	Face 5, vertex 3 and enter: **−2**
prompt	Face 5, vertex 4 and <RETURN>
prompt	Face 6, vertex 1 and <RETURN>.

16 Now View-Hide to display the model with the hidden edge option of the PFACE command.

17 The negative (−1, etc.) entry for the face/vertex prompt is the invisible edge option. Think this out for the vertices being entered.

18 Save if required, but this model will not be used again.

Summary

1 The 3DFACE and PFACE commands allow **surface models** to be created by drawing 'skins' over wire-frame models.

2 The HIDE command allows surface models to be displayed with hidden line removal.

3 The 3DFACE command can only be used with three or four sided 'shapes' although continuous faces can be created.

4 The PFACE command can be used with multi-sided figures.

5 Both commands have an invisible edge option.

6 The commands can be activated:
 a) 3DFACE: command line, menu bar or icon
 b) PFACE: command line only.

7 Using separate coloured layers for different faces allows models to be displayed in colour using the SHADE command.

8 If the HIDE command has been used, the original model can be restored with:
 a) View-Regen: in the active viewport
 b) View-Regenall for all viewports.

9 If the SHADE command has been used then REGEN will not restore the original model. The menu bar sequence View-Shade-2D Wireframe must be selected. This must be applied in all the viewports which used the SHADE command.

Assignment

One of MACFARAMUS's structures was a temple created from a series of hexagonal prisms, these prisms having two different sloped surfaces. It is one of these columns which you have to create as a 3DFACED surface model.

Activity 10: Hexagonal column of MACFARAMUS

1 Start with your MV3DSTD template/drawing file.

2 Layer MODEL current and UCS BASE.

3 Create a wire-frame model of the hexagonal prism using the sizes given and zoom-centre about 0,0,75 at 200 magnification.

4 Make three new coloured layers:
   a) verticals: blue
   b) slopes: green and magenta.

5 Use the 3DFACE command with the coloured layers to convert the wire-frame model into a surface model.

6 The base has not been surfaced – up to you?

7 Freeze layer MODEL, then hide and shade.

8 Save as always.

9 Try the 3D Orbit command in the 3D viewport and the unfaced base will be very obvious.

Chapter 15

3DMESH

A 3D mesh (or more correctly, a 3D polygon mesh) consists of a series of 3D faces in a rectangular array pattern. This mesh matrix is defined by **M** × **N vertices** and:
a) M is the mesh size in the x direction
b) N is the mesh size in the y direction
c) the user enters the x,y,z coordinates of every vertex in the matrix.

3D mesh example

1 Open your MV3DSTD template file with layer MODEL, UCS BASE and the lower right viewport active.

2 Display the Surfaces toolbar and refer to Fig. 15.1.

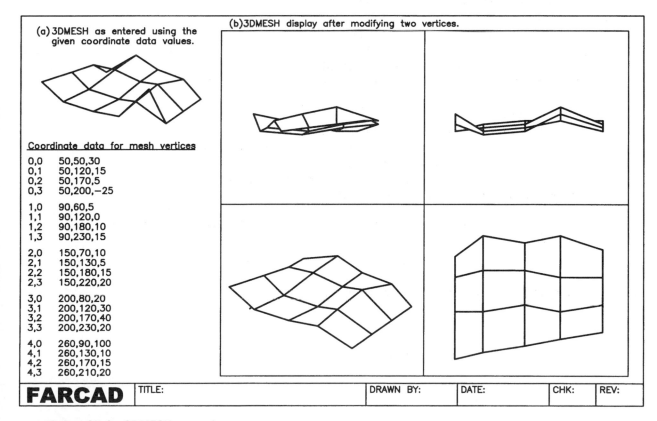

(a) 3DMESH as entered using the given coordinate data values.

(b) 3DMESH display after modifying two vertices.

Coordinate data for mesh vertices

0,0	50,50,30
0,1	50,120,15
0,2	50,170,5
0,3	50,200,−25
1,0	90,60,5
1,1	90,120,0
1,2	90,180,10
1,3	90,230,15
2,0	150,70,10
2,1	150,130,5
2,2	150,180,15
2,3	150,220,20
3,0	200,80,20
3,1	200,120,30
3,2	200,170,40
3,3	200,230,20
4,0	260,90,100
4,1	260,130,10
4,2	260,170,15
4,3	260,210,20

FARCAD | TITLE: | DRAWN BY: | DATE: | CHK: | REV:

Figure 15.1 3DMESH example.

3   Zoom-centre about the point 150,150,25 at 250 magnification.

4   Select the 3DMESH icon from the Surfaces toolbar and:
    prompt   `Enter size of mesh in M direction` and enter: **5 <R>**
    prompt   `Enter size of mesh in N direction` and enter: **4 <R>**
    prompt   `Specify location for vertex (0,0)` and enter: **50,50,30 <R>**
    prompt   `Specify location for vertex (0,1)` and enter: **50,120,15 <R>**
    prompt   `Specify location for vertex (0,2)` and:
    respond refer to Fig. 15.1 and enter the required coordinates in response to the vertex prompts.

5   When the last vertex coordinate is entered – Vertex (4,3), the 3D mesh will be displayed as fig(a).

6   Two of the vertices have been entered wrongly, these being:
    vertex (0,3): entered value of (50,200,–25)
    vertex (4,0): entered value of (260,90,100).

7   Menu bar with **Modify-Object-Polyline** and:
    prompt   `Select polyline`
    respond **pick any point on the mesh**
    prompt   `Enter an option [Edit vertex/Smooth surface/..`
    enter   **E <R>** – the edit vertex option
    prompt   `Current vertex (0,0)` and a small X displayed at vertex (0,0)
    and   `Enter an option [Next/Previous/Left/Right/..`
    enter   **N <R>** until current vertex is (0,3) and:
    prompt   `Enter an option [Next/Previous/..`
    enter   **M <R>** – the move vertex option
    prompt   `Specify new location for marked vertex`
    enter   **50,50,5 <R>** – absolute coordinate entry
    prompt   `Current vertex (0,3) Enter an option [Next/Previous..`
    enter   **N <R>** until current vertex is (4,0) and:
    prompt   `Enter an option [Next/Previous/..`
    enter   **M <R>**
    prompt   `Specify new location for marked vertex`
    enter   **@0,0,-95 <R>** – relative coordinate entry
    prompt   `Current vertex (4,0) Enter an option [Next/Previous/..`
    enter   **X <R>** – to exit edit vertex options
    prompt   `Enter an option [Edit vertex/Smooth surface/..`
    and   **right-click/enter** – to exit command.

8   The mesh will be displayed as fig(b), with the two wrong vertices have been 'repositioned'.

9   Use the hide command.

10 Save if required, as this exercise is now complete.

Notes.

1. This example has been a brief introduction to the 3DMESH command.
2. The command requires the user to enter all vertex values as coordinates and is therefore very tedious to use. You can also reference existing objects if these are displayed.
3. The Modify-Polyline command can be used with 3D meshes. This is the same as the 2D modify-polyline command.
4. Selecting MESH from the 3D Objects dialogue box, will allow the user to create a 2D mesh by:
   a) specifying the four corners of the mesh
   b) entering the M and N sizes.
5. The 3D MESH values M and N can be between 2 and 256.
6. A 3D MESH is a single object.
7. The command can be activated:
   a) by icon selection from the Surfaces toolbar
   b) from the menu bar with Draw-Surfaces
   c) by entering 3DMESH at the command line.

Chapter 16

Ruled surface

A ruled surface is a polygon mesh created between two defined boundaries selected by the user. The objects which can be used to define the boundaries are lines, arcs, circles, points and 2D/3D polylines. The surface created is a 'onc-way' mesh of straight lines drawn between the two selected boundaries. The number of straight line meshes is controlled by the system variable **SURFTAB1** which has an initial value of 6.

The ruled surface effect will be demonstrated by worked examples, the first being in 2D to allow the user to become familiar with the basic terminology.

Example 1

1 Begin a new 2D drawing from scratch (metric) and create two layers, MOD (red) and RULSUR (blue). Refer to Fig. 16.1.

2 Display the Draw, Modify and Surfaces toolbars.

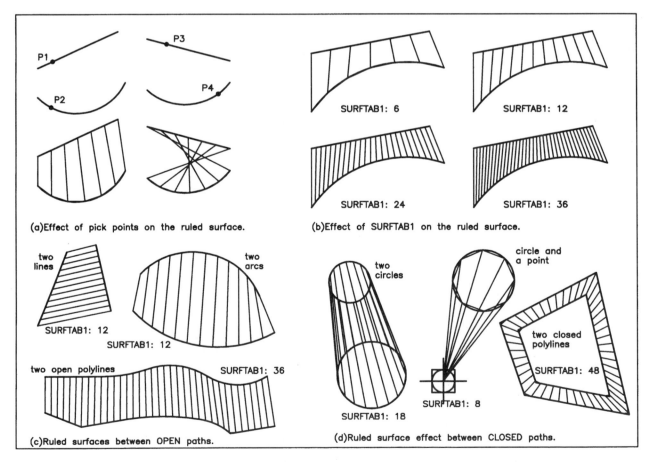

Figure 16.1 Ruled surface example 1 – usage and basic terminology.

Pick points effect

1 With layer MOD current, draw two lines and two three point arcs as fig(a) then make layer RULSUR current.

2 Select the RULED SURFACE icon from the Surfaces toolbar and
prompt   Select first defining curve
respond   **pick a point P1 on the first line**
prompt   Select second defining curve
respond   **pick a point P2 on the first arc**
and   a blue ruled surface is drawn between the two objects.

3 Menu bar with Draw-Surfaces-Ruled Surface and:
  a) first defining curve prompt: pick point P3 on second line
  b) second defining curve prompt: pick point P4 on second arc
  c) ruled surface drawn between the line and arc.

4 The ruled surface drawn between selected objects is dependent on the pick point positions.

Effect of the SURFTAB1 system variable

1 With layer MOD current draw a line and three point arc as fig(b).

2 Copy the line and arc to three other places on screen.

3 Make layer RULSUR current.

4 At the command line enter **SURFTAB1 <R>** and:
prompt   Enter new value for SURFTAB1<?>
enter   **6 <R>**.

5 At the command line enter **RULESURF <R>** and:
prompt   Select first defining curve
respond   **pick a point on the first line**
prompt   Select second defining curve
respond   **pick a point on the first arc**.

6 By entering SURFTAB1 at the command line, enter new values of 12, 24 and 36 and add a ruled surface between the other lines and arcs.

7 The system variable **SURFTAB1** controls the display of the ruled surface effect, i.e. the number of 'strips' added between the selected boundaries. The default value is 6. The value of SURFTAB1 to be used is dependent on the 'size' of the defining curves.

Open paths

1 An open path is defined as a line, arc or open polyline.

2 With layer MOD current draw some open paths as fig(c).

3 Using the ruled surface command and with SURTFAB1 set to your own value, add ruled surfaces between the drawn open paths.

Closed paths

1 A closed path is defined as a circle, point or closed polyline.

2 Draw some closed paths as fig(d) and add ruled surfaces between them.

Note

1 A ruled surface can only be drawn:
   a) between TWO OPEN paths
   b) between TWO CLOSED paths.

2 A ruled surface **cannot** be created between an open and a closed path. If a line and a circle are selected as the defining curves, the following message will be displayed:

   Cannot mix closed and open paths

3 This first exercise is now complete and need not be saved.

Example 2

1 Open your MV3DSTD template file and refer to Fig. 16.2. Note that I have only displayed the 3D viewport.

2 With layer MODEL current and UCS BASE, zoom centre about the 70,40,25 at 150 magnification in all viewports, then create the model base from lines and trimmed circles using the sizes given in fig(a). Use the (0,0) start point.

3 Make a new layer RULSRF, colour blue and current.

4 Set the SURFTAB1 system variable to 18.

5 Using the ruled surface icon (three times) from the Surfaces toolbar, select the following defining curves:
   a) lines 1 and 2
   b) arcs a and b
   c) lines v and w
   d) effect as fig(b).

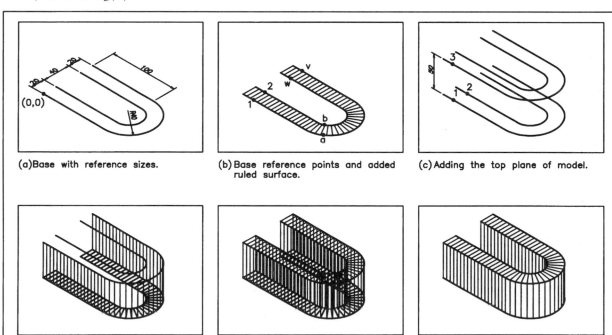

(a) Base with reference sizes.

(b) Base reference points and added ruled surface.

(c) Adding the top plane of model.

(d) Ruled surfaces added to the base on layer R1 and the outside of model on layer R2.

(e) Complete ruled surface model displayed without hide.

(f) Complete ruled surface model displayed with hide effect.

FARCAD | TITLE: | DRAWN BY: | DATE: | CHK: | REV:

Figure 16.2 Ruled surface example 2.

6 Erase the ruled surface and create the top surface of the model by copying the base objects:
   a) from the point 0,0,0
   b) by @0,0,50 – fig(c).

7 With layer RULSRF still current, select the ruled surface icon and select the following defining curves as fig(c):
   a) lines 1 and 2 – ruled surface added
   b) lines 3 and 1 – no ruled surface added and following message displayed:
   Object not usable to define ruled surface – why?
   c) Explanation: when the second set of defined curves were being selected:
      i) point 3 was picked satisfactorily
      ii) point 1 could not be picked – you were picking the previous ruled surface added between lines 1 and 2
   d) cancel the ruled surface command (ESC) and erase the added ruled surface.

8 Make the following four new layers:
   R1 – red; R2 – blue; R3 – green; R4 – magenta.

9 *a*) Make layer R1 current
   b) Add a ruled surface to the base of the model (three needed).

10 *a*) Make layer R2 current
   b) Freeze layer R1
   c) Add a ruled surface to the three 'outside' vertical planes of the model
   d) Thaw layer R1 – fig(d).

11 a) Make layer R3 current
   b) Freeze layers R1 and R2
   c) Rule surface the top three defining curves of the model.

12 a) Make layer R4 current and freeze layer R3
   b) Add a ruled surface to the three 'inside' vertical planes.

13 a) Thaw layers R1, R2 and R3
   b) Model displayed a fig(e).

14 Menu bar with **View-Hide** to give fig(f).

15 Menu bar with **View-Shade-Flat Shaded** – impressive?

16 Return the model to wire-frame then save as **MODR2000\RSRF1**, it may be used in a later exercise.

17 *Note.*
   When the ruled surface command is being used with adjacent surfaces, it is recommended that:
   a) a layer be made for each ruled surface to be added
   b) once a ruled surface has been added, that layer should be frozen before the next surface is added
   c) the new surface layers should be coloured for effect.

18 *Task.*
   a) Try the 3D orbit with the 3D viewport active
   b) The two 'ends' of the model are 'open'. A 3DFACE could be added to these ends?
   c) The original model was created from lines and circles/arcs. The base could have been created from a single polyline and then offset. Try this and add a ruled surface and note that only one set of defining curves is required. What about SURFTAB1?

Example 3

This example will investigate how a ruled surface can be added to a surface which has a circular/slotted hole in it. The example will be in 2D, but the procedure is identical for a 3D model.

1 Begin a new 2D metric drawing from scratch and refer to Fig. 16.3.

2 Make two new layers, MOD red (current) and RULSRF blue.

3 Set SURFTAB1 to 24.

4 Using the LINE icon draw a square of side 60 with a 15 radius circle at the square 'centre' – snap on helps.

5 Using the Ruled Surface icon, pick any line of the square and the circle as the defining curves. No ruled surface can be added because of the open/closed path effect – fig(a).

6 With the Polyline icon, draw a 60 sided square from 1-2-3-4-<R> as fig(b) and draw the 15 radius circle. Add a ruled surface and the open/closed path message is displayed and no ruled surface is added.

7 Draw a closed polyline square using the points 1-2-3-4-c in the order given in fig(c). Draw the circle. With the ruled surface icon pick the defining curves indicated and the a ruled surface is added, but not as expected.

8 Draw a 60 sided square as a closed polyline with points 1-2-3-4-c in the order given in fig(d). Draw the circle then add a ruled surface picking the defining curves indicated. The added ruled surface is not quite 'correct' at the circle.

9 Erase the ruled surface effect, set SURFTAB1 to 48 and repeat the ruled surface command – fig(e). Set SURFTAB1 back to 24.

10 *Note*.
    a) When a ruled surface is added between two defined curves, the surface 'begins at the defined curve start points'. It is thus essential that the defined curves are:
    1. **DRAWN IN THE SAME DIRECTION**
    2. **DRAWN FROM THE SAME 'RELATIVE' START POINT**
    b) Circular holes require to be drawn as two closed polyarcs.

11 *Task*.
    Using the information given in step 10, add ruled surfaces to the following models displayed in Fig. 16.3:
    a) fig(p): square drawn as a closed polyline and circle drawn as two closed polyarcs. Note start points
    b) fig(q): square drawn as a closed polyline and circle drawn as two closed polyarcs. Note that the start points differ from those in fig(p)
    c) fig(r): both the outer and inner perimeters are drawn as closed polylines/polyarcs. Note the start points
    d) fig(s): the outer perimeter is drawn as four lines, and the inner as two arcs and two lines.

12 When this task is complete, this exercise is finished. Save?

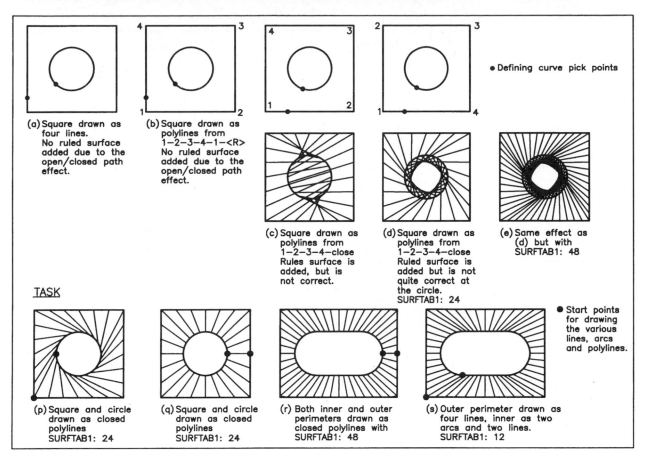

Figure 16.3 Ruled surface example 3.

Example 4

A ruled surface is one of the most effective surface modelling techniques, and I have included another 3D model to demonstrate how it is used. The procedure when adding a ruled surface is basically the same with all models, this being:

a) create the 3D wire-frame model

b) make new coloured layers for the surfaces to be added

c) use the ruled surface command with layers current as required.

1 Open your MV3DSTD template file and refer to Fig. 16.4.

2 Make four new layers, R1 red, R2 blue, R3 green and R4 magenta.

3 With layer MODEL current, restore UCS FRONT and make the lower left (3D) viewport active.

4 Select the POLYLINE icon and draw:

Start point	0,0
Next point	@0,100
Next point	Arc option, and enter A <R>
Arc endpt	@50,50 then right-click/enter.

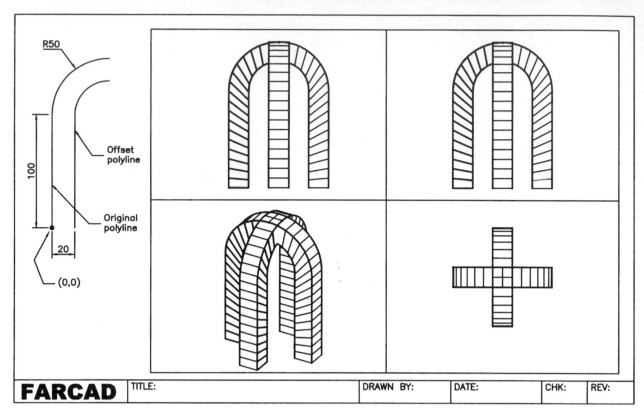

Figure 16.4

5 Centre each viewport about the point 50,75,0 at 175 magnification.

6 Offset the polyline by 20 'inwards'.

7 Copy the two polylines from: 0,0, by: @0,0,–20.

8 Change the viewpoint in the lower left viewport with the rotate option and angles:
   first prompt   300
   second prompt   30.

9 Set SURFTAB1 to 18.

10 Making each layer R1-R4 current, add a ruled surface to each 'side' of the model, remembering to freeze layers as in the second example.

11 Restore UCS BASE and polar array the complete model (crossing selection) using:
   a) centre point: 50,10
   b) number of items: 4
   c) angle: 360 with rotation.

12 Hide, shade, etc. – impressive result?

13 Save the complete model as **MODR2000\ARCHES** for future recall.

14 *Note*.
   The top 'square' of the arrayed arches – comments?

Summary

1 A ruled surface can be added between lines, circles, arcs, points and polylines.

2 The command can be activated in icon form, from the menu bar or by keyboard entry.

3 The command can be used in 2D or 3D.

4 A ruled surface **CAN ONLY** be added between:
   a) two open paths e.g. lines, arcs, polylines (not closed)
   b) two closed paths e.g. circles, points, closed polylines.

5 With closed paths, the correct effect can only be obtained if:
   a) the paths are drawn in the same direction
   b) the paths start at the 'same relative point'.

6 The system variable SURFTAB1 controls the number of ruled surface 'strips' added between the two defining curves. The default is 6.

Assignment

Activity 11: Ornamental flower bed of MACFARAMUS

MACFARAMUS designed some interesting artefacts for the famous lost city of CADOPOLIS. One of his least known creations has the 'hanging gardens' for which he made several unusual ornamental flower beds. It is this which you have to create as a 3D ruled surface model, the procedure being the same as in the examples:

1 Open your MV3DSTD template file.

2 Create the wire-frame model from lines and trimmed circles using the sizes given with the (0,0) start point. The vertical R50 arch requires the UCS RIGHT to be current and the R30 side curve requires UCS FRONT. Use your discretion for any sizes omitted.

3 With UCS BASE, zoom centre about 90,50,50 at 200 mag.

4 Make four coloured layers.

5 Add ruled surfaces to the 'four sides' of the model using the four new layers correctly. Use a SURFTAB1 value of 18 for most of the defining curves, but 6 for the 'side' line/arc selection.

6 Hide, shade, 3D orbit, save.

7 *Note.* I suggest that you enter paper space and zoom-window the lower left viewport then return to model space. This will make creating the wire-frame model and selecting the defining curves easier. When complete, paper space and zoom-previous, then model space.

Chapter 17

Tabulated surface

A tabulated surface is a parallel polygon mesh created along a path, the user defining:
a) the **path curve** – the profile of the final model
b) the **direction vector** – the 'depth' of the profile.

The path curve can be created from lines, arcs, circles, ellipses, splines or 2D/3D polylines, The direction vector **MUST** be a line or an open 2D/3D polyline. The system variable SURFTAB1 determines the 'appearance' of curved tabulated surfaces.

Example

1   Open your MV3DSTD template file with layer MODEL current, lower left viewport active and UCS BASE. Display toolbars to suit.

2   Refer to Fig. 17.1 and draw two lines:
a) start point: 0,0,0 next point: @0,0,120
b) start point: 0,0,0 next point: @−150,0,0.

Note.
Only the 3D viewport is displayed in Fig. 17.1.

3   Restore the appropriate UCS and draw two closed polylines with the following coordinate data:

UCS BASE		*UCS RIGHT*	
Start	70,50,0	*Start*	20,20,−50
Next	@50,0	*Next*	@100,0
Next	@0,20	*Next*	@0,30
Next	@−20,0	*Next*	@−40,0
Next	@0,30	*Next*	@0,80
Next	@50,0	*Next*	@−20,0
Next	@0,20	*Next*	@0,−80
Next	@−80,0	*Next*	@−40,0
Next	close	*Next*	close.

4   Restore UCS BASE and zoom centre about −35,70,60 at 250 mag.

5   Select the TABULATED SURFACE icon from the Surfaces toolbar and:
prompt   Select object for path curve
respond   **pick polyline 1 as fig(a)**
prompt   Select object for direction vector
respond   **pick line 1 at the end indicated**
and   a tabulated surface is added to the path curve.

6   The added tabulated surface has a 'depth' equal to the length of the direction vector.

7   Menu bar with Draw-Surfaces-Tabulated Surface and:
prompt   Select object for path curve
respond   **pick polyline 2 as fig(a)**
prompt   Select object for direction vector
respond   **pick line 2 at the end indicated**.

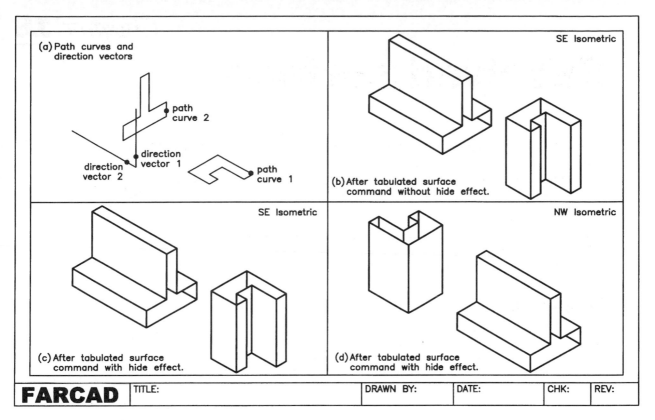

Figure 17.1 Tabulated surface example.

8 Figure 17.1 displays the results of the tabulated surface commands:
  a) reference information
  b) tabulated surfaces without hide
  c) tabulated surfaces with hide
  d) at a NW Isometric viewpoint with hide.

9 *Task*.
  a) Erase the tabulated surfaces to display the original path curves
  b) Repeat the tabulated surface commands, but pick the direction vector lines at the 'opposite ends' from the exercise. The path curve will be 'extruded' in the opposite sense.

Summary

1 A tabulated surface is a parallel polygon mesh.

2 The command requires:
  a) a path curve – a single object
  b) a direction vector – generally a line.

3 The command can be used in 2D or 3D.

4 The final surface orientation is dependent on the direction vector 'pick point'.

5 SURFTAB1 determines the surface appearance with curved objects.

6 The command can be activated:
  a) in icon form from the Surfaces toolbar
  b) from the menu bar with Draw-Surfaces
  c) by entering **TABSURF <R>** at the command line.

Chapter 18

Revolved surface

A revolved surface is a polygon mesh generated by rotating a path curve (profile) about an axis, the user selecting:
a) the **path curve** – a single object e.g. a line, arc, circle or 2D/3D polyline
b) the **axis of revolution** – generally a line, but can be an open or closed polyline.

The generated mesh is controlled by two system variables:
a) SURFTAB1: controls the mesh in the direction of the revolution
b) SURFTAB2: defines any curved elements in the profile
c) the default value for both variables is 6.

Example 1

1 Open the MV3DSTD template file, layer MODEL current, UCS BASE and refer to Fig. 18.1

2 Make the lower right viewport active and display toolbars.

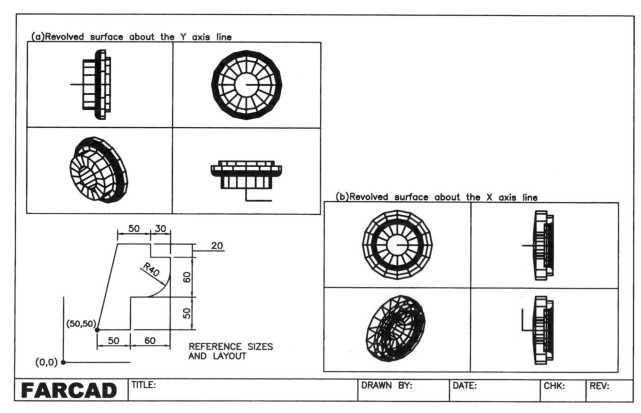

Figure 18.1 Revolved surface example 1.

3 Draw two lines:
   a) *start*: 0,0   *next*: @100,0
   b) *start*: 0,0   *next*: @0,100.

4 Set SURFTAB1 to 18 and SURFTAB2 to 6 – command line entry.

5 Using the polyline icon from the Draw toolbar, create a **CLOSED** polyline shape using the reference sizes given in Fig. 18.1. The start point is to be 50,50.

   Note.
   The actual polyline shape is not that important. Use your discretion/own design, but try and keep the overall reference sizes given.

6 Select the REVOLVED SURFACE icon from the Surfaces toolbar and:
   prompt   `Select object to revolve`
   respond   **pick any point on the polyline**
   prompt   `Select object that defines the axis of revolution`
   respond   **pick the Y axis line**
   prompt   `Specify start angle<0>` and enter: **0 <R>**
   prompt   `Specify included angle (+ = ccw, - = cw)<Full circle>`
   enter   **360 <R>**.

7 A revolved surface model will be displayed in each viewport.

8 In all viewport, zoom centre about 0,120,0 at 350 magnification.

9 Hide each viewport – fig(a).

10 Erase the revolved surface (regen needed?) to display the original polyline shape and from the menu bar select **Draw-Surfaces-Revolved Surface** and:
   a) object to revolve: pick the polyline shape
   b) object to define axis of revolution: pick the X axis line
   c) start angle: 0
   d) included angle: 360.

11 Zoom centre about 100,0,0 at 400 magnification.

12 Hide the viewports – fig(b).

13 Save if required.

Example 2

1 Open the MV3DSTD template file, layer MODEL, UCS BASE with the the lower right viewport active and refer to Fig. 18.2.

2 Draw a line from 0,0 to @0,250.

3 With the polyline icon, draw an **OPEN** polyline shape using the sizes in fig(a) as a reference. The start point is to be (0,50) but the final polyline shape is at your discretion – it is your wine glass design.

4 Set SURFTAB1 to 18 and SURFTAB2 to 6.

5 At the command line enter **REVSURF <R>** and:
   a) object to revolve: pick the polyline shape
   b) object to define axis of revolution: pick the line
   c) start angle: enter 0
   d) included angle: enter 270.

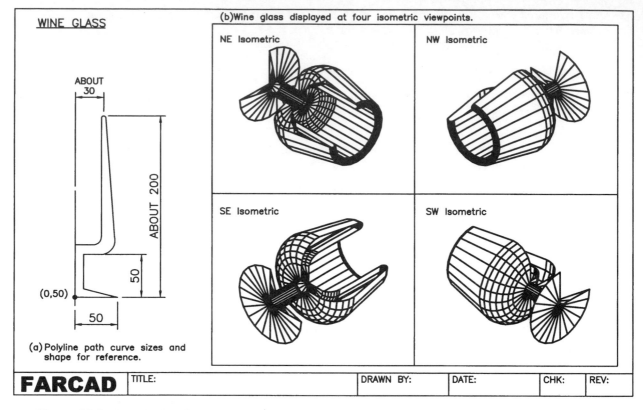

Figure 18.2 Revolved surface example – 2.

6 Set the following 3D viewpoints in the named viewports:
Top left: NE Isometric   Top right: NW Isometric
Lower left: SE Isometric   Lower right: SW Isometric.

7 Zoom centre about 0,120,0 at 200 magnification.

8 Hide the viewports – fig(b).

9 Save if required.

Summary

1 The revolved surface command can be used to produce very complex surface models from relatively simple profiles.

2 The resultant polygon mesh is controlled by the two system variables SURFTAB1 and SURFTAB2 and:
SURFTAB1: controls the mesh in the direction of rotation
SURFTAB2: controls the display of curved elements in the profile.

3 The start angle can vary between 0 and 360. A start angle of 0 means that that the surface is to begin on the current drawing plane. This is generally what is required.

4 The included angle allows the user to define the angle the path curve is to be revolved through. The 360 default value gives a complete revolution, but 'cut-away' models can be obtained with angles less than 360.

5 The direction of the revolved surface is controlled by the sign of the included angle and:
   a) +ve for anti-clockwise revolved surfaces
   b) −ve for a clockwise revolution.

6 The command can be activated by icon, from the menu bar or by command line entry.

Assignment

MACFARAMUS designed a garden furniture arrangement for the gardens in CADOPOLIS. This garden furniture set complemented the ornamental flower bed created as a ruled surface. You need to create two profiles (path curves) and revolve them about two different axes. Adding colour to the revolved surfaces greatly enhances the model appearance with shading and rendering.

Activity 12: Garden furniture set of MACFARAMUS

1 Use your MV3DSTD template file.

2 Make the top right viewport active and restore UCS FRONT.

3 Draw two polyline profiles using the reference data given. Use your discretion for sizes not given, or design your own table and chair. Also draw two vertical lines for the axes of revolution.

4 Set SURFTAB1 to 18 and SURFTAB2 to 6.

5 Revolve the profiles about vertical lines.

6 Change the colour of the revolved chair to green and the table to blue.

7 Restore UCS BASE and make the lower left viewport active.

8 Polar array the chair for five items about the point (0,0) with rotation.

9 Hide the viewports, then REGENALL and save as MODR2000\GARDEN.

10 Try the following:
   a) Flat shade the model in the 3D viewport
   b) Paper space and zoom in on the 3D viewport then model space
   c) Using the 3D orbit command, interactively rotate the model – quite impressive?
   d) Exit the 3D orbit command then select the undo icon to restore the original 3D view.
   e) make sure this model has been saved.

Chapter 19

Edge surface

An edge surface is a 3D polygon mesh stretched between four **touching** edges. The edges can be combinations of lines, arcs, polylines or splines but **must form a closed loop**.

The edge surface mesh is controlled by the system variables:
a) SURFTAB1: the M facets in the direction of the first edge selected
b) SURFTAB2: the N facets in the direction of the edges adjacent to the first selected edge.

Three examples will be used to demonstrate the command, the first being in 2D, the second to allow us to use the editing features of a polygon mesh, and the third will use splines as the four touching edges.

Example 1 – 2D edge surfaces

1 Open any 2D drawing and make two layers, EDGE colour red and MESH colour blue – refer to Fig. 19.1. Display toolbars as needed.

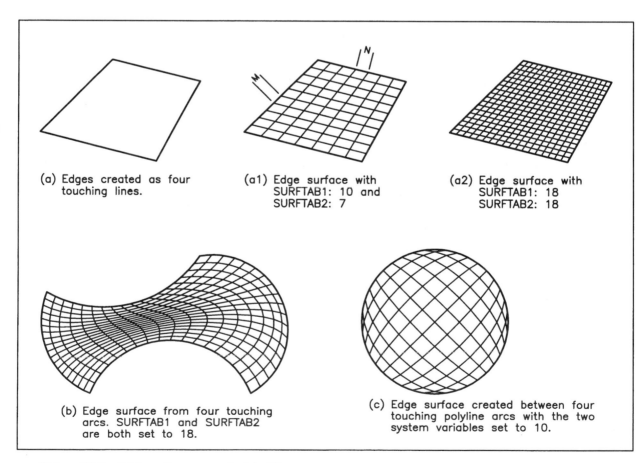

(a) Edges created as four touching lines.

(a1) Edge surface with SURFTAB1: 10 and SURFTAB2: 7

(a2) Edge surface with SURFTAB1: 18 SURFTAB2: 18

(b) Edge surface from four touching arcs. SURFTAB1 and SURFTAB2 are both set to 18.

(c) Edge surface created between four touching polyline arcs with the two system variables set to 10.

Figure 19.1 Edge surface example 1 in 2D.

2 With layer EDGE current, create the following touching edges:
   a) four lines – fig(a)
   b) four three point arcs – fig(b)
   c) four single 90° polyline arcs (use CE option) – fig(c).

3 Set SURFTAB1 to 10 and SURFTAB2 to 7

4 Select the EDGE SURFACE icon from the Surfaces toolbar and:
   prompt   Select object 1 for surface edge and pick a line
   prompt   Select object 2 for surface edge and pick another line
   prompt   Select object 3 for surface edge and pick a third line
   prompt   Select object 4 for surface edge and pick the fourth line.

5 A 10 × 7 surface mesh is stretched between the four touching lines as fig(a1).

6 *a*) Erase the added edge surface
   b) Set SURFTAB1 and SURFTAB2 to 18
   c) Menu bar with **Draw-Surfaces-Edge Surface** and pick the four touching lines in any order
   d) The edge surface mesh is displayed as fig(a2).

7 At the command line enter **EDGESURF <R>** and pick the four arcs to display the edge surface mesh as fig(b).

8 Set both SURFTAB1 and SURFTAB2 to 10 and add an edge surface mesh between to four touching polyarcs – fig(c). The result of this mesh is quite interesting?

9 This completes the first exercise and it need not be saved.

Example 2 – a 3D edge surface mesh

1 Open your MV3DSTD template file and refer to Fig. 19.2.

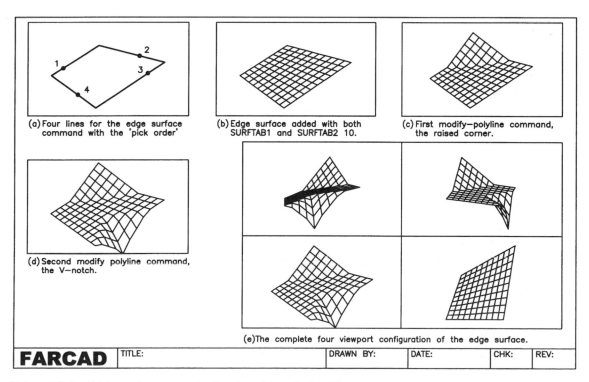

Figure 19.2   Edge surface example 2 – 3D with edited vertices.

2   With layer MODEL, UCS BASE and the lower left viewport active, use the LINE icon
    and draw:
    Start point   0,0,0   *Next*   150,0,–20   *Next point*   180,200,30
    Next   40,120,50   *Next*   close.

3   The four lines will be displayed as fig(a).

4   Centre each viewport about the point 90,100,25 at 250 mag.

5   Make a new layer, MESH colour blue and current.

6   Set both SURFTAB1 and SURFTAB2 to 10.

7   Using the edge surface icon, pick the four lines in the order 1-2-3-4 as fig(a).

8   An edge surface mesh will be stretched between the four lines as fig(b).

9   In paper space, zoom the 3D viewport and return to model space.

10 Menu bar with **Modify-Polyline** and:
    prompt   `Select polyline`
    respond   **pick any point on mesh**
    prompt   `Enter an option [Edit vertex/Smooth surface/..`
    enter   **E <R>** – the edit vertex option
    prompt   `Current vertex (0,0). Enter an option [Next/Previous/..`
    and   an X is displayed at the 0,0 vertex – leftmost?
    enter   **U <R>** until X is at vertex (10,0) and:
    prompt   `Current vertex (10,0). Enter an option [Next/Previous/..`
    enter   **M <R>** – the move option
    prompt   `Specify new location for marked vertex`
    enter   **@0,0,60 <R>**
    and   **DO NOT EXIT COMMAND**.

11 We now want to alter other vertices of the mesh to create a raised effect. This will be
    achieved by:
    a) moving the X to the required vertices
    b) using the M option
    c) entering the required relative vertex coordinates.

12 Use the N/D/L/R/U options and enter the following new locations for the named vertices:
relative movement	*vertices*				
@0,0,50	9,0	10,1			
@0,0,40	8,0	9,1	10,2		
@0,0,30	7,0	8,1	9,2	10,3	
@0,0,20	6,0	7,1	8,2	9,3	10,4
@0,0,10	5,0	6,1	7,2	8,3	9,4	10,5.

13 When all the new vertex locations have been entered:
    a) enter X <R> to exit the edit vertex option
    b) then enter X <R> to end the command.

14 The mesh will be displayed with a 'raised corner' as fig(c).

15 At the command line enter **PEDIT <R>** then:
    a) pick any point on the mesh
    b) enter E <R> for the edit vertex option
    c) use the N/U/R/L/D entries to move the X to the following named vertices and with
        the M (move option), enter the following new locations:

relative movement	vertices					
@0,0,−80	4,10					
@0,0,−50	3,10	4,9	5,10			
@0,0,−30	2,10	3,9	4,8	5,9	6,10	
@0,0,−10	1,10	2,9	3,8	4,7	5,8	6,9	7,10

d) exit the vertex option with X <R>

e) exit the polyline edit command with X <R>.

16　These vertex modifications have produced a v-type notch in the mesh as fig(d).

17　Paper space and zoom-previous then model space. Freeze the MODEL layer.

18　The complete four viewport configuration of the edge surface mesh is displayed in fig(e).

19　The exercise is now complete – save if required.

20　*Investigate*.
　　The effect of the smooth surface option (S) on the mesh.

Example 3 – an edge surface mesh created from splines

This example will demonstrate how an edge surface can be stretched between four spline curves to simulate a car body panel.

1　Open your MV3DSTD template file with layer MODEL, UCS BASE.

2　Zoom centre about the point −100,50,50 at 2225 magnification in the 3D viewport and 200 in the other three.

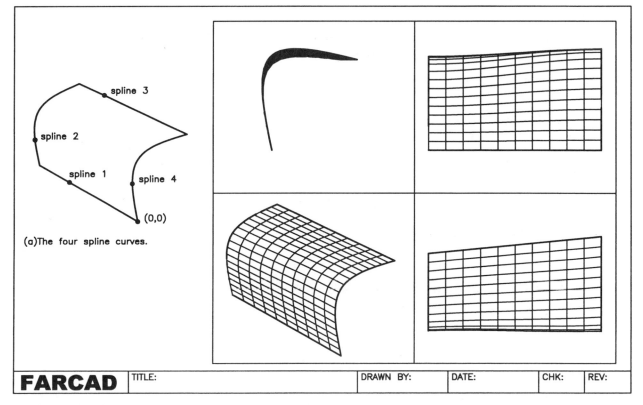

Figure 19.3　Edge surface example 3 – using splines.

3 With the lower left viewport active, refer to Fig. 19.3 and by selecting the SPLINE icon from the Draw toolbar, draw four spline curves using the following coordinate information. Use the start and end coordinates as the start and end tangents.

spline 1	*spline 2*	*spline 3*	*spline 4*
0,0,0	−200,0,0	−200,80,105	0,0,0
−200,0,0	−200,0,100	0,100,105	0,0,110
<RETURN>	−200,80,105	<RETURN>	0,100,105
	<RETURN>		<RETURN>.

4 The four spline curves will be displayed as fig(a).

5 Make a new layer, MESH colour blue and current.

6 Set both SURFTAB1 and SURFTAB2 to 18.

7 Using the Edge Surface icon, pick the four spline curves.

8 *Task*.
   a) Use the View-Hide sequence in the four viewports, and you will probably not notice any difference
   b) Flat shade the four viewports and the effect is impressive
   c) Use the 3D orbit command in the 3D viewport, and real-time rotate the shaded model. This is really impressive.

9 Save if required, as this completes the edge surface exercises.

Summary

1 An edge surface is a polygon mesh stretched between four **touching** objects – lines, arcs, splines or polylines.

2 An edge surface mesh can be edited with the polyline edit command.

3 The added surface is a **COONS** patch and is **bicubic**, i.e. one curve is defined in the mesh M direction and the other is defined in the mesh N direction.

4 The first curve (edge) selected determines the mesh M direction and the adjoining curves define the mesh N direction.

5 The mesh density is controlled by the system variables:
   a) SURFTAB1: in the mesh M direction
   b) SURFTAB2: in the mesh N direction.

6 The default value for SURFTAB1 and SURFTAB2 is 6.

7 The type of mesh stretched between the four curves is controlled by the **SURFTYPE** system variable and:
   a) SURFTYPE 5 – Quadratic B-spline
   b) SURFTYPE 6 – Cubic B-spline (default)
   c) SURFTYPE 8 – Bezier curve.

8 The SURFTYPE variable controls the appearance of all mesh curves.

Assignment

MACFARAMUS was contracted by the Emperor TOOTENCADUM to create a flat-topped hill for a future project.

The activity is very similar to the second example, i.e. an edge surface has to have several of its vertices modified to give a 'flat-top hill' effect. The process is quite tedious, but persevere with it as it is needed for another activity in a later chapter.

Activity 13: The flat-topped hill made by MACFARAMUS

1   Use your MV3DSTD template file with UCS BASE.

2   Zoom centre about 0,0,50 at 400 magnification originally.

3   With layer MODEL, create four touching polyline arcs of radius 200 with 0,0 as the arc centre point. If you are unsure of this, use the Centre, Start, End ARC option.

4   Make a new layer called HILL, colour green and current.

5   Set SURFTAB1 and SURFTAB2 to 20.

6   Add an edge surface to the four touching arcs.

7   In paper space, zoom the 3D viewport then return to model space.

8   Use the Modify-Polyline command with the Edit Vertex option to move the following vertices by **@0,0,100**:

a)			6,9	6,10	6,11			
b)		7,7	7,8	7,9	7,10	7,11	7,12	7,13
c)		8,7	8,8	8,9	8,10	8,11	8,12	8,13
d)	9,6	9,7	9,8	9,9	9,10	9,11	9,12	9,13	9,14
e)	10,6	10,7	10,8	10,9	10,10	10,11	10,12	10,13	10,14
f)	11,6	11,7	11,8	11,9	11,10	11,11	11,12	11,13	11,14
g)		12,7	12,8	12,9	12,10	12,11	12,12	12,13
h)		13,7	13,8	13,9	13,10	13,11	13,12	13,13
i)				14,9	14,10	14,11			

9   *Note.*
   a) The named vertices all lie within a circle of radius 100
   b) Use the N/U/D/L/R entries of the edit vertex option until the named vertex is displayed then use the M option with an entry of @0,0,100.

10   When all the vertices have been modified, optimize your viewpoints. I used four different VPOINT-ROTATE values and the effect with hide was quite 'pleasing'.

11   Save this drawing as **MODR2000\HILL** as it will be used with a later activity.

12   The View-Shade-Flat Shaded effect in any 3D viewport with the 3D orbit command is very interesting. You can rotate the model to 'see inside' the raised part of the edge surface.

3D polyline

A 3D polyline is a continuous object created in 3D space. It is similar to a 2D polyline, but does not possess the 2D versatility, i.e. there are no variable width or arc options available with a 3D polyline.

Example

This exercise will create a series of hill contours from splined 3D polylines, so:

1 Open your MV3DSTD template file with the lower left viewport active and UCS BASE. Refer to Fig. 20.1.

2 Make the following new layers
LEVEL1, LEVEL2, LEVEL3, LEVEL4 – all colour green
PATH1: red; PATH2: blue; PATH3: magenta.

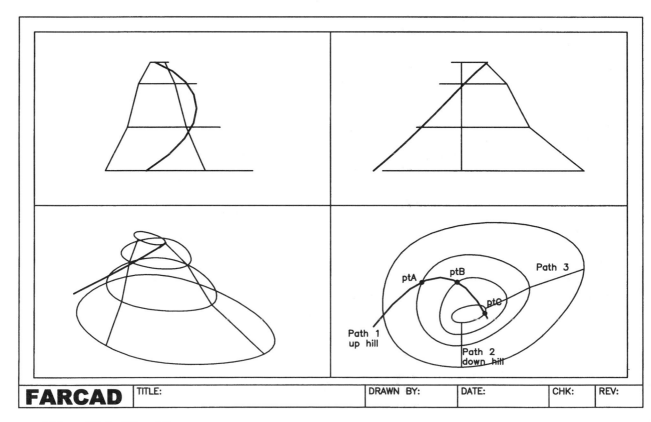

Figure 20.1 3D polyline.

3 With layer LEVEL1 current, menu bar with **Draw-3Dpolyline** and:
   prompt   Specify start point of polyline and enter: **0,50,0 <R>**
   prompt   Specify endpoint of line and enter: **50,0,0 <R>**
   prompt   Specify endpoint of line and enter: **150,0,0 <R>**
   prompt   Specify endpoint of line and enter: **220,60,0 <R>**
   prompt   Specify endpoint of line and enter: **260,140,0 <R>**
   prompt   Specify endpoint of line and enter: **170,180,0 <R>**
   prompt   Specify endpoint of line and enter: **20,160,0 <R>**
   prompt   Specify endpoint of line and enter: **c <R>**.

4 Make layer LEVEL2 current and at the command line enter **3DPOLY <R>** and:
   prompt   Specify start point of polyline and enter: **40,60,50 <R>**
   prompt   Specify endpoint of line and enter: **80,20,50 <R>**
   prompt   Specify endpoint of line and enter: **140,35,50 <R>**
   prompt   Specify endpoint of line and enter: **200,100,50 <R>**
   prompt   Specify endpoint of line and enter: **130,140,50 <R>**
   prompt   Specify endpoint of line and enter: **60,130,50 <R>**
   prompt   Specify endpoint of line and enter: **c <R>**.

5 With layers LEVEL3 and LEVEL4 current, use the 3D polyline command with the following coordinate values:

	Level 3	*Level 4*
Start point	70,70,100	85,70,125
Endpoint	80,35,100	90,50,125
Endpoint	130,45,100	130,60,125
Endpoint	170,90,100	130,80,125
Endpoint	100,120,100	close
Endpoint	close.	

6 Menu bar with **Modify-Polyline** and:
   prompt   Select polyline
   respond **pick the 3D polyline created at level 1**
   prompt   Enter an option
   enter   **S <R>** – the spline option
   prompt   Enter an option
   enter   **X <R>** – the exit command option.

7 The selected polyline will be displayed as a splined curve.

8 Use the S option of the Edit Polyline command to spline the other three 3D polylines.

9 Zoom centre about 120,90,60 at 200 magnification in all viewports.

10 With layer PATH1 current, use the 3D polyline command with the following entries:
   Start   0,50,0   – level 1 point
   Endpoint   60,130,50   – level 2 point
   Endpoint   100,120,100   – level 3 point
   Endpoint   130,60,125   – level 4 point
   Endpoint   <R>.

11 This 3D polyline is a path 'up the hill' and each entered coordinate value is a point on the level 2,3,4 contours.

12 Spline this polyline, and it does not pass through the entered coordinates.

13 *Task*.

    a) Using the ID command, identify the coordinates of points A, B and C where PATH1 'crosses' the contours. My values were:

      ptA: 55.06, 101.57, 50

      ptB: 95.42, 101.91, 100

      ptC: 127.07, 65.65, 125.

    b) With layer PATH2 current, create a 3D polyline as a 'path down the hill', this path to be drawn as a vertical line in the top viewport. It has to 'touch' each contour, and if possible, be the shortest distance (ortho on helps, as does OSNAP nearest). Do not spline this path. Find the distance from top to bottom for this path. My value was 135.51.

    c) With layer PATH3 current, create another un-splined 3D polyline which is to 'join the four level right-ends' in the top right viewport. Find the distance between each level for this path.

    My three values were:

    1-2: 82.81

    2-3: 57.69

    3-4: 38.26.

15 The exercise is now complete. Save if required.

Summary

1 A 3D polyline is a single object and can be used with x,y,z coordinate entry.

2 A 3D polyline can be edited with options of Edit vertex, Spline and Decurve.

3 3D polylines cannot be displayed with varying width or with arc segments.

4 The command is activated from the menu bar or by command line entry.

Chapter 21

3D objects

AutoCAD has nine predefined 3D objects, these being box, pyramid, wedge, dome, sphere, cone (and cylinder), torus, dish and mesh. They are considered as 'meshes' but can be displayed with hide, shade and render.

To demonstrate some of these objects:

1 Open your MV3DSTD template file, with layer MODEL, UCS BASE and the lower left viewport active. Refer to Fig. 21.1 and display the Surfaces toolbar.

2 In the steps which follow, reason out the coordinate entry values.

3 Select the BOX icon from the Surfaces toolbar and:
prompt   Specify corner point of box and enter: **0,0,0 <R>**
prompt   Specify length of box and enter: **150 <R>**
prompt   Specify width of box and enter: **120 <R>**
prompt   Specify height of box and enter: **100 <R>**
prompt   Specify rotation angle of box about Z axis and enter: **0 <R>**.

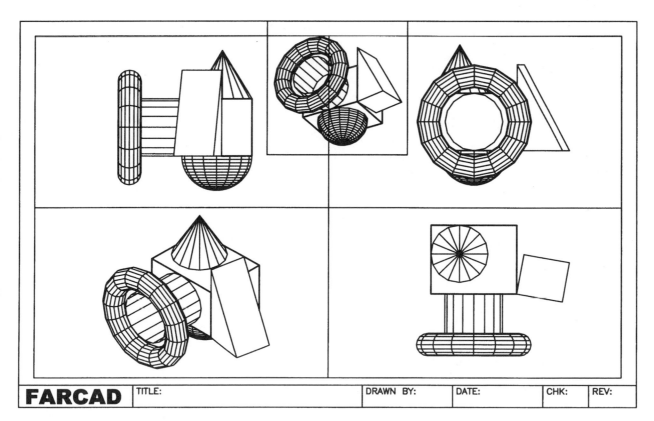

FARCAD | TITLE: | DRAWN BY: | DATE: | CHK: | REV:

Figure 21.1 3D object.

4   A red box will be displayed at the 0,0,0 origin point.

5   Menu bar with **Draw-Surfaces-3D Surfaces** and:
    prompt   3D Objects dialogue box
    respond   **pick Wedge then OK**
    prompt   Specify corner point of wedge and enter: **150,0,0 <R>**
    prompt   Specify length of wedge and enter: **80 <R>**
    prompt   Specify width of wedge and enter: **70 <R>**
    prompt   Specify height of wedge and enter: **150 <R>**
    prompt   Specify rotation angle of wedge about Z axis and enter:
                −10 <R>.

6   At the command line enter **CHANGE <R>** and:
    prompt   Select objects and pick the wedge then right-click
    prompt   Specify change point or [Properties] and enter: **P <R>**
    prompt   Enter property to change and enter: **C <R>** – colour option
    prompt   Enter new colour and enter: **14 <R>**
    prompt   Enter property to change and <RETURN>.

7   Using the icons from the Surfaces toolbar, or the 3D Objects dialogue box, create the
    following two 3D objects:

Cone	*Cylinder* – using cone
Base centre: 50,70,100	Base centre: 75,0,50
Radius for base: 50	Radius for base: 50
Radius for top: 0	Radius for top: 50
Height: 85	Height: 90
Number of segments: 16	Number of segments: 16
Colour: green	Colour: blue.

8   Restore UCS RIGHT and with the ROTATE icon from the Modify toolbar:
    a) pick the blue cylinder then right-click
    b) base point: 0,50
    c) rotation angle: 90.

9   Restore UCS BASE.

10 Create the following two 3D objects:

Dish	*Torus*
Centre of dish: 75,60,0	Centre of torus: 75,−90,50
Radius: 60	Radius of torus: 100
Longitudinal segments: 16	Radius of tube: 20
Latitudinal segments: 16	Tube segments: 16
Colour: magenta	Torus segments: 16.

11 Change the colour of the torus to CYAN, then restore UCS RIGHT.

12 With the ROTATE icon:
    a) pick the cyan torus then right-click
    b) base point: −90,50
    c) angle: 90.

13 Restore UCS BASE.

14 Zoom centre about 75,0,50 at 300 magnification.

15 Hide and shade to display the model with 'bright' colours.

16 *Task*.
   a) Enter paper space and make layer VP current
   b) menu bar with View-Viewports-1 Viewport and make a new viewport selecting one of the points 'outwith' the original four as shown in Fig. 21.1
   c) display the model in this new viewport from below and zoom centre about the same point as before
   d) *Question*: why did we pick one of the new viewport points outwith the original viewports?
   e) Flat shade the model in each viewport, then convert back to 2D wireframe.

17 Save the layout, although we will not use it again.

Summary

1 The nine 3D objects are displayed as either faced or meshed surface models.

2 The hide and shade (and render) commands can be used with 3D objects.

3 3D objects are created from a reference point (corner/centre, etc.) and certain model geometry, e.g. length, width and height.

4 A cylinder is created from a cone with the base and top radii the same.

5 Activating 3D objects is available from the Surfaces toolbar or from the 3D Objects dialogue box. The various objects can also be created by command line entry, although this is **NOT** recommended.

6 *Note*.
   In the 3D objects exercise, I used the command line CHANGE to alter the colour of the added objects. Changing object colour is an essential user requirement, especially when dealing with solid models. With R2000, there are two ways in which an objects colour can be altered, these being governed by the PICKFIRST system variable as follows:
   a) PICKFIRST set to 0: CHANGE at the command line then pick the objects to be modified
   b) PICKFIRST set to 1: select the objects to be modified then pick the Properties icon
   c) the user must decide which method is to be used. Either method is perfectly valid
   d) I will generally refer to this type of operation as:
       1. change the colour of the box to blue
       2. make the added cylinder green.

Assignment

MACFARAMUS was commissioned by the Emperor TOOTENCADUM to design and build a palace for Queen NEFERSAYDY in the city of CADOPOLIS. With his knowledge of CAD, MACFARAMUS decided to build the palace from 3D objects, and this is your assignment. You have to use your imagination and initiative when designing the palace from 3D objects. Remember that the polar array command is very useful.

Activity 14: Palace of Queen NEFERSAYDY by MACFARAMUS

1 Use your MV3DSTD template file with UCS BASE.

2 The 3D objects have to be positioned in a circle with an 85 **maximum** radius. This circle has to be:
   a) created from four touching polyarcs – as a previous exercise
   b) edge surfaced with both SURFTAB1 and SURFTAB2 set to 16. The edge surface mesh should be on its own layer with a colour number of 42.

3 The 3D objects have to be created on layer MODEL and can be to your own specification and layout. Some of my 3D objects were:

box	*wedge*	*dome*
corner: –40,–40,0	corner: 40,–40,0	centre: 0,0,60
length: 80	length: 20	radius: 25
width: 80	width: 10	colour: magenta
height: 60	height: 60	
colour: red	colour: blue	

cylinder	*cone*
centre: 50,–50,0	centre: 50,–50,70
radius: 8	radius: 12
height: 70	height: 20
colour: green	colour: green.

4 When the palace layout is complete, hide and shade.

5 Save the complete model as **MODR2000\PALACE**. It will be used in a later activity.

Chapter 22

3D geometry commands

All AutoCAD commands can be used in 3D but there are three commands which are specific to 3D models, these being 3D Array, Mirror 3D and Rotate 3D. In this chapter we will investigate these three commands and how to use the Align, Extend and Trim commands with 3D models.

Getting started

To investigate the 3D commands, we will create a new model from 3D Objects, so:

1 Begin a new drawing with your MV3DSTD template file, with layer MODEL, UCS BASE and the lower left viewport active. Refer to Fig. 22.1.

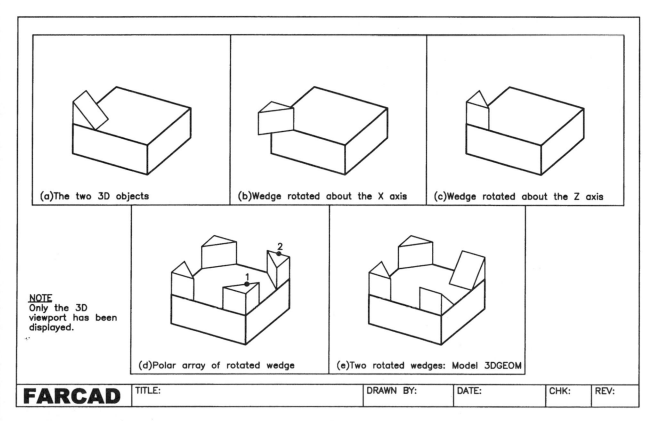

(a)The two 3D objects

(b)Wedge rotated about the X axis

(c)Wedge rotated about the Z axis

NOTE
Only the 3D
viewport has been
displayed.

(d)Polar array of rotated wedge

(e)Two rotated wedges: Model 3DGEOM

FARCAD | TITLE: | | DRAWN BY: | DATE: | CHK: | REV:

Figure 22.1 The 3DGEOM model for the 3D commands.

2   Select the BOX icon from the Surfaces toolbar and:
    a) corner: 0,0,0
    b) length: 100; width: 100; height: 40; Z rotation: 0
    c) colour: red.

3   Select the WEDGE icon from the Surfaces toolbar and:
    a) corner: 0,0,40
    b) length: 30; width: 30; height: 30; Z rotation: 0
    c) colour: blue.

4   Alter the 3D viewport viewpoint with VPOINT-ROTATE and enter angles of 300 and 30.

5   In each viewport, zoom centre about 50,50,35 at 200 magnification.

6   The two 3D objects will be displayed as fig(a).

Rotate 3D

Using the menu bar sequence Modify-Rotate or selecting the ROTATE icon from the Modify toolbar results in a 2D command, i.e. the selected objects are rotated in the current XY plane. Objects can be rotated in 3D relative to the X, Y and Z axes with the Rotate 3D command. The command will be demonstrated by:
a) rotating the blue wedge in the first instance
b) rotating the complete model.

Rotating the wedge

1   From the menu bar select **Modify-3D Operation-Rotate 3D** and:
    prompt   Select objects
    respond   **pick the blue wedge then right-click**
    prompt   Specify first point on axis or define axis by [Object/Last/..
    enter   **X <R>** – the X axis option
    prompt   Specify a point on the X axis<0,0,0>
    enter   **0,0,40 <R>** – why these coordinates?
    prompt   Specify rotation angle
    enter   **90 <R>**.

2   The blue wedge is rotated about the x-axis as fig(b)

3   Activate the Rotate 3D command and:
    prompt   Select objects
    enter   **pick the blue wedge the right-click**
    prompt   Rotate 3D options
    enter   **Z <R>** – the Z axis option
    prompt   Specify a point on Z axis<0,0,0>
    enter   **0,0,0 <R>**
    prompt   Specify rotation angle
    enter   **90 <R>**.

4   The blue wedge is now aligned as required – fig(c).

5   Select the ARRAY icon from the Modify toolbar and:
    a) pick the blue wedge then right-click
    b) enter P <R> for the polar array option
    c) enter the centre point as 50,50
    d) number of items: 4
    e) angle to fill of 360 with rotation.

6 The blue wedge is arrayed to the four corners of the box – fig(d).

7 With the Rotate 3D command:
   a) pick wedges 1 and 2 then right-click
   b) enter Y <R> as the defined axis
   c) enter 100,0,40 <R> as a point on axis – why this entry?
   d) enter 90 <R> as the rotation angle.

8 Now move these two rotated wedges from 0,0 by @–30,0.

9 The final result is fig(e) and can be saved as **MODR2000\3DGEOM** for future recall.

Rotating the model

1 Model 3DGEOM on screen with lower left viewport active, UCS BASE and layer MODEL current. Refer to Fig. 22.2

2 Menu bar with Modify-3D Operation-Rotate 3D and:
   prompt   Select objects
   respond   **window the complete model then right-click**
   prompt   Specify first point on axis or define axis
   enter   **X <R>** – the X axis option
   prompt   Specify a point on the X axis
   respond   **right-click**, i.e. accept the 0,0,0 default point
   prompt   Specify rotation angle and enter: **45 <R>**
   then   PAN to suit – fig(b).

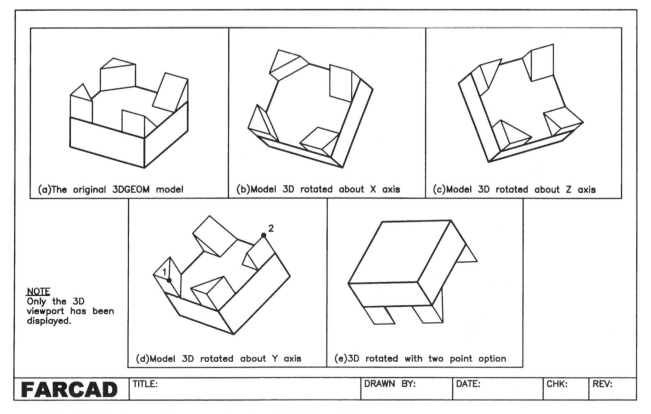

(a)The original 3DGEOM model

(b)Model 3D rotated about X axis

(c)Model 3D rotated about Z axis

NOTE
Only the 3D viewport has been displayed.

(d)Model 3D rotated about Y axis

(e)3D rotated with two point option

FARCAD | TITLE: | | DRAWN BY: | DATE: | CHK: | REV: |

Figure 22.2 Rotate 3D command using 3DGEOM model.

3 At the command line enter **ROTATE3D <R>** and:

prompt Select objects
respond **window the model then right-click**
prompt Specify first point on axis or define axis
enter **Z <R>** – the Z axis option
prompt Specify a point on Z axis<0,0,0> and: right-click
prompt Specify rotation angle and enter: **60 <R>**
then PAN to suit – fig(c).

4 Activate the Rotate 3D command and:

a) window the model
b) select the Y axis option
c) accept the default 0,0,0 point on Y axis
d) enter –60 as the rotation angle and pan to suit – fig(d).

5 Rotate 3D again, window the model and:

prompt Specify first point on axis
respond **Intersection icon and pick pt1**
prompt Specify second point on axis
respond **Intersection icon and pick pt2**
prompt Specify rotation angle and enter: **180 <R>**
then PAN to suit – fig(e).

6 Hide the viewports.

7 Save layout if required, but we will not use it again.

Mirror 3D

This command allows objects to be mirrored about selected points or about any of the three X-Y-Z planes.

1 Open model 3DGEOM, UCS BASE, lower left viewport active and refer to Fig. 22.3.

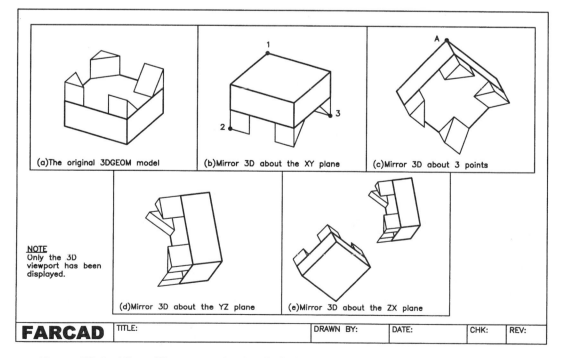

(a)The original 3DGEOM model
(b)Mirror 3D about the XY plane
(c)Mirror 3D about 3 points

NOTE
Only the 3D viewport has been displayed.

(d)Mirror 3D about the YZ plane
(e)Mirror 3D about the ZX plane

FARCAD | TITLE: | | DRAWN BY: | DATE: | CHK: | REV: |

Figure 22.3 Mirror 3D command using 3DGEOM model.

2 Menu bar with **Modify-3D Operation-Mirror 3D** and:
  prompt Select objects
  respond **window the model then right-click**
  prompt Specify first point on mirror plane (3 points) or [Object/Last/..
  enter **XY <R>** – the XY plane option
  prompt Specify point on XY plane<0,0,0> and: **right click**
  prompt Delete source objects<Yes/No> and enter: **Y <R>**
  then PAN to suit – fig(b).

  Note.
  The model at this stage has the AMBIGUITY effect of all 3D models, i.e. are you looking down or looking up? Hence HIDE!

3 At the command line enter **MIRROR3D <R>** and:
  prompt Select objects
  respond **window the model then right-click**
  prompt Specify first point on mirror plane
  respond **Intersection icon and pick pt1**
  prompt Specify second point on mirror plane
  respond **Intersection icon and pick pt2**
  prompt Specify third point on mirror plane
  respond **Intersection icon and pick pt3**
  prompt Delete source object<Yes/No> and enter: **Y <R>**
  then PAN to suit – fig(c).

4 Activate the Mirror 3D command and:
  a) window the model the right-click
  b) select the YZ plane option
  c) pick intersection of point A as a point on the plane
  d) enter Y to delete source objects prompt
  e) pan to suit – fig(d).

5 Using the Mirror 3D command:
  a) window the model the right-click
  b) select the ZX option
  c) enter –50,–50 as a point on the ZX plane
  d) accept the N default delete source objects option
  e) pan as required – fig(e).

6 Hide the viewports then save if required. We will not refer to this drawing again.

3D Array

The 3D array command is similar in operation to the 2D array. Both rectangular and polar arrays are possible, the rectangular array having rows and columns as well as levels in the Z direction. The result of a 3D polar array requires some thought!

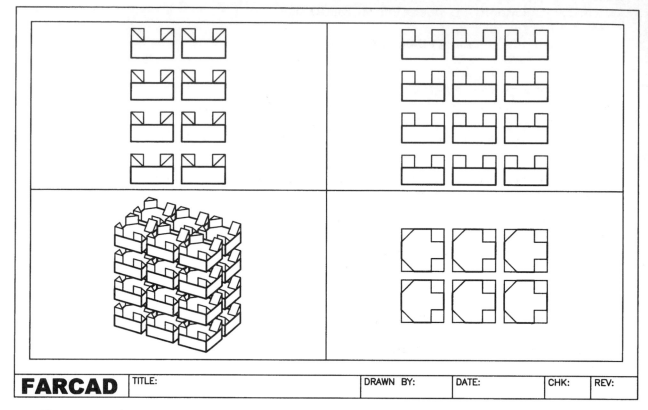

Figure 22.4 3D ARRAY (rectangular) using 3DGEOM.

Rectangular

1 Open the 3DGEOM drawing, UCS BASE, lower left viewport active and refer to Fig. 22.4.

2 Menu bar with **Modify-3D Operation-3D Array** and:

prompt Select objects

respond **window the model then right-click**

prompt Enter the type of array [Rectangular/Polar] and enter: **R <R>**

prompt Enter the number of rows(---)<1> and enter: **2 <R>**

prompt Enter the number of columns(||||)<1> and enter: **3 <R>**

prompt Enter the number of levels(...)<1> and enter: **4 <R>**

prompt Specify the distance between rows(---) and enter: **120 <R>**

prompt Specify the distance between columns(||||) and enter: **120 <R>**

prompt Specify the distance between levels(...) and enter: **100 <R>**.

3 The model will be displayed in a 2 × 3 × 4 rectangular matrix pattern but will probably need to be re-centred. Zoom centre about the point 170,110,185 (why these coordinates?) at 400 magnification but 550 in the 3D viewport.

4 Hide the model – Fig. 22.4 then flat shade the 3D viewport. Try the 3D orbit command with the shaded model.

5 This exercise does not need to be saved.

Polar

1 Open 3DGEOM, UCS BASE and lower left viewport active.

2 At the command line enter **3DARRAY <R>** and:

prompt	Select objects
respond	**window the model then right-click**
prompt	Enter the type of array and enter: **P <R>**
prompt	Enter the number of items and enter: **5 <R>**
prompt	Specify the angle to fill and enter: **360 <R>**
prompt	Rotate arrayed objects and enter: **Y <R>**
prompt	Specify center point of array
enter	**150,150,0 <R>**
prompt	Specify second point on axis of rotation
enter	**@0,0,100 <R>**, i.e. a line in Z axis direction.

3 Zoom centre about 150,160,50 at 300 magnification in the 3D viewport and 450 in the others, then hide each viewport – fig(a).

4 Undo this 3D polar array.

5 Activate the 3D array command and:
   a) window the original model then right-click
   b) enter a polar array type
   c) number of items: 5
   d) angle to fill: 360
   e) rotate as copied: Y
   f) centre point of array and enter: −50,0,0 <R>
   g) second point on axis and enter: @0,100,0 <R>.

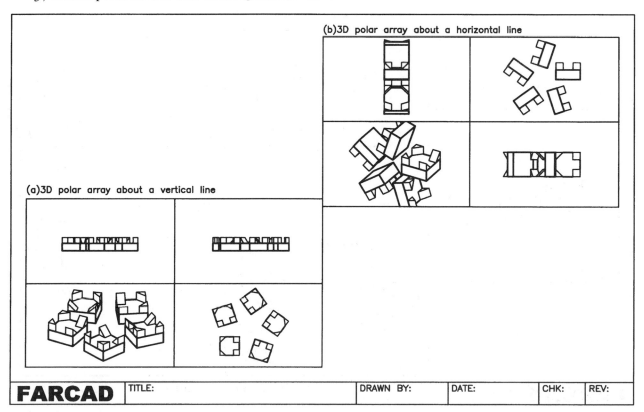

(b)3D polar array about a horizontal line

(a)3D polar array about a vertical line

FARCAD TITLE: DRAWN BY: DATE: CHK: REV:

Figure 22.5 3D ARRAY (polar) using 3DGEOM model.

6   Zoom centre about the point –50,50,0 at 300 magnification in the 3D viewport and 350 in the others.

7   Hide the model – fig(b).

8   *Note*. The first polar array was about a Z axis line, the second about a Y axis line. Think about the entered coordinates.

9   This exercise is complete and need not be saved.

Align

The align commands can be used in 2D or 3D and allows objects (models) to be aligned with each other.

1   Open your MV3DSTD template file with UCS BASE and layer MODEL current. Refer to Fig. 22.6.

2   Using the Surfaces toolbar create the following objects:

	Box	Wedge
corner	0,0,0	160,0,0
length	100	100
wedge	80	80
height	50	50
rotation	0	0
colour	red	blue

3   Copy the box and wedge:
    a) start point: 0,0,0
    b) next point: @150,150.

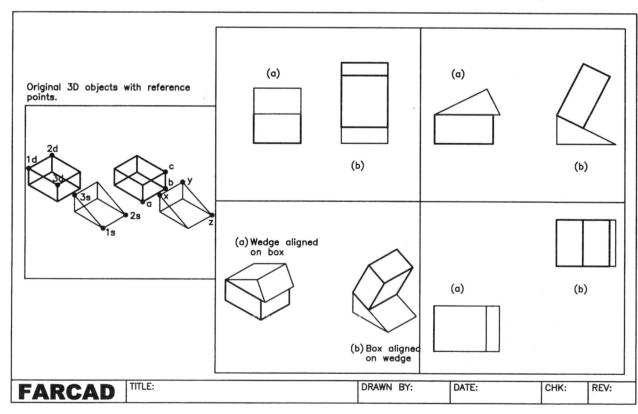

Figure 22.6   The ALIGN command with 3D objects.

4 Set the running object snap to Intersection.

5 Menu bar with **Modify-3D Operation-Align** and:
    prompt   Select objects
    respond   **pick a blue wedge then right-click**
    prompt   Specify first source point and pick point 1s
    prompt   Specify first destination point and pick point 1d
    prompt   Specify second source point and pick point 2s
    prompt   Specify second destination point and pick point 2d
    prompt   Specify third source point and pick point 3s
    prompt   Specify third destination point and pick point 3d.

6 The green wedge will be aligned with its sloped surface on the top of the box as (a).

7 At the command line enter **ALIGN <R>** and:
   a) pick the other red box then right-click
   b) pick first source/destination points a and x
   c) pick second source/destination points b and y
   d) pick third source/destination points c and z
   e) the red box will be aligned onto the sloped surface of the wedge as (b).

8 This completes the align exercise.

3D extend and trim

Objects can be trimmed and extended in 3D irrespective of the objects' alignment. The two commands are very dependent on the UCS position.

1 Open your MV3DSTD template file and refer to Fig. 22.7.

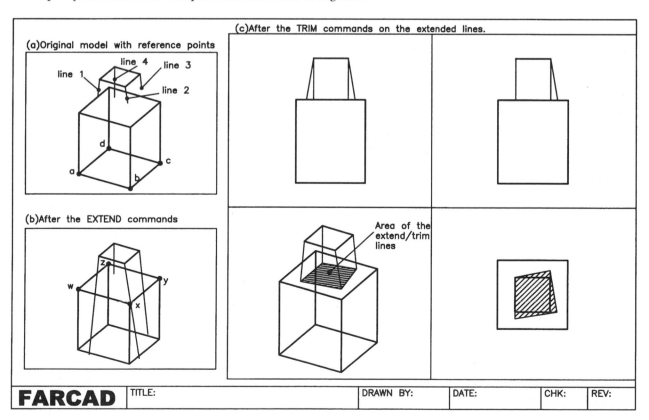

Figure 22.7 EXTEND and TRIM in 3D.

2 Using the LINE icon draw a square with:
  Start point: 0,0;   *next point*: @100,0;   *next point*: @0,100
  Next point: @−100,0;   *next point*: close.

3 Multiple copy the square with:
  a) base point: 0,0
  b) second point: @0,0,120 and: @0,0,180.

4 Scale the top square about the point 50,50,180 by 0.5.

5 Draw in the four vertical lines between the two large squares, then draw the following four lines:

line	start point	next point	colour
1	25,25,180	@0,−5,−30	blue
2	75,25,180	@5,0,−30	green
3	75,75,180	@0,5,−30	cyan
4	25,75,180	@0,0,−60	magenta.

6 Change the viewpoint in the 3D viewport with VPOINT-ROTATE and angles of 300 and 30. The model will be displayed as fig(a).

Extend

1 With the 3D viewport active, restore UCS RIGHT and select the EXTEND icon from the Modify toolbar and:

prompt	`Select objects`
respond	**pick line ab then right-click**
prompt	`Select object to extend or [Project/Edge/Undo]`
enter	**E <R>** – the edge option
prompt	`Enter an implied edge extension mode [Extend/No extend]`
enter	**E <R>** – the extend option
prompt	`Select object to extend or [Project/Edge/Undo]`
enter	**P <R>** – the project option
prompt	`Enter a projection mode [None/Ucs/View]`
enter	**U <R>** – the current UCS option
prompt	`Select object to extend`
respond	**pick blue line 1 then right-click**.

2 Repeat the EXTEND command using the entries E,E,P,U as step 1 and:
  a) extend the green line 2 to edge bc with UCS RIGHT
  b) extend the cyan line 3 to edge cd with UCS FRONT.

3 The extended lines are displayed as fig(b).

Trim

1 Still with the 3D viewport active, restore UCS BASE and select the TRIM icon from the modify toolbar and:

prompt	`Select objects`
respond	**pick line wx then right-click**
prompt	`Select object to trim or [Project/Edge/Undo]`
enter	**P <R>** – the project option
prompt	`Enter a projection option [None/Ucs/View]`
enter	**V <R>** – the view option
prompt	`Select object to trim`
respond	*a*) make the top right viewport active
	b) pick the blue line then right-click/enter.

2 Repeat the TRIM command with P and V entries as step 1 and:
  a) trim the green line to edge xy, picking the green line in the top left viewport at the select object to trim prompt
  b) trim the cyan line to edge yz, picking the cyan line in the top right viewport at the select object to trim prompt.

3 The coloured lines have now been extended and trimmed 'to the top surface' of the large red box – fig(c).

4 *Task*.
  a) draw four lines connecting the 'bottom ends' of the blue, green, cyan and magenta lines
  b) hatch this area
  c) find the hatched area and perimeter. My values were:
    Area: 3350 Perimeter: 232.65.

Summary

1 The commands Rotate3D, Mirror3D and 3Darray are specific to 3D models.

2 Rotate 3D allows models to be rotated about the X,Y and Z axes as well as two specified points and about objects.

3 Mirror 3D allows models to be mirrored about the XY, YZ and ZX axes as well as three specified points and objects.

4 3D Array is similar to the 2D command but has 'levels' in the Z direction. The result of the polar 3D array can be difficult to 'visualize'.

5 3D models can be aligned with each other.

6 The trim and extend commands can be used in 3D, the result being dependent on the UCS position. Generally objects are trimmed or extended 'to a plane'.

Chapter 23

Blocks and wblocks in 3D

3D blocks and wblocks are created and inserted into a drawing in a similar manner as 2D blocks and wblocks. The UCS position and orientation is critical. In this chapter we will:
a) create a chess set using blocks
b) create a wall-clock as wblocks
c) use both the models for rendering exercises.

Creating the models for the blocks

1   Open your MV3DSTD template file, layer MODEL, UCS BASE and lower left viewport active. In each viewport, zoom centre about the point 120,90,50 at 275 magnification. Refer to Fig. 23.1.

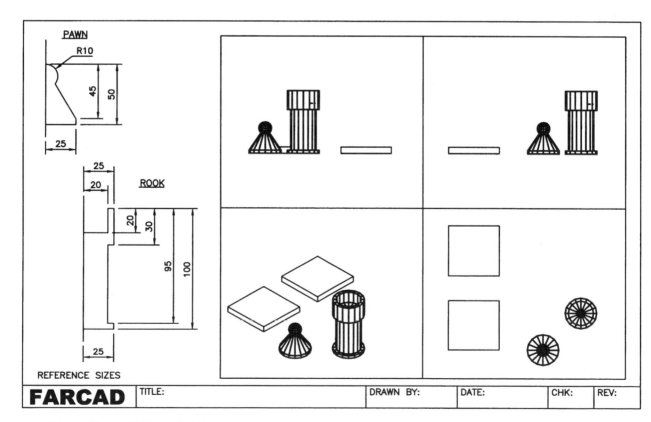

Figure 23.1   3D block details.

2 With the lower left viewport active, create the following two 3D box objects:

	box 1	*box 2*
corner	0,0,0	0,120,0
length	80	80
width	80	80
height	10	10
rotation	0	0
colour	number 126	number 220.

3 Restore UCS FRONT and make the upper right viewport active. Draw a line, first point: 150,−10 and next point: @0,80.

4 In paper space, zoom-window the top right viewport, then return to model space.

5 *a*) Draw the pawn outline as a polyline from: 150,0 using your own design but with the 'overall' sizes given as reference.
  b) Set SURFTAB1 to 16
  c) With the REVOLVED SURFACE icon from the Surfaces toolbar, revolve the pawn outline about the vertical line – full circle
  d) The pawn colour is to be red.

6 Still with UCS FRONT, draw a line, first point: 210,−10,−60 and next point: @0,120.

7 *a*) Draw the rook outline as a polyline from: 210,0,−60 using the reference sizes given but your own design.
  b) Revolve the rook polyline about the vertical line for a full circle.
  c) The rook colour is to be red.

8 Erase the two vertical lines.

9 Restore UCS BASE and models displayed as Fig. 23.1.

Making the blocks

1 With the lower left viewport active and UCS BASE, menu bar with **Draw-Block-Make** and:

  prompt Block Definition dialogue box
  respond 1 enter name: SQ1
        2 enter base point as X: 0; Y:0; Z: 0
        3 pick Select objects and pick the green coloured box then right-click
        4 enter description: FIRST SQUARE
        5 ensure insert units: millimeters
        6 dialogue box as Fig. 23.2.

2 Using the Block Definition dialogue box, make the other three blocks using the same method as step 1 with the following information:

	first	*second*	*third*
name:	SQ2	PAWN	ROOK
inscrtion pt	0,120,0	150,0,0	210,60,0
object	purple box	3D pawn	3D rook
description	SECOND SQUARE	PAWN PIECE	ROOK PIECE

3 Now erase the four chess pieces and the original polyline outlines should be displayed. Erase them.

4 Activate the block definition dialogue box and scroll at name. The four created blocks will be listed – PAWN, ROOK, SQ1 and SQ2 in alphabetical order.

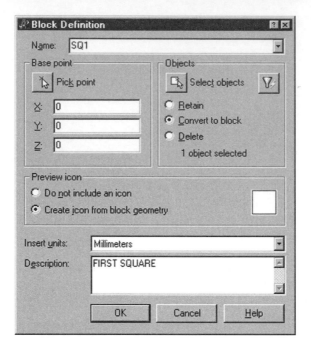

Figure 23.2 Block Definition dialogue box for SQ1.

5 *Note*.
  a) The command line BLOCK entry will display the Block Definition dialogue box
  b) The command line entry – BLOCK will allow block creation from the command line.
  c) Enter -BLOCK <R> and:
    prompt   Enter block name or [?] and enter: **? <R>** – query option
    prompt   Enter block(s) to list and enter: *** <R>**
    prompt   Text window with four defined blocks
    respond   cancel the text window.

Inserting the blocks

1 Four 'blank' viewports displayed with UCS BASE, layer MODEL and the 3D viewport active.

2 Menu bar with **Insert-Block** and:
  prompt   Insert dialogue box
  respond   1 scroll at name and pick SQ1
              2 activate all on-screen prompts, i.e. no tick
              3 enter insertion point as X: 0; Y: 0; Z: 0
              4 enter scale as X: 1; Y: 1; Z: 1
              5 enter rotation as 0
              6 dialogue box as Fig. 23.3
              7 pick OK
  and   the green 3D box block will be displayed at the 0,0,0 insertion point.

3 Repeat the Insert-Block sequence with:
  a) scroll and pick SQ2
  b) ensure on-screen prompts are active
  c) insertion point of X: 80; Y: 0; Z: 0
  d) scale of X: 1; Y: 1; Z: 1 and rotation: 0
  e) purple 3D box block displayed adjacent to the green 3D box.

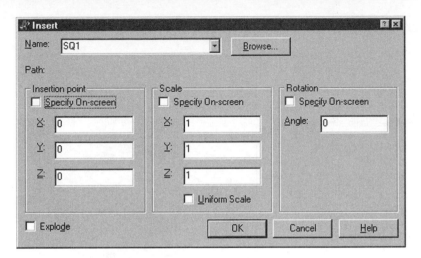

Figure 23.2 Block Definition dialogue box for SQ1.

4 Zoom centre about 320,320,100 at 700 in all viewports and with the 3D viewport active, complete the 64 square chess board using one of the following methods:
   a) inserting each block SQ1 and SQ2
   b) multiple copy the two inserted boxes
   c) rectangular array
   d) note: I used multiple copy.

5 At the command line enter **-INSERT <R>** and:
   prompt Enter block name and enter: **PAWN <R>**
   prompt Enter insertion point and enter: **40,120,10 <R>**
   prompt Enter X scale factor and enter: **1 <R>**
   prompt Enter Y scale factor and enter: **1 <R>**
   prompt Specify rotation angle and enter: **0 <R>**
   and   the red pawn piece will be displayed on top of the left second row square.

6 Now insert the ROOK full-size with 0 rotation at the insertion point of 40,40,10 using either the Insert dialogue box or the – INSERT command line entry.

7 *a*) Rectangular array the red pawn for: 1 row; 8 columns; column distance 80.
   b) Copy the eight pawns from: 40,80,10 to: @0,400,0.
   c) Multiple copy the rook from a base point of 40,40,10 to second points of: @560,0,0; @0,560,0; @560,560,0.

8 *Task*.
   a) Alter the layout to display a three viewport configuration, remembering to make layer VP current.
   b) set the viewpoints to display a 3D, top and front view.
   c) Change the colour of one set of prawns and rooks to blue. This may not be as simple as you think. The inserted blocks must be exploded before the colour can be changed. Decide whether to use the PICKFIRST variable set to:
      i) 0: CHANGE at command line then pick the objects
      ii) 1: pick the objects then the Properties icon.
   d) Re-centre the model in each viewport about 320,320,100 at 1100 magnification in the 3D viewport and 700 in the other two.

9 When complete, the layout should resemble Fig. 23.4 and should be saved as **MODR2000\CHESS** for the activity part of the chapter.

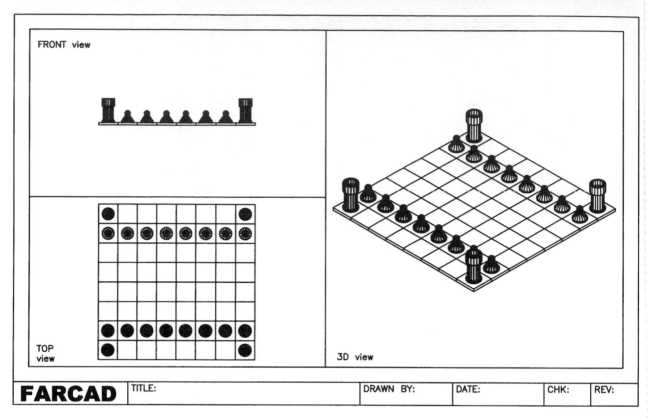

Figure 23.4 Inserting the blocks.

Creating the models for the Wblocks

1 Open the MV3DSTD template file and zoom centre about 125,0,100 at 300 magnification in all viewports.

2 The wblocks will be created using the WCS, so menu bar with **Tools-New UCS-World**.

3 With the top right viewport active, layer MODEL current rotate the WCS about the X axis with menu bar sequence **Tools-New UCS-X** and enter 90 as the rotation angle.

4 Create the three outlines for parts of a wall clock with:
   a) draw the body as lines using the 0,0,0 start point and the reference sizes given. Use the Modify-Polyline command to 'convert' the five lines into a single polyline object
   b) draw the face as an octagon circumscribed in a circle with centre at 90,90,0 and radius 30
   c) draw the dial as a 30 radius circle, centre at 90,10,0.

4 Draw the following three lines:
   a) line 1, start point: 150,0 next point: @0,0,40
   b) line 2, start point: 200,0 next point: @0,0,15
   c) line 3, start point: 250,0 next point: @0,0,8.

5 The three wall clock components will be created as tabulated surface models, so set SURFTAB1 to 16.

6 With the TABULATED SURFACE icon from the Surfaces toolbar:
   prompt   Select object for path curve
   respond   **pick the BODY polyline**
   prompt   Select object for direction vector
   respond   **pick line 1 at end indicated by the donut**
   and   extruded red tabulated surface model of wall clock body.

7 Repeat the tabulated surface command and:
   a) select the FACE octagon as the path curve and line 2 as the direction vector at end indicated
   b) select the DIAL circle as the path curve and line 3 as the direction vector at end indicated.

8 Change the colour of the tabulated surface models:
   a) FACE: blue
   b) DIAL: green.

9 The layout at this stage should resemble Fig. 23.5.

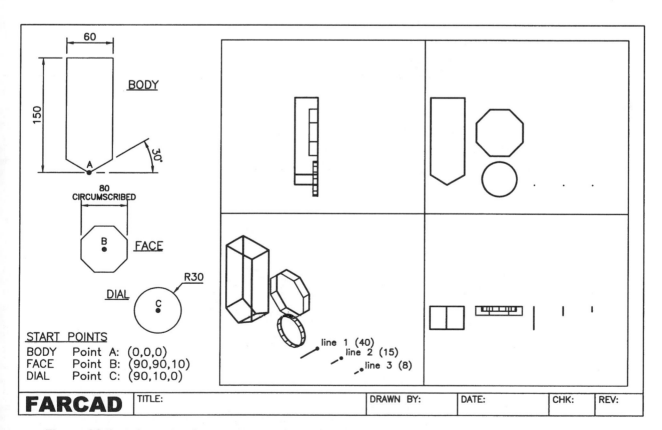

Figure 23.5 Information for creating the three wblocks.

Making the wblocks

1 Menu bar with **Tools-New UCS-World** to restore the WCS and make the lower left viewport active.

2 At the command line enter **WBLOCK <R>** and:
   prompt   Write Block dialogue box
   respond   1 Source: Objects
                   2 Base point: X: 0; Y: 0; Z: 0
                   3 Objects: Retain
                   4 pick Select objects and:
   prompt   Select objects
   respond   pick the red body then right-click
   prompt   Write Block dialogue box
   respond   1 Destination file name: BODY
                   2 Location: C:\modr2000 (or your named folder)
                   3 Insert units: Millimeters
                   4 dialogue box as Fig. 23.6
                   5 pick OK.

3 Create another two wblocks using the same procedure as step 2 with the following information:

	wblock2	wblock3
Insertion base point	90,0,90	90,0,10
Objects	blue object	green object
File name	FACE	DIAL
Location	C:\modr2000	C:\modr2000.

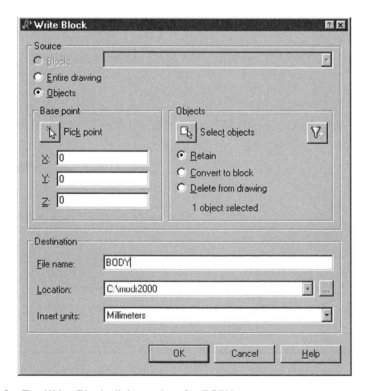

Figure 23.6 The Write Block dialogue box for BODY.

Inserting the three wblocks

1 Menu bar with **File-Close** and pick No to save changes.

2 Menu bar with **File-New** and 'open' your MV3DSTD template file with UCS BASE, layer MODEL and lower left viewport active.

3 Restore the WCS.

4 Menu bar with **Insert-Block** and:

prompt	Insert dialogue box
respond	**pick Browse**
prompt	Select Drawing File dialogue box
respond	1 scroll and pick the C: drive
	2 scroll and pick C:\modr2000 (or your named folder)
	3 pick BODY and note the preview
	4 pick Open
prompt	Insert dialogue box
respond	1 cancel the on-screen prompts
	2 enter insertion point as X: 0; Y: 0; Z: 0
	3 all scale factors 1 and rotation angle 0
	4 pick OK
and	the red body will be displayed at the 0,0,0 insertion point.

5 Activate the Insert dialogue, select the Browse option and insert the other wblocks with the following information:

File name:	FACE	DIAL
Insertion point:	0,−40,130	0,−55,130
X and Y scale:	1	1
Rotation angle:	0	0.

6 Zoom centre about the point 0,−30,80 at 200 magnification in all viewports – Fig. 23.7.

7 Hide and shade the model. Try the 3D orbit in the 3D viewport.

8 Save as this exercise as **MODR2000\WALL**.

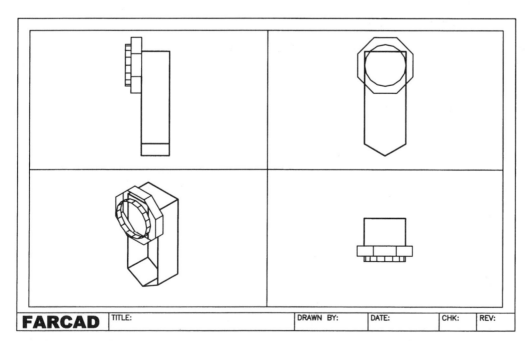

Figure 23.7 Inserting the three WBLOCKS to create the clock 'assembly'.

Summary

1 3D blocks and wblocks are created and inserted in a similar manner to 2D blocks and wblocks.

2 With 3D blocks, the position of the UCS is important.

3 With 3D wblocks, it is **strongly recommended** that the WCS be used when creating and inserting the wblocks.

4 Wblocks which are inserted 'unexploded' into a drawing become blocks within that drawing. It is therefore recommended that wblocks are exploded as they are inserted.

Assignments

Two activities have been included for you to attempt, one with blocks using the chess set partially completed, and the other using two previously saved drawings, one of which will be inserted as a wblock.

Activity 15: Chess set

1 Recall the drawing CHESS saved earlier in this chapter to display the 64 square chess board with the two sets of red and blue pawns and rooks.

2 Design the other chess pieces – KNIGHT, BISHOP, KING and QUEEN using the same method as the worked example:
   a) draw the outline as a polyline
   b) use the revolved surface command to create the piece as a 3D surface model
   c) *Note*: the actual shape of the pieces is at your discretion. The information given in the activity 15 drawing is for reference purposes only
   d) ensure that your start point for the outline is known – it will be useful as the block insertion point.

3 Create a block of each created piece.

4 Insert the created blocks onto the chess board.

5 Complete the chess set layout, remembering to change the colours of the pieces to red and blue as appropriate.

6 Save as MODR2000\CHESS.

7 Investigate the various shade options with the completed model.

8 *Note*.
   The model layout displayed in activity 15 was produced by Craig Matthewman. Craig was a full-time student on the HNC CADD course at Motherwell College and his design was interesting. He gave his permission for the layout to be included as an activity.

Activity 16: Palace of Queen NEFERSAYDY built by MACFARAMUS

MACFARAMUS was last encountered building the palace for Queen NEFERSAYDY. Unfortunately this palace was to be built on a flat-topped hill and you have to create the layout using an existing drawing and inserting another drawing into it as a wblock.

1 Open the drawing MODR2000\HILL of the edge surface model created as activity 13.

2 Insert the wblock drawing file MODR2000\PALACE of the 3D objects created as activity 14.

3 The palace has to be positioned at the centre point of the hill top, and the coordinates of this point as 0,0,100. This is the only help given.

4 Optimize the viewport layout for maximum effect.

5 When complete save the layout as MODR2000\HILLPAL.

Chapter 24

Dynamic viewing

Dynamic viewing is a powerful (yet underused) command which is very useful with 3D modelling as it allows models to be viewed from a perspective viewpoint. The command also allows objects to be 'cut-away' enabling the user to 'see inside' models. Dynamic viewing has its own terminology which is obvious when you are familiar with the command, but can be confusing to new users.

The basic concept of dynamic viewing is that the user has a **CAMERA** which is positioned at a certain **DISTANCE** from the model – called the **TARGET**. The user is looking through the camera lens at the model and can **ZOOM** in/out as required. The viewing direction is from the camera lens to a **TARGET POINT** on the model. The camera can be moved relative to the stationary target, and both the camera and target can be turned relative to each other. The target can also be **TWISTED** relative to the camera. Two other concepts which the user will encounter with the dynamic view command are the **slider bar** and the **perspective icon**. The slider bar allows the user to 'scale' the variable which is current, while the perspective icon is displayed when the perspective view is 'on'.

Figure 24.1(A) displays the various dynamic view concepts of:
a) the basic terminology
b) the slider bar
c) the perspective icon.

The dynamic view command has twelve options, these being:

CAmera,TArget,Distance,POints,Pan,Zoom,TWist,CLip,Hide,Off,Undo,eXit

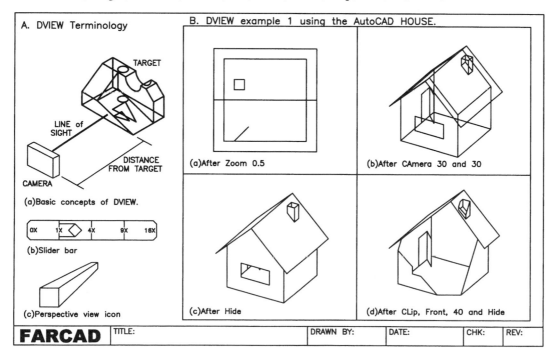

Figure 24.1 Dynamic view terminology and AutoCAD's 'House block'.

The option required is activated by entering the CAPITAL letters at the command line, e.g. CA for the camera option, TW for twist etc. The various options will be investigated with two examples:

a) AutoCAD's dynamic view 'house'

b) a previously saved drawing.

Note.

1 Dynamic view is a model space concept, and cannot be used in paper space.

2 Dynamic view is **viewport independent**, i.e. if the command is used in a specific viewport, the model display in the other viewports will not be affected.

3 The command is activated by entering **DVIEW <R>** at the command line.

Example 1 – AutoCAD's 'house'

AutoCAD has a 'drawing' – actually a type of block – which can be used as an interactive aid with the dynamic view command. We will use this house block to demonstrate some of the options so:

1 Open your 3DSTDA3 template/drawing file to display a black border in 3D and menu bar with View-3D Views-Plan View-Current UCS.

2 The black border will be displayed in plan view.

3 Refer to Fig. 24.1(b).

4 At the command line enter **DVIEW <R>** and:

	prompt	`Select objects or <use DVIEWBLOCK>`
	respond	**right-click**, i.e. accept the DVIEWBLOCK default
a)	*prompt*	`Enter option [Camera/Target/..`
	and	some coloured lines appear on the screen
	enter	**Z <R>** – the zoom option
	prompt	`slider bar with scale displayed at top of screen`
	and	`Specify zoom scale factor`
	enter	**0.5 <R>**
	and	full plan view of house – fig(a)
b)	*prompt*	`Enter option [CAmera/TArget/..`
	enter	**CA <R>** – the camera option
	prompt	***ghost image of house*** which moves as mouse moved
	and	`Specify camera location or enter angle from XY plane`
	enter	**30 <R>**
	prompt	`Specify camera location or enter angle in XY plane from X axis`
	enter	**30 <R>**
	and	3D view of house – fig(b)
c)	*prompt*	`Enter option [CAmera/TArget/..`
	enter	**H <R>** – the hide option
	and	house displayed with hidden line removal – fig(c)
d)	*prompt*	`Enter option [CAmera/TArget/..`
	enter	**CL <R>** – the clip option
	prompt	`Enter clipping option [Back/Front/Off]`
	enter	**F <R>** – the front clip option
	prompt	`Specify distance from target or [set to..`
	enter	**40 <R>**
	prompt	`Enter option [CAmera/TArget/..`
	enter	**H <R>** – the hide option
	and	house displayed 'cut-away' at front similar to fig(d)

e)	*enter*	**U <R>** – undoes the hide effect of (d)
	enter	**U <R>** – undoes the clip effect of (d)
	enter	**U <R>** – undoes the hide effect of (c)
	and	**leave house with Camera option displayed**
	and	**command prompt line options**
	then	**read the explanation before proceeding**.

Explanation of the command

Dynamic view is an **interactive** command and the various options can be used one after the other. The undo (U) option will undo the last option performed, and can be used repeatedly until all the options entered have been 'undone'. Some of the options have been used to demonstrate how the command is used, these options being zoom, camera, clip, hide and undo. The hide option is very useful as it allows the model to be displayed when other options have been entered, and removes the 'ambiguity' effect from the model. The command can be used with all 3D models, i.e. extruded, wire-frame, surface and solid. The command is also **viewport independent**, i.e. it can be used in any viewport without affecting the display in other viewports. The AutoCAD 'house' is a user-reference, and if a model is displayed on the screen, this model will assume the house orientation when the dynamic view command is completed. This will be investigated during the next example.

The house displayed on the screen has been left with the Camera option with entered angles of 30 and 30. We will continue with the screen display and investigate the other dynamic view options. This means that you have to enter the various options and values as prompted.

Refer to Fig. 24.2 during the following exercise.

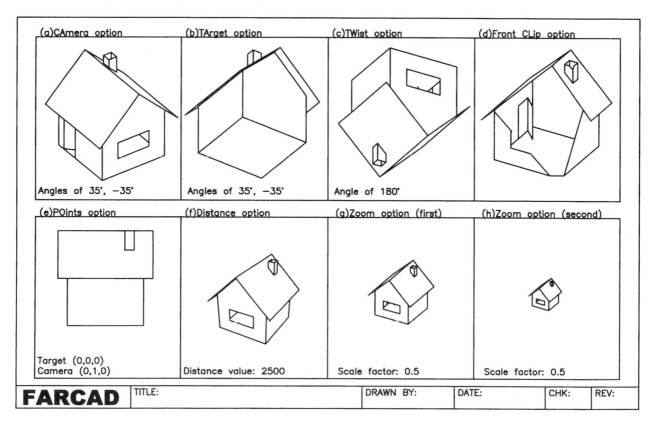

Figure 24.2 The various DVIEW options with DVIEWBLOCK – AutoCAD's house.

CAmera

1 This option is used to direct the camera at the target and the camera can be 'tilted' relative to two planes with two angles:
prompt 1   angle in the XY plane, between −90° and +90°
prompt 2   angle from the XY plane, between −180° and +180°.

2 The angles can be:
a) toggled using the ghost image as a guide
b) entered directly from the keyboard.

3 Using the CAmera option enter the following angle values:

angle in XY plane	*angle from XY plane*
a) 35	35
b) 35	−35
c) −35	35
d) −35	−35

4 The option can be considered similar to the **VPOINT ROTATE**.

5 When all the above entries have been completed, return the camera angles to the original 30 and 30, but do not exit the command.

TArget

1 This option allows the target (the model) to be tilted relative to the camera. The two angle prompts are the same as the camera option:
prompt 1 angle in the XY plane
prompt 2 angle from the XY plane.

2 The angles can be toggled or entered from the keyboard.

3 Using the TArget option enter the following angle values:

angle in XY plane	*angle from XY plane*
a) 35	35
b) 35	−35
c) −35	35
d) −35	−35.

4 The option can be used to give the same effect as the camera option, but it should be remembered that the camera and target are being 'tilted' in the 'opposite sense' to each other.

5 When all angles have been entered, undo until original 30,30 camera angles, but do not exit the command.

TWist

1 A very useful option as it allows the 'plane' on which the target is 'resting' to be twisted through an entered angle. This angle can be positive or negative and have values between 0 and 360°.

2 The prompt with this option is **Specify new view twist angle**.

3 The result of the option is dependent on the CAmera/TArget angles.

4 Using the TWist option enter angle values of:

a) 35   *b*) −35   *c*) 180   *d*) −90.

5 This is one of the few AutoCAD commands which allows models to be 'flipped' over by 180°.

6 When the four twist angles have been viewed with the hide effect, restore the original twist angle of 0, with the camera options of 30 and 30. Do not exit the command.

CLip

1 The clip option of the dynamic view command is probably of the most useful of all the options, as it allows models to be 'cut-away', thus allowing the user to 'see inside' the model.

2 The user selects a (F)ront or (B)ack clip and then decides on the clip distance either:
   a) using the slider bar
   b) entering a value at the command line.

3 The result of the clip option is dependent on the CAmera/TArget angles as well as the 'size' of the model on the screen.

4 With the CAmera angles set to 30 and 30, activate the front clip option and move the slider bar until the ghost image displays a clip effect then right-click.

5 When some clip options have been attempted, undo the various effects with **U <R>** until the house is again displayed with the CAmera settings of 30 and 30.

POints

1 This option allows the model (the target) to be viewed from a specific 'stand point', the user looking at a specific point on the target.

2 Two sets of coordinates need to be specified:
   a) the target point coordinates to be looked at
   b) the coordinates of the camera – the user.

3 The coordinate entries can be absolute or relative.

4 When this option is used, the PAn option is also usually needed.

5 The result does not depend on the CAmera or TArget options.

6 Use the Point option with the following entries:

	target point	*camera point*
a)	0,0,0	1,0,0
b)	0,0,0	0,1,0
c)	0,0,0	0,0,1
d)	0,0,0	1,1,0
e)	0,0,0	1,0,1
f)	0,0,0	1,1,1
g)	1,2,3	0,0,0
h)	0,0,0	1,2,3.

7 The option is similar to the **VPOINT VECTOR** command.

8 When all the points entries have been entered, restore the camera angles of 30 and 30, but do not exit the command.

Distance

1 Alters the distance between the camera and the target.

2 The distance can be:
   a) entered as a value from the command line
   b) toggled using the slider bar.

3 With the distance option, enter some values e.g.:
   a) 1000   *b*) 1500   *c*) 2500   *d*) 5000.

4 The distance option introduces **true perspective** to the model.

5 When the distance option has been used, and the command is exited, the zoom command cannot be used.

6 Restore the original CAmera option of 30 and 30.

Zoom

1 This option does what you would expect – it 'zooms the model'.

2 The zoom factor can be:
   a) entered as a value from the keyboard
   b) toggled using the slider bar.

3 Try some zoom entries e.g.:
   a) 1   *b*) 0.75   *c*) 0.5   *d*) 0.25.

4 Restore the original CAmera effect (30,30) and use the zoom option with a 0.5 scale factor three times.

Pan

1 This option is similar to the AutoCAD PAN command, but the 'real-time' pan effect is not available.

2 The user selects (or enters) the pan displacement.

Hide

1 Will display the model with a hide effect.

2 Removes any ambiguity.

Undo

1 Entering **U <R>** will undo the last option of the DVIEW command.

2 Can be used repetitively until all the option entries have been undone.

eXit

1 The **X <R>** option will end the dynamic view command and a blank screen will be returned.

2 The blank screen results because we did not have any drawing displayed, the AutoCAD 'house' being a visual aid indicating what any model would 'look like'.

3 With 'real models', the model orientation will be similar to the 'house' orientation when the DVIEW command has been exited, as will now be investigated.

4 If the DVIEW command is still active, enter X <R> to display the black border in plan view.

5 This first exercise is now complete..

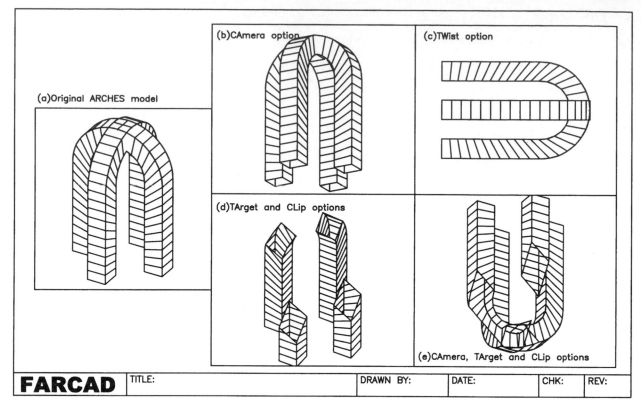

Figure 24.3 Dynamic view example 2 using R14MOD\ARCHES.

Example 2

In this example we will use the dynamic view command with a previously created model.

1 Open the ruled surface model MODR2000\ARCHES created during Chapter 16 with UCS BASE, layer MODEL. Re-centre the model about the point 50,10,75 at 150 mag.

2 Make the upper left viewport active and refer to Fig. 24.3.

3 At the command line enter **DVIEW <R>** and:
> *prompt*　Select objects or use <DVIEWBLOCK> and right-click
> *prompt*　AutoCAD's house as an 'end view' in the active viewport
> *and*　dynamic view options
> *enter*　**CA <R>**
> *prompt*　Angle from XY plane and enter: **20 <R>**
> *prompt*　Angle in XY plane and enter: **–30 <R>**
> *prompt*　dynamic view options and enter: **X <R>**.

4 The model will be displayed with house CAmera configuration as fig(b).

5 With the top right viewport active, enter **DVIEW <R>** at the command line and:
> *prompt*　Select objects or use <DVIEWBLOCK>
> *respond*　**window the model then right-click**
> *prompt*　dynamic view options
> *enter*　**TW <R>**
> *prompt*　Specify view twist angle and enter: **–90 <R>**
> *prompt*　dynamic view options and enter: **X <R>**
> *and*　Model displayed with new twist as fig(c).

6 Use the dynamic view command in the lower viewports with the following entries:

lower left	*lower right*
options: TArget	options: CAmera
angles: −40 and 30	angles: 30 and 30
options: CLip, Front	options: TWist, angle: 180
distance: 10	options: CLip, Front, Distance: 30
options: X	options: X
fig(d)	fig(e).

7 Save the new viewport configuration, but we will not refer to this exercise again.

Summary

1 The dynamic view command is viewport specific, i.e. it only affects the active viewport

2 The command has several useful options:
CAmera, TArget: similar to VPOINT rotate
TWist: allows models to be 'inverted'
Distance: introduces true perspective
CLip: useful to 'see inside' models.

3 The command can only be activated with DVIEW <R> at the command line.

4 The command can be used:
a) directly on models
b) interactively using AutoCAD's house.

5 The command is used relative to the WCS – observe the prompt line when the command is activated.

Assignment

No specific activity, but investigate DVIEW with some previously created models.

Chapter 25

Viewport specific layers

When layers are used with multiple viewports they are generally **GLOBAL**, i.e. what is drawn on a layer in one viewport will be displayed in the other viewports. This is quite acceptable for creating models but is unacceptable for certain other concepts, e.g. when dimensions have to be added to a model, or if the model is to be sectioned. If dimensions are to be added to a multi-view drawing, then these dimensions should only be visible in the active viewport.

In this chapter we will investigate how to create and use viewport specific layers.

Global layers

1 Open the 3D faced model MODR2000\CHEESE from Chapter 14 and refer to Fig. 25.1.

2 With UCS BASE, lower right viewport active make layer DIM current and display the Dimension toolbar.

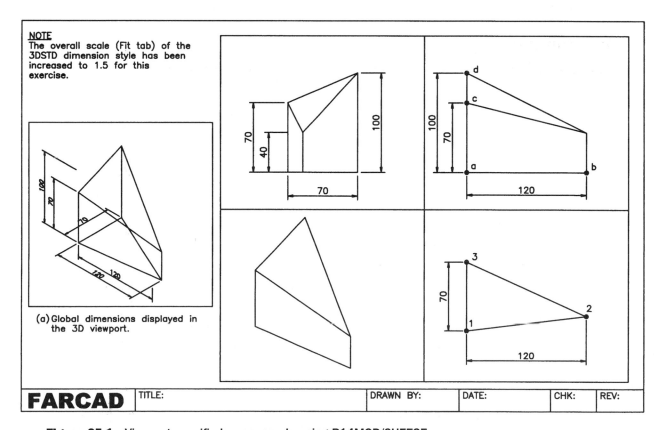

Figure 25.1 Viewport specific layer example using R14MOD/CHEESE.

3 Select the LINEAR DIMENSION icon from the Dimension toolbar and dimension lines 1-2 and 1-3.

4 Make the upper right viewport active and restore UCS FRONT.

5 Linear dimension line a-b and baseline dimension lines a-c and a-d.

6 The five dimensions will be displayed in all four viewports due to the GLOBAL nature of layer DIM. Figure 25.1(a) displays the five dimensions as added to the 3D viewport.

7 Now erase the five dimensions and restore UCS BASE.

8 Remember that dimensioning is a 2D concept, the result depending on the orientation of the UCS.

Viewport specific layers

1 Still with the 3D faced model displayed on screen?

2 Menu bar with **Format-Layer** and:
   prompt   Layer Properties Manager dialogue box
   respond 1. pick the DIM layer line – becomes highlighted
   2. pick New three times to make three new magenta layers: Layer1, Layer2 and Layer3
   3. alter the new layer names to:
      Layer1: DIMTL   Layer2: DIMTR   Layer3: DIMBR
   4. The nomenclature for these new layer names is for individual viewports, e.g. TL: top left, BR: bottom right, TR: top right
   5. pick OK.

3 In model space make the top left viewport active and:
   a) activate the Layer Properties manager dialogue box
   b) select the Show Details option
   c) hold down the control key (Ctrl) and pick the DIMTR and DIMBR layer lines
   d) pick the Freeze in Active viewport option (tick)
   e) note the Active icon changes from yellow to blue
   f) pick OK.

4 With the top right viewport active:
   a) activate the Layer Properties Manager dialogue box
   b) by selecting the Active VP Freeze icon, freeze in the active viewports the new layers DIMTL and DIMBR
   c) pick OK.

5 With the lower right viewport active use the Layer Properties Manager dialogue box to freeze layers DIMTL and DIMTR in the active viewport.

6 In the lower left viewport freeze in the active viewport, the three new layers DIMTL, DIMTR and DIMBR

7 Re-centre the model in top left, top right and lower right viewports about the point 60,35,50 at 175 magnification. This will allow additional 'space' for the dimensions.

8 With UCS BASE and the lower right viewport active:
   a) make layer DIMBR current
   b) linear dimension lines 1-2 and 1-3
   c) the two dimensions should only be displayed in the lower right viewport?

9 Restore UCS FRONT and make the upper right viewport active and:
   a) make layer DIMTR current
   b) linear dimension line a-b and baseline dimension lines a-c and a-d
   c) the three dimensions are only displayed in the top right viewport.

10 *a*) restore UCS RIGHT
   b) make the upper left viewport active
   c) make layer DIMTL current
   d) add the four dimensions as Fig. 25.1.

11 *Notes*.
   a) All dimensions should have been added to the viewport which was active when the command was used.
   b) The dimensions have been added to a viewport specific layer which was made current in the viewport where the dimensions had to be added.
   c) Generally the 3D viewport does not require a dimension layer as dimensions are not usually added to a 3D viewport.
   d) In the 3D viewport the three viewport specific layers were all currently frozen.
   e) The Overall Dimension Scale (Fit tab) of the 3DSTD dimension style was set to 1.5 for this exercise.

Layer states

1 Layers can have different **states** depending on whether they are global or viewport specific, these states being easily controlled:
   a) from the Layer Properties Manager dialogue box
   b) from the icons displayed in the Object Properties toolbar.

2 The different states are:

Global	Viewport specific
On/Off	On/Off
Freeze/Thaw	Freeze/Thaw in all viewports
Lock/Unlock	Freeze/Thaw in active viewports
Plot/non-plot	Freeze/Thaw in new viewports
Lock/Unlock	
Plot/non-plot.	

3 Layers can have more than one state active at a time, e.g. on and locked.

4 Figure 25.2 displays the Layer Properties Manager dialogue box layers icons and names.

5 *a*) An icon displayed in yellow is on or thawed
   b) an icon displayed in blue is off or frozen.

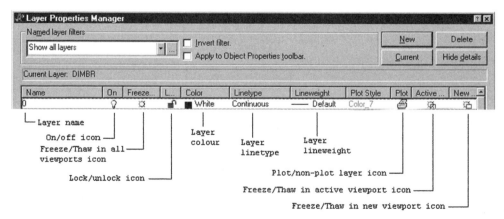

Figure 25.2 The Layer Properties Manager dialogue box layer states.

Summary

1 Viewport specific layers are layers which are specific to a named viewport.

2 Viewport specific layers are used with multi-view drawings and are essential for such concepts as dimensioning a 3D model.

3 Viewport specific layers can **ONLY BE CREATED** if the TILEMODE variable is set to 0, i.e. if paper space is active.

4 Viewport specific layers can be created using the:
   a) Layer Properties Manager dialogue box – recommended
   b) VPLAYER command – not considered in this exercise.

5 The most commonly used state with viewports specific layers is 'Freeze in active viewport'.

Assignment
Activity 17: Dimensioning a 3D model

1 Recall the 3D faced hexagonal prism from activity 10.

2 Make three new dimension layers as the exercise, e.g. DIMTL, etc.

3 Freeze in active viewports layers which have not to be 'displayed' using the same method as the exercise.

4 Making the appropriate viewport active:
   a) restore the required UCS
   b) make the correct DIM layer current
   c) add the dimensions as shown – or your own.

5 Save the completed activity with a different name.

Chapter 26

Shading and 3D orbit

The shading and 3D orbit topics have been used in previous chapters without any discussion. In this chapter we will investigate both topics in greater detail.

Shading

Shading allows certain models to be displayed on the screen as more realistic coloured images. The models which can be shaded (and rendered) are $2\frac{1}{2}$D extruded models, 3D objects, 3D surface models and solid models. We will use some previously created 3D surface models to investigate the topic.

1 Open the ruled surface model MODR2000\ARCHES from Chapter 14.

2 In model space restore UCS BASE and make the 3D viewport active.

3 In paper space, zoom-window the 3D viewport then return to model space.

4 *a*) Menu bar with **View-Hide** to display the model with hidden line removal. Note the 2D icon is still displayed
   b) Menu bar with **View-Regen** to restore original model.

5 *a*) Menu bar with **View-Shade-Hidden** and the model will be displayed with hidden line removal, but note the coloured 3D icon with X-axis red, Y-axis green and Z-axis blue.
   b) Menu bar with View-Regen and model is unchanged.
   c) Menu bar with **View-Shade-3D Wireframe** and the model will be displayed without hidden line removal, but the coloured 3D icon is still displayed.
   d) Menu bar with **View-Shade-2D Wireframe** to restore the original model with the 2D icon.

6 Using the menu bar sequence View-Shade, activate the four shade options returning the display to 3D Wireframe before activating the next option. Note the difference in the shading between the Flat and Gouraud options, evident at the arch curved 'shoulders'.

Explanation of the shade options

Activating SHADE from the View pull-down menu allows the user access to seven options. These options allow models to be displayed as shaded/wireframe images as follows:

1 2D Wireframe: The model is displayed with the boundaries as lines and curves with the 'normal' 2D icon. This option is generally used to restore shaded models to their original appearance.

2 3D Wireframe: Models are displayed as lines and curves for their boundaries but with a coloured 3D icon. When used, this option restores shaded models to their original appearance but retains the coloured 3D icon.

3 Hidden: Displays models with hidden line removal and displays the coloured 3D icon. The REGEN command will not work when this option has been used, and models are restored to their original appearance with either the 2D Wireframe or 3D Wireframe options.

4 Flat Shaded: Models are shaded between their polygon mesh faces and appear flatter and less smooth than the Gouraud shaded models. Any materials (later chapter) which have been applied are also displayed flat shaded.

5 Gouraud Shaded: Models are shaded with the edges between the polygon mesh faces smoothed. This option gives models a realistic appearance. Added materials are also Gouraud shaded.

6 Flat Shaded, Edges On: Models are flat shaded with the wireframe showing through the shade effect.

7 Gouraud Shaded, Edges On: Models displayed with the Gouraud shading effect and the wireframe shows through.

8 General:
   a) Both the Flat and Gouraud shading options display the coloured 3D icon.
   b) The Flat and Gouraud shading use the 2D wireframe or the 3D Wireframe options to restore the model to its original appearance.
   c) The REDRAW/REGEN/REGENALL commands cannot be used if the View-Shade sequence is activated.
   d) If HIDE <R> is entered from the command line to display any model with hidden line removal, the REGEN can be used.

This completes the shading part of the chapter. Ensure that the ARCHES drawing is still displayed with the zoomed 3D viewport for the 3D orbit exercise.

3D orbit

The 3D orbit command is new to R2000 and allows (for the first time in any AutoCAD release) real-time 3D rotation, the user controlling this rotation with the pointing device. The basic concept is that you are viewing the model (the target) with a camera (the user), the target remaining stationary while the camera moves around the target. The opposite effect is displayed on the screen, i.e. the models appears to 'rotate' The 3D orbit concept has its own terminology, the most common being the arcball and icons – Fig. 26.1.

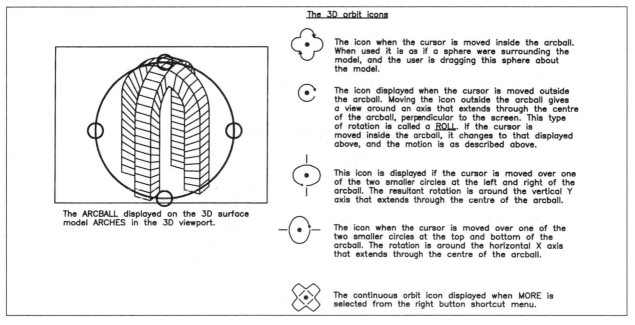

The 3D orbit icons

The ARCBALL displayed on the 3D surface model ARCHES in the 3D viewport.

The icon when the cursor is moved inside the arcball. When used it is as if a sphere were surrounding the model, and the user is dragging this sphere about the model.

The icon displayed when the cursor is moved outside the arcball. Moving the icon outside the arcball gives a view around an axis that extends through the centre of the arcball, perpendicular to the screen. This type of rotation is called a ROLL. If the cursor is moved inside the arcball, it changes to that displayed above, and the motion is as described above.

This icon is displayed if the cursor is moved over one of the two smaller circles at the left and right of the arcball. The resultant rotation is around the vertical Y axis that extends through the centre of the arcball.

The icon when the cursor is moved over one of the two smaller circles at the top and bottom of the arcball. The rotation is around the horizontal X axis that extends through the centre of the arcball.

The continuous orbit icon displayed when MORE is selected from the right button shortcut menu.

Figure 26.1 The 3D orbit icons.

Arcball: is a circle with smaller circles at the quadrants.

Icons: which alter in appearance dependent on were the pointing device is positioned relative to the arcball.

Click and drag: the term for holding down the left button of the mouse and moving the mouse to give rotation of the model.

Roll: a type of rotation when the icon is outside the arcball. It is a rotation about an axis through the centre of the arcball perpendicular to the screen.

Using 3D orbit

1 The ARCHES model still displayed with a zoom-window effect of the 3D viewport in Model space?

2 Pick the 3D Orbit icon from the Standard toolbar and:

prompt	Press ESC or ENTER to exit, or right-click to display shortcut menu
and	arcball displayed
with	a 3D orbit icon depending on where the pointing device is positioned
respond	1. move the icon outside the arcball
	2. hold down the left button
	3. move the mouse in a clockwise direction around the arcball and note model
	4. move icon inside the arcball (still holding down the left button) and continue with the clockwise motion
	5. become familiar with moving the 3D icon around the arcball and note the model rotation
then	**right-click the mouse**
prompt	3D orbit shortcut menu – Fig. 26.2(a)
respond	pick Exit
and	model is displayed in the orientation when the 3D orbit command was exited.

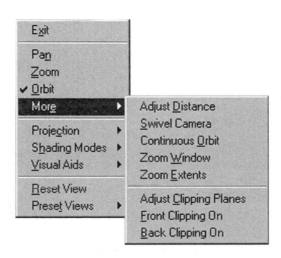

(a) Shortcut menu   (b) The MORE shortcut menu

Figure 26.2 The 3D orbit right-click menu.

3 At the command line enter **U <R>** to restore the model to its original orientation.

4 Menu bar with View-Shade-Flat Shaded.

5 At the command line enter **3DORBIT <R>** and:
  prompt   arcball and 3D orbit icon displayed
  respond 1. move icon around arcball – inside or outside
       2. right-click
  prompt   Shortcut menu
  respond **pick More**
  prompt   cascade shortcut menu
  respond **pick Continuous Orbit**
  prompt   continuous icon displayed
  respond 1. move mouse slightly then leave it alone
       2. model be displayed shaded with continuous rotation
       3. use the mouse left button to alter the rotation
       4. practice the continuous rotation
       5. right-click, pick Exit, then enter U <R>.

The 3D orbit shortcut menu

The right button shortcut menu has been used in the above exercise with the Exit and Continuous orbit options. The user has several useful and powerful options available from this shortcut menu, the complete list being:

Exit: does what it says, it exits the command

Pan: the real-time AutoCAD pan command

Zoom: the real-time AutoCAD zoom command, i.e. movement upwards gives magnification of model, movement downwards gives a reduction

Orbit: indicated that the command is active

More: allows the user access to additional options which include Adjust Distance, Swivel Camera, Continuous Orbit, Clipping Planes options

Projection: allows parallel or perspective selections

Shading Modes: allows selection of the normal AutoCAD shading

Visual Aids: compass, grid and UCS icon

Reset View: a useful selection as it restores the model to its original orientation prior to using the orbit command and should be used instead of the U <R> used previously

Preset Views: allows the normal 3D views to be activated.

Selecting one of the above options is quite straightforward:

1 Activate the 3D orbit command and start rotating the model.

2 Press the right button.

3 Select the required option, e.g. Shading Modes-Flat Shaded.

4 Display restored and the 3D rotation can continue.

The visual aids selection allows the user to display:
  a) a compass: a sphere is displayed inside the arcball consisting of three lines representing the X, Y and Z axes. This sphere rotates with the model
  b) a grid: draws an array of lines on a plane parallel to the current X and Y axes, perpendicular to the Z axis.

The clipping planes

The clipping plane options in 3D orbit are similar to the clip option of the DVIEW command, i.e. the clipping plane is an invisible plane set by the user. Parts of the model can be clipped, i.e. 'cut-away' relative to this clipping plane. To demonstrate the option:

1 Start the model rotating with the 3D orbit command.

2 Activate the shortcut menu and select the Hidden shading mode.

3 Activate the shortcut menu and select More-Adjust Clipping Plane and:
   prompt   Adjust Clipping Plane dialogue box
   respond 1. pick the Adjust Front Clipping icon
           2. drag the datum plane downwards – Fig. 26.3(a)
           3. right-click and close.

4 Continue with the 3D orbit and the model will be rotated with a front clip effect – Fig. 26.3(b).

5 When you are satisfied with the display:
   a) right-click and reset view
   b) right-click and exit.

6 The model should be restored to its original orientation.

7 Try this clipping plane option a few times. It is relatively easy to use.

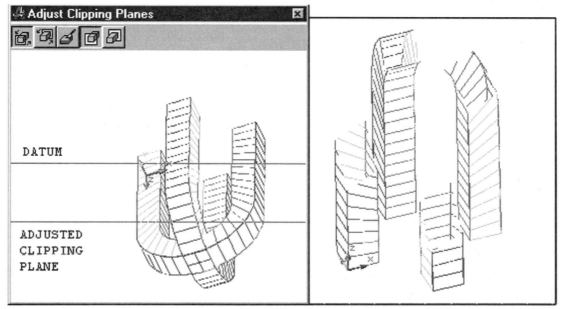

(a) The Adjust Clipping Planes dialogue box, with Front Clipping selection.

(b) The model display in 3D orbit with front clipping on.

Figure 26.3 Using the Adjust Clipping Planes option.

The 3D Orbit toolbar

The toolbar for the 3D orbit command is displayed in Fig. 26.4 and allows the user access to:
a) pan and zoom
b) the 3D orbit, swivel and continuous rotations
c) the 3D adjust distance
d) the clipping plane options: adjust, front and back
e) selecting the current 3D view.

This completes the chapter on shading and 3D orbit.

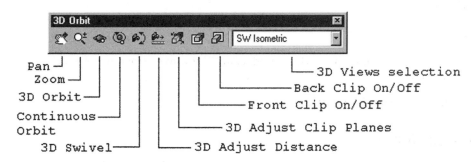

Figure 26.4 The 3D orbit toolbar.

Summary

1 Surface and solid models can be shaded, the two options being Flat and Gouraud.

2 Gouraud shaded models appear smoother than flat shaded models.

3 The 3D orbit command allows interactive real-time 3D rotation of shaded models.

4 The user has access to several useful options when the 3D orbit command is being used. These include parallel and perspective views of the model, front and back clipping and continuous 3D orbit.

5 The user should become familiar with using the 3D orbit command as it will be used with solid modelling.

Chapter 27

Introduction to solid modelling

Three dimensional modelling with computer-aided draughting and design (CADD) can be considered as three categories:
- wire-frame modelling
- surface modelling
- solid modelling.

We have already created wire-frame and surface models and will now concentrated on how solid models are created.

This chapter will summarize the three model types.

Wire-frame modelling

1 Wire-frame models are defined by points and lines and are the simplest possible representation of a 3D component. They may be adequate for certain 3D model representation and require less memory than the other two 3D model types, but wire-frame models have several limitations:

   a) *Ambiguity*: it is difficult to know how a wire-frame model is being viewed, i.e. from above or from below?

   b) *No curved surfaces*: while curves can be added to a wire-frame model as arcs or trimmed circles, an actual curved surface cannot. Lines may be added to give a 'curved effect' but the computer does not recognize these as being part of the model.

   c) *No interference*: as wire-frame models have no surfaces, they cannot detect interference between adjacent components. This makes them unsuitable for kinematic displays, simulations, etc.

   d) *No physical properties*: mass, volume, centre of gravity, moments of inertia, etc. cannot be calculated

   e) *No shading*: as there are no surfaces, a wire-frame model cannot be shaded or rendered.

   f) *No hidden line removal*: as there are no surfaces, it is not possible to display the model with hidden line removal.

2 AutoCAD R2000 allows wire-frame models to be created.

Surface modelling

1 A surface model is defined by points, lines and faces. A wire-frame model can be 'converted' into a surface model by adding these 'faces'. Surface models have several advantages when compared to wire-frame models, some of these being:
   a) recognition and display of curved profiles
   b) shading, rendering and hidden line removal are all possible, i.e. no ambiguity
   c) recognition of holes.

2 Surface models are suited to many applications but they have some limitations which include:
   a) *No physical properties*: other than surface area, a surface model does not allow the calculation of mass, volume, centre of gravity, moments of inertia, etc.
   b) *No detail*: a surface model does not allow section detail to be obtained.

3 Several types of surface model can be generated including:
   a) plane and curved swept surfaces
   b) swept area surfaces
   c) rotated or revolved surfaces
   d) splined curve surfaces
   e) nets or meshes.

4 AutoCAD R2000 allows surface models of all types to be created.

Solid modelling

1 A solid model is defined by the volume the component occupies and is thus a real 3D representation of the component. Solid modelling has many advantages which include:
   a) complete physical properties of mass, volume, centre of gravity, moments of inertia, etc.
   b) dynamic properties of momentum, angular momentum, radius of gyration etc
   c) material properties of stress–strain
   d) full shading, rendering and hidden detail removal
   e) section views and profile extraction
   f) interference between adjacent components can be highlighted
   g) simulation for kinematics, robotics, etc.

2 Solid models are created using a **solid modeller** and there are several types of solid modeller, the two most common being:
   a) constructive solid geometry or constructive representation, i.e. CSG/CREP. The model is created from solid primitives and/or swept surfaces using Boolean operations
   b) boundary representation (BREP). The model is represented by the edges and faces making up the surface, i.e. the topology of the component.

3 AutoCAD R2000 supports solid models of the CSG/CREP type.

4 The AutoCAD R2000 modeller is based on the **ACIS** solid modeller which has certain advantages over the original AME modeller introduced with R12.

Comparison of the model types

The three model types are displayed in:
a) Fig. 27.1: as models with hidden line removal
b) Fig. 27.2: as model cross-sections.

3D WIRE–FRAME MODEL	3D SURFACE MODEL	3D SOLID MODEL
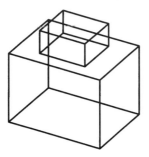		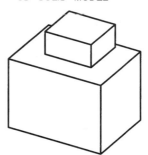
1. Model has length, width and height 2. There are no surfaces on the model. 3. The model does not have area, volume or mass 4. HIDE has no effect on the appearance of the model 5. The model displays AMBIGUITY ie it is difficult to know if the model is being viewed from above or from below.	1. Model has length, width and height 2. Surfaces have been added 3. The model has a surface area but no volume or mass 4. The HIDE command displays the model with hidden line removal 5. There is no ambiguity 6. No details can be extracted from the model. 7. The model can be shaded and rendered.	1. The model has length, width and height 2. The model has a surface area, a volume and a mass 3. The HIDE command will display the model with hidden line removal and there is no ambiguity 4. The model has mass properties eg centroid, moment of inertia, radius of gyration etc 5. Details can be extracted from the model eg sections 6. The model can be shaded and rendered

Figure 27.1 Simple comparison between wire-frame, surface and solid models.

3D WIRE–FRAME MODEL	3D SURFACE MODEL	3D SOLID MODEL
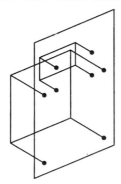	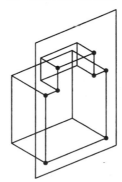	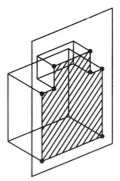
The model is represented as a series of corner points and edge lines. The cross–section of the model is a series of points which are not connected. The model is useful for general shapes, appearance and position only.	The model is represented as a series of corner points, edge lines and face surfaces. The cross–section of the model is a series of points and connected face lines. The model is useful for external surface display and can be displayed with hidden line removal and shading. Materials can be applied to the surfaces for rendering.	The model is represented as a series of corner points, edge lines, face surfaces and interior volume. The cross–section of the model is a series of points, face lines and section planes. The model is useful for mass properties, dynamic properties and material properties with hidden line removal and shading. Materials can be applied for rendering.

Figure 27.2 Further comparison of model types as cross-section.

The solid model standard sheet

A solid model standard sheet (prototype drawing) will be created as a template and drawing file using the layout from the surface model exercises, i.e. MV3DSTD. This standard sheet will:
a) be for A3 paper
b) have a four viewport (paper space) configuration.

1 Menu bar with **File-New** and open your MV3DSTD template file.

2 Check the following:
   a) Tool-Named UCS: BASE, FRONT, RIGHT displayed
   b) Layers 0,DIM,MODEL,OBJECTS,SECT,SHEET,TEXT,VP
   c) Sheet layout to your own specification
   d) Text style: ST1 with romans.shx font
   e) Dimension style 3DSTD with various settings.

3 At the command line enter **PURGE <R>** and:
prompt	Enter type of unused objects to purge
enter	**LA <R>** – layer option
prompt	Enter names to purge<*> and right-click
prompt	Verify each name to be purges [Yes/No] and right-click
prompt	Purge layer "DIM" and enter: **N <R>**
prompt	Purge layer "OBJECTS" and enter: **Y <R>**
prompt	Purge layer "SECT" and enter: N <R>
prompt	Purge layer "TEXT" and enter: N <R>.

4 Repeat the command line PURGE command with the following entries:
   a) B (blocks) and purge all (if any) blocks
   b) D (dimstyles) and purge all dimension styles except 3DSTD
   c) ST (textstyles) and purge any text styles except ST1.

5 At the command line enter **ISOLINES <R>** and:
prompt	Enter new value for ISOLINES<4>
enter	**18 <R>**.

6 At the command line enter **FACETRES <R>** and:
prompt	Enter new value for FACETRES<0.5000>
enter	**1 <R>**.

7 Display the Draw, Modify, Object Snap and Solids toolbars.

8 Make the lower left viewport active, restore UCS BASE with layer MODEL current.

9 Menu bar with **File-Save As** and:
prompt	Save Drawing As dialogue box
respond	1. scroll at Save as Type
	2. pick **AutoCAD Drawing Template File (*.dwt)**
	3. enter file name as: **A3SOL.dwt**
	4. pick **Save**
prompt	Template Description dialogue box
enter	**My solid model prototype layout created on ???**
then	pick OK.

10 Menu bar with **File-Save As** and:
   prompt   Save Drawing As dialogue box
   respond   1. scroll at Save as Type
        2. pick **AutoCAD 2000 Drawing (*.dwg)**
        3. enter file name: **A3SOL.dwg**
        4. scroll and pick your named folder
        5. pick **Save**.

11 You are now ready to start creating solid models.

   Notes.

1 The new A3SOL solid model standard sheet has been saved as both a template file and a drawing file.

2 The A3Sol drawing file has been saved to your named folder, while the template file has been saved to the AutoCAD Template folder. You can save the template file to your named folder if required.

3 Two new system variables have been introduced in the creation of the A3SOL template/drawing file, these being:
   ISOLINES: specifies the number of isolines per surface on objects. It is an integer with values between 0 and 2047. The default value is 4.
   FACETRES: adjusts the smoothness of shaded and rendered objects and objects with hidden line. The value can be between 0.01 and 10.00, the default being 0.5.

4 The ISOLINES and FACETRES values may be altered when creating some models.

5 The viewports have not been zoom-centred, as this will depend on the model being created.

6 Solid modelling consists of creating 'composites' from 'primitives' and R2000 supports the following types of primitive:
   a) basic   *b*) swept   *c*) edge.

7 All three types of primitive will be investigated with examples and the various options for each will be discussed.

Solid modelling is a fascinating topic, and should give the user a great deal of satisfaction as the various models are created and rendered.

Chapter 28

The basic solid primitives

AutoCAD R2000 supports the six basic solid primitives of box, wedge, cylinder, cone, sphere and torus. In this chapter we will create (interesting?) layouts using each primitive and also investigate the various options which are available.

Note. During the exercises do not just accept the coordinate values given, try and reason out why they are being used.

The BOX primitive – Fig. 28.1

1 Open your A3SOL template file with layer MODEL, UCS BASE and the lower left viewport active. Display the Object Snap and Solids toolbars.

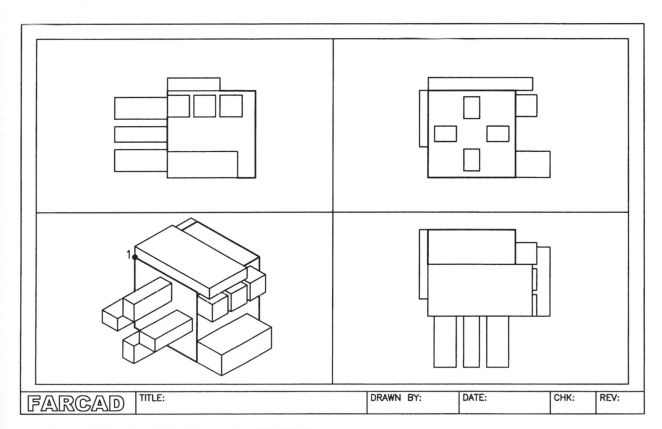

Figure 28.1 The BOX solid primitive (BOXPRIM).

2 Select the BOX icon from the Solids toolbar and:
   prompt   Specify corner of box or [CEnter]<0,0,0>
   enter   **0,0,0 <R>**
   prompt   Specify corner or [Cube/Length]
   enter   **C <R>** – the cube option
   prompt   Specify length
   enter   **100 <R>**
   and   a red cube is displayed in all viewports.

3 Select from the menu bar **Draw-Solids-Box** and:
   prompt   Specify corner of box or [CEnter]<0,0,0>
   enter   **100,0,0 <R>**
   prompt   Specify corner or [Cube/Length]
   enter   **L <R>** – the length option
   prompt   Specify length and enter: **40 <R>**
   prompt   Specify width and enter: **80 <R>**
   prompt   Specify height and enter: **30 <R>**
   and   another red cuboid is displayed in all viewports.

4 At the command line enter **CHANGE <R>** and:
   prompt   Select objects
   respond **pick the smaller box then right-click**
   prompt   Specify change point or [Properties] and enter: **P <R>**
   prompt   Enter property to change and enter: **C <R>**
   prompt   Enter new color and enter: **3 <R> or green <R>**
   prompt   Enter property to change and right-click/enter.

5 Now zoom centre about 60,20,60 at 200 magnification in all viewports, then make the lower left again active.

6 At the command line enter **BOX <R>** and:
   prompt   Specify corner of box or [CEnter]<0,0,0>
   respond **Endpoint icon and pick pt1** – first corner point
   prompt   Specify corner or [Cube/Length]
   enter   **@120,60,15 <R>** – the diagonally opposite corner point.

7 Change the colour of this box to blue, with CHANGE <R> at the command line as step 4.

8 Restore UCS RIGHT.

9 Create a solid box with the following information:
   a) corner: 0,70,100
   b) cube option with length: 25.

10 *a*) At the command line enter **CHANGE <R>** and:
       prompt   Select objects
       respond   pick the last box created
       prompt   1 was not parallel to the UCS
       respond   right-click to end the command
    b) At the command line enter **CHPROP <R>** and:
       prompt   Select objects
       respond   pick the last box created and right-click
       prompt   Enter property to change and enter: **C <R>**
       prompt   Enter new color and enter: **MAGENTA <R>**
       prompt   Enter property to change and right-click/enter.

c) *Note.*

The CHANGE and CHPROP commands will be discussed at the end of the chapter. In future, when an object has to have its colour changed use the CHPROP command from the command line.

11 Rectangular array the magenta box:
a) for 1 row and 3 columns
b) with column distance: 30.

12 Restore UCS FRONT.

13 Activate the solid BOX command and:
prompt Specify corner of box or [CEntre]<0,0,0>
enter **CE <R>** – the box center point option
prompt Specify center of box and enter: **50,80,30 <R>**
prompt Specify corner of box or [Cube/Length] and enter: **L <R>**
prompt Specify length and enter: **18 <R>**
prompt Specify width and enter: **25 <R>**
prompt Specify height and enter: **60 <R>**.

14 With CHPROP, change the colour of this last box to suit yourself. I used colour number 76.

15 Polar array this last box with:
a) center point: 50,50
b) items: 4
c) 360 angle with rotation.

16 Finally restore UCS BASE and create another solid box with:
a) corner: 0,100,100
b) length: −10   width: −80   height: −65
c) colour: number 234.

17 The model is now complete so save as **MODR2000\BOXPRIM**

18 *Investigate.*
a) The model with hide – menu bar or command line.
b) Shading the viewports.
c) The 3D orbit command with the 3D viewport active, and the model shaded.
d) Restoring the model to the original 3D wirefame display.

19 *Changing properties.*
When solid model layouts are being created the user will be asked to change some properties, especially the colour. All primitives will be originally displayed as red (due to layer MODEL being current) and thus require to be changed to another colour. This is to give a coloured image for shading, rendering and for the 3D orbit command. Changing the colour of a primitive depends on the value of the PICKFIRST system variable and:
a) if PICKFIRST is set to 0, then use CHANGE <R> at the command line as step 4, i.e. activate the command then pick the object which is to have its colour changed.
b) If PICKFIRST is set to 1 then:
1. select the object to be changed
2. pick the Properties icon from the Standard toolbar
3. pick the Color line
4. scroll and pick the required colour
5. cancel the Properties dialogue box and press ESC.

20 *CHANGE or CHPROP?*
These two commands are similar but:
a) CHANGE can only be used for objects created with the current UCS, hence the step 10(a) message.
b) CHPROP can be used with **ANY** UCS setting, and should be used for all future change colour operations.

21 The user must now decide whether to set PICKFIRST to 0 or 1. My personal preference is to have PICKFIRST set to 0 and use the CHPROP command.

The WEDGE primitive – Fig. 28.2

1 Open the A3SOL template file with layer MODEL, UCS BASE and lower left viewport active.

2 Menu bar with **Draw-Solids-Wedge** and:
prompt Specify corner of wedge or [CEnter]<0,0,0>
enter **0,0,0 <R>**
prompt Specify corner or [Cube/Length]
enter **C <R>** – the cube option
prompt Specify length
enter **100 <R>**
and red wedge displayed in all viewports.

3 Select the WEDGE icon from the Solids toolbar and:
prompt Specify corner of wedge or [CEnter]
enter **0,0,0 <R>**
prompt Specify corner or [Cube/Length]
enter **@80,–60 <R>** – the other corner option
prompt Specify height and enter: **50 <R>**.

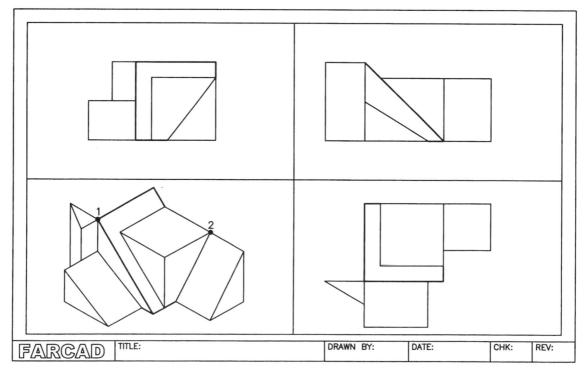

Figure 28.2 The wedge solid primitive (WEDPRIM).

4 Change the colour of this wedge to blue.

5 In each viewport, zoom centre about 80,30,50 at 200 magnification and pan to suit if needed.

6 At the command line enter **WEDGE <R>** and create a solid wedge with:
   a) corner: 100,100,0
   b) length: 60   width: 60   height: 80
   c) colour: green
   d) 2D rotate the green wedge about the point 100,100 by **−90°**.

7 Restore UCS FRONT and create a wedge:
   a) corner: **endpoint icon and pick pt1**
   b) length: −50
   c) width: −100
   d) height: 30
   e) colour: magenta (CHPROP command).

8 Restore UCS BASE.

9 The final wedge is to be created with:
   a) corner: **endpoint of pt2**
   b) cube option with length: −80
   c) colour: number 14.

10 Save the model layout as **MODR2000\WEDPRIM.**.

11 Hide and shade the model in each viewport.

12 Use 3D orbit with the shaded model in the 3D viewport.

The CYLINDER primitive – Fig. 28.3

1 Open A3SOL, UCS BASE, layer MODEL, lower left active.

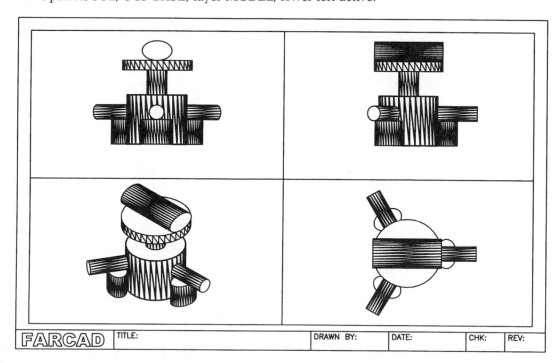

Figure 28.3 The CYLINDER solid primitive (CYLPRIM).

2 Menu bar with **Draw-Solids-Cylinder** and:
   prompt   `Specify center point for base of cylinder or [Elliptical]`
   enter   **0,0,0 <R>** – the cylinder base centre point
   prompt   `Specify radius for base of cylinder or [Diameter]`
   enter   **60 <R>** – the cylinder radius
   prompt   `Specify height of cylinder or [Center of other end]`
   enter   **100 <R>** – the cylinder height
   and   a red cylinder is displayed, centred on 0,0,0.

3 Select the CYLINDER icon from the Solids toolbar and:
   prompt   `Specify center point for base of cylinder or [Elliptical]`
   enter   **E <R>** – the elliptical option
   prompt   `Specify axis endpoint of ellipse for base of cylinder or`
              `[Center]`
   enter   **C <R>** – the centre option
   prompt   `Specify center point of ellipse for base of cylinder`
   enter   **80,0,0 <R>**
   prompt   `Specify axis endpoint of ellipse for base of cylinder`
   enter   **@20,0,0 <R>**
   prompt   `Specify length of other axis for base of cylinder`
   enter   **@0,30,0 <R>**
   prompt   `Specify height of cylinder or [Center of other end]`
   enter   **50 <R>**.

4 Change the colour of this cylinder to green, then polar array it:
   a) about the point 0,0
   b) for 3 items, full angle with rotation.

5 Zoom centre about 0,0,80 at 300 magnification in all viewports.

6 At the command line enter **CYLINDER <R>** and:
   prompt   `Specify center point for base of cylinder or [Elliptical]`
   enter   **60,0,65 <R>** – the cylinder base centre point
   prompt   `Specify radius for base of cylinder` and enter: **15 <R>**
   prompt   `Specify height of cylinder or [Center of other end]`
   enter   **C <R>** – centre of other end option
   prompt   `Specify center of other end of cylinder`
   enter   **@80,0,0 <R>**.

7 Change the colour of this cylinder to magenta and polar array it with the same entries as step 4.

8 Create another two cylinders:

centre pt	rad	ht	colour
0,0,100	20	50	number 15
0,0,150	70	20	blue.

9 Finally create an elliptical cylinder:
   a) centre: 70,0,190
   b) axis endpoint: @30,0
   c) length of other axis: @0,20
   d) centre of other end: @–140,0,0
   e) colour to suit.

10 Save the model as MODR2000\CYLPRIM.

11 Hide the model and note the triangular facets which are not displayed when the cylinder primitives are created. Shade then return the model to wireframe representation.

12 *Investigate*.
    a) With the 3D viewport active, enter ISOLINES at the command line and enter a value of 6. Enter REGEN <R> and note model display
    b) change the ISOLINES value to 48 and regen
    c) return the ISOLINES value to the original 18
    d) enter FACETRES at the command line and alter the value to 2, then enter HIDE <R>. Note the effect then regen
    e) alter FACTRES to 5, hide then regen
    f) return FACETRES to 1.

13 *Note*.
The ISOLINES system variable controls the appearance of primitive curved surfaces when they are created. The triangulation effect, or *FACETS*, is controlled by the system variable FACETRES. The higher the value of FACETRES (max 10) then the 'better the appearance' of curved surfaces, but the longer it takes for hide and shade. At our level, the values of 18 for ISOLINES and 1 for FACETRES are sufficient.

The CONE primitive – Fig. 28.4

1 Open the A3SOL template file, UCS BASE, etc.

2 Menu bar with **Draw-Solid-Cone** and:
    prompt   Specify center point for base of cone or [Elliptical]
    enter   **0,0,0 <R>** – the cone base centre point
    prompt   Specify radius for base of cone or [Diameter]
    enter   **50<R>**
    prompt   Specify height of cone or [Apex]
    enter   **60 <R>**.

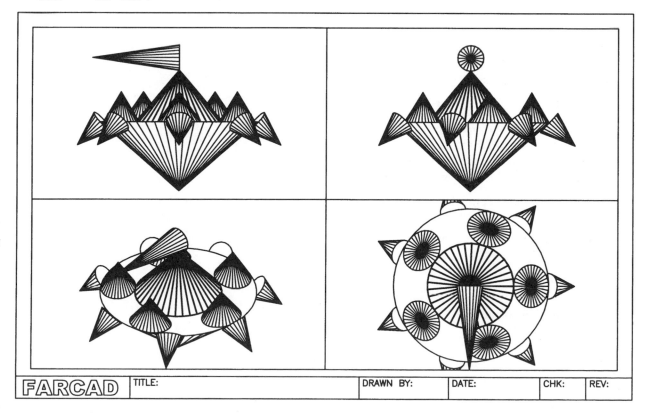

Figure 28.4 The CONE solid primitive (CONPRIM).

3 Create another cone with:
   a) centre: 0,0,0
   b) radius: 90
   c) height: −80
   d) colour: green.

4 Centre each viewport about the point 0,0,10 at 200 mag.

5 Select the CONE icon from the Solids toolbar and:
   prompt   Specify center point for base of cone or [Elliptical]
   enter   **E <R>** – the elliptical option
   prompt   Specify axis endpoint of ellipse for base of cone or [Center]
   enter   **C <R>** – the centre point option
   prompt   Specify center point of ellipse for base of cone
   enter   **70,0,0 <R>**
   prompt   Specify axis endpoint of ellipse for base of cone and enter: **@20,0,0 <R>**
   prompt   Specify length of other axis for base of cone and enter: **@0,25,0 <R>**
   prompt   Specify height of cone or [Apex] and enter: **35 <R>**.

6 Change the colour of this cone to blue, then polar array it with:
   a) centre point: 0,0
   b) items: 5
   c) full angle to fill, with rotation.

7 At the command line enter **CONE <R>** and:
   prompt   Specify center point for base of cone and enter: **90,0,0 <R>**
   prompt   Specify radius for base of cone and enter: **15 <R>**
   prompt   Specify height of cone or [Apex]
   enter   **A <R>** – the apex option
   prompt   Specify apex point
   enter   **@40,0,0 <R>**.

8 Change the colour of this last cone to colour number 235.

9 Use the ROTATE 3D command with the last cone and:
   a) enter a Y axis rotation
   b) enter 90,0,0 as the point on the Y axis
   c) enter 41.63 as the rotation angle – why this figure?

10 Polar array the last cone about the point 0,0 for seven items, full angle with rotation.

11 Create the final cone with:
   a) centre: 0,0,75
   b) radius: 15
   c) apex option: @0,−100,0
   d) colour to suit.

12 Hide, shade, 3D orbit then save as MODR2000\CONPRIM.

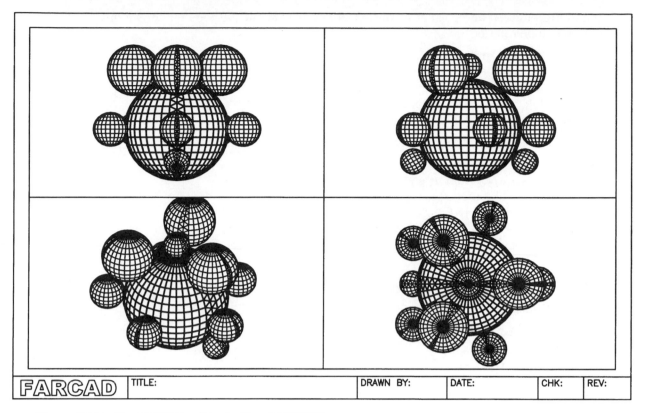

FARCAD | TITLE: | | DRAWN BY: | DATE: | CHK: | REV:

Figure 28.5 The SPHERE solid primitive (SPHPRIM).

The SPHERE primitive – Fig. 28.5

1 Open the A3SOL template file, UCS BASE, etc.

2 Menu bar with **Draw-Solids-Sphere** and:
   prompt   Specify center of sphere<0,0,0>
   enter   **0,0,0 <R>**
   prompt   Specify radius of sphere or [Diameter]
   enter   **60 <R>**.

3 Centre each viewport about 0,0,20 at 200 magnification.

4 Select the SPHERE icon from the Solids toolbar and:
   prompt   Specify center of sphere<0,0,0>
   enter   **80,0,0 <R>**
   prompt   Specify radius of sphere or [Diameter]
   enter   **D <R>** – the diameter option
   prompt   Specify diameter and enter: **40 <R>**.

5 Change the colour of this sphere to green, then polar array it:
   a) about the point: 0,0
   b) for five items
   c) full angle with rotation.

6 At the command line enter **SPHERE <R>** and create a sphere with:
   a) centre: 0,0,75
   b) radius: 15
   c) colour: magenta.

7 Restore UCS FRONT and polar array the magenta sphere about the point 0,0 for 3 items with full angle rotation.

8 Restore UCS BASE and create the final sphere with:
   a) centre: 58,0,70
   b) radius: 30
   c) colour blue
   d) polar arrayed about 0,0 for 3 items, full angle rotation.

9 Hide, shade, save as MODR2000\SPHPRIM.

10 *Investigate.*
   a) ISOLINES set to 48 then regen
   b) ISOLINES set to 5 then regen
   c) restore original ISOLINES 18
   d) FACETRES set to 10 then hide and regen
   e) Note the appearance of the sphere primitives with these system variable values.

The TORUS primitive – Fig. 28.6

1 A3SOL template file with UCS BASE

2 Menu bar with **Draw-Solids-Torus** and:
   prompt   Specify center of torus<0,0,0>
   enter   **0,0,0 <R>**
   prompt   Specify radius of torus or [Diameter]
   enter   **80 <R>**
   prompt   Specify radius of tube or [Diameter]
   enter   **15 <R>**.

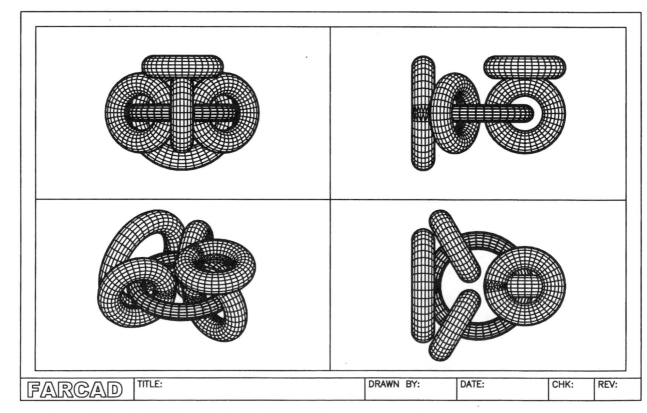

FARCAD	TITLE:		DRAWN BY:	DATE:	CHK:	REV:

Figure 28.6 The TORUS solid primitive (TORPRIM).

3 Zoom centre about 0,0,0 at 300 magnification in all viewports.

4 Restore UCS FRONT and select the TORUS icon from the Solids toolbar and:
   prompt `Specify center of torus<0,0,0>`
   enter   **80,0,0 <R>**
   prompt `Specify radius of torus` and enter: **50 <R>**
   prompt `Specify radius of tube` and enter: **20 <R>**.

5 Change the colour of this torus to blue.

6 Restore UCS BASE and polar array the blue torus about 0,0 for 3. Items with full circle rotation.

7 Restore UCS RIGHT, enter **TORUS <R>** at the command line and create a torus with:
   a) centre: 0,0,−95
   b) radius of torus: 80
   c) radius of tube: 20
   d) colour: green.

8 Restore UCS BASE and create the final torus with:
   a) centre: 80,0,80
   b) radius of torus: 50
   c) radius of tube: 20
   d) colour: to suit.

9 Hide, shade and save as MODR2000\TORPRIM.

10 *Investigate*.
   The effect of ISOLINES and FACETRES on the layout.

Summary

1 The six solid primitives can be activated:
   a) from the menu bar with Draw-Solids
   b) by icon selection from the Solids toolbar
   c) by entering the solid name at the command line.

2 The corner/centre start points can be:
   a) entered as coordinates from the keyboard
   b) referenced to existing objects
   c) picking suitable points on the screen.

3 All six primitives have options:
   box: *a*) corner; centre
             b) cube; length, width, height; other corner
   wedge: *a*) corner; centre
             b) cube; length, width, height; other corner
   cylinder: *a*) circular; elliptical
             b) radius; diameter
             c) height; centre of other end
   cone: *a*) circular; elliptical
             b) radius; diameter
             c) height; apex point
   sphere: *a*) centre only
             b) diameter; radius
   torus: *a*) centre only
             b) radius of torus; diameter
             c) radius of tube; diameter.

Assignment

A single activity for your imaginative mind.

Activity 18: A solid primitive layout

Create a layout **of your own design** with the six basic primitives using the following information and with your own colours:

Box: length: 100   *Wedge*: length: 50   *Cylinder*: radius: 20
width: 40   width: 60   height: 80
height: 30   height: 50

Cone: radius: 50   *Sphere*: radius: 40   *Torus*: torus rad: 50
height: 120   tube rad: 20

Chapter 29

The swept solid primitives

Solid models can be generated by extruding or revolving 'shapes' and in this chapter we will use several exercises to demonstrate how complex solids can be created from relatively simple shapes.

Extruded solids

Solid models can be created by extruding **CLOSED OBJECTS** such as polyline shapes, polygons, circles, ellipses, splines and regions:
a) to a specified height and taper angle
b) along a path.

Extruded example 1: letters

1 Open your A3SOL template file, layer MODEL, Solids toolbar.

2 *a*) change the viewpoint in lower left viewport with VPOINT-ROTATE and angles of 30 and 30
   b) upper left viewport active and restore UCS RIGHT.

3 Using the reference sizes given in Fig. 29.1:
   a) draw the three letters M, T and C as polyline shapes
   b) use Modify-Polyline to 'convert' the letter C into a single polyline
   c) use your discretion for sizes not given (a snap of 5 helps)
   d) use the start points A, B and C given.

4 Still with UCS RIGHT, zoom centre about 0,50,0 at 200 in 3D viewport and 300 in the other three viewports.

5 Menu bar with **Draw-Solids-Extrude** and:
   prompt   Select objects
   respond **pick the letter M then right-click**
   prompt   Specify height of extrusion or [Path]
   enter   **80 <R>**
   prompt   Specify angle of taper for extrusion
   enter   **0 <R>**.

6 The letter M will be extruded for a height of 80 in the positive Z direction.

7 Select the EXTRUDE icon from the Solids toolbar and:
   prompt   Select objects
   respond **pick the letter T then right-click**
   prompt   Specify height of extrusion or [Path]
   enter   **50 <R>**
   prompt   Specify angle of taper for extrusion and enter: **5<R>**.

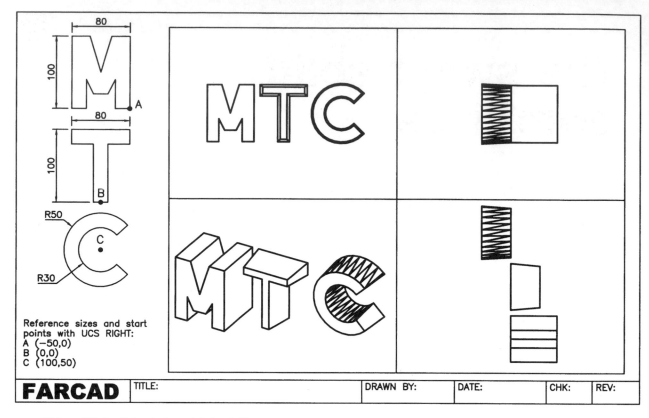

Figure 29.1 Extruded model 1 – letters.

8 At the command then enter **EXTRUDE <R>** and:
   a) objects: pick the letter C then right-click
   b) height: enter **–50**
   c) taper angle: enter **–3**.

9 Hide and shade each viewport, then save if required.

Extruded example 2: keyed splined shaft

1 Open the A3SOL template file, layer MODEL, UCS BASE and the lower right viewport active.

2 Zoom centre about 0,0,–20 at 150 magnification in all viewports.

3 Refer to Fig. 29.2 and create two profiles:
   a) an outer tooth profile from two circles and an arrayed line, then trim as required. The circle centres should be at 0,0
   b) an inner shaft profile to your own specification.

4 Use the menu bar sequence Modify-Polyline (or PEDIT at the command line) to convert each profile into a single polyline using the Join option.

5 Alter the system variables ISOLINES to 6 and FACETRES to 0.5.

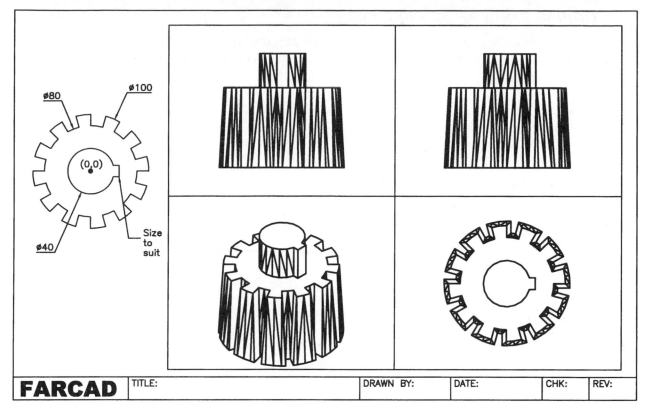

Figure 29.2 Extruded model 2 – splined shaft.

6 Select the EXTRUDE icon from the Solids toolbar and:
   prompt   Select objects
   respond **pick the outer tooth profile then right-click**
   prompt   Specify height of extrusion or [Path]
   enter   **–70 <R>**
   prompt   Specify angle of taper for extrusion
   enter   **–3 <R>**.

7 Repeat the Extrude icon selection and:
   a) objects: pick the inner shaft profile then right-click
   b) height: enter 30
   c) taper: enter 0.

8 Gouraud shade the model and use 3D orbit in the 3d viewport.

9 *Note:* the 'dense' display of the model without the hide effect.

10 Save the model layout if required.

Extruded example 3: a moulding

1 Open the A3SOL template file with UCS BASE, layer MODEL and with the lower right viewport active. Centre the viewports about the point 120,75,35 at 300 magnification.

2 Draw a polyline with:
start point: 0,0
next point: @0,100
arc option with endpoint: @100,0
arc endpoint: @100,–100
line option with endpoint: @100,0 then right-click/enter.

3 Change the colour of the polyline to bluc.

4 Restore UCS FRONT and make the top right viewport active.

5 Use the reference sizes in Fig. 29.3 to create the moulding as a single polyline or create your own outline design if required.

6 Make the lower left viewport active.

7 Set ISOLINES to 12.

8 Select the EXTRUDE icon from the Solids toolbar and:
prompt   Select objects
respond **pick the red polyline then right-click**
prompt   Specify height of extrusion or [Path]
enter   **P <R>** – the path option
prompt   Select extrusion path
respond **pick the blue polyline**
and   the red outline is extruded along the blue path.

9 Shade the model, 3D orbit then restore to original wireframe.

10 Save the model if required.

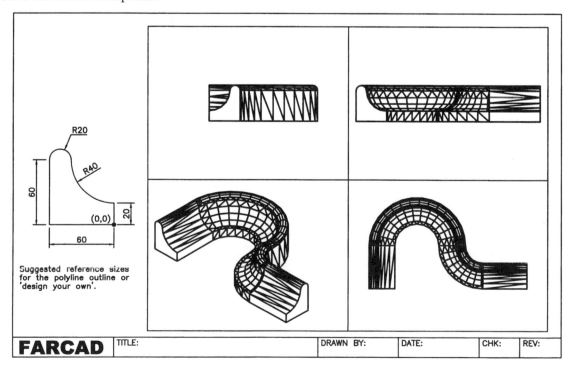

Figure 29.3 Extruded model 3 – the moulding.

Extruded example 4: a polygon type duct arrangement

1 Open the A3SOL template file with UCS BASE, layer MODEL and the lower left viewport active.

2 Create a five segment 3D polyline with the menu bar sequence **Draw-3D Polyline** and:
   prompt   From point and enter: **0,0 <R>**
   prompt   Start point and enter: **@0,0,100 <R>**
   prompt   Specify endpoint of line and enter: **@100,0,100 <R>**
   prompt   Specify endpoint of line and enter: **@100,100,0 <R>**
   prompt   Specify endpoint of line and enter: **@0,100,100 <R>**
   prompt   Specify endpoint of line and enter: **@100,100,-100 <R>**
   prompt   Specify endpoint of line and: right-click/enter.

3 Change the colour of the 3D polyline to green.

4 In each viewport, zoom centre about 150,150,175 at 400 mag.

5 Draw a polygon with:
   a) sides: 6
   b) centre: 0,0
   c) inscribed in a circle of radius 40.

6 Select the EXTRUDE icon and:
   a) objects: pick the red polygon then right-click
   b) enter P <R> for the path option
   c) path: pick the green 3D polyline.

7 The polygon will be extruded along the green path to give a ducting effect.

8 Shade, 3D orbit then save the model if required.

9 This completes the extrusion exercises.

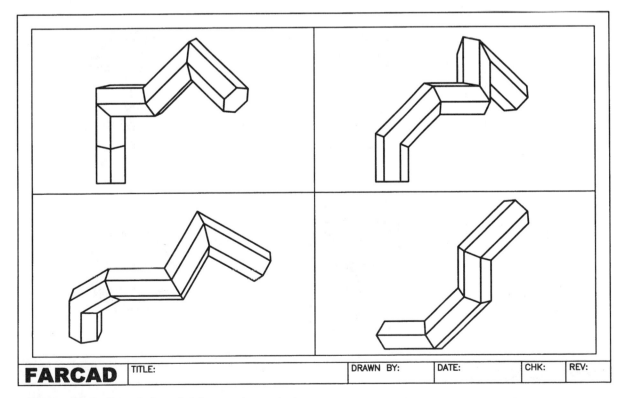

Figure 29.4 Extruded model 4 – a polygon duct.

Revolved solids

Solid models can be created by revolving objects (closed polylines, polygons, circles, ellipses, closed splines, regions) about the X and Y axes or selected objects by a specified angle. As with extrusions, very complex models can be obtained from relatively simple shapes.

Revolved example 1: a flagon

1 Open the A3SOL template file, UCS BASE and layer MODEL current and in each viewport zoom centre about 0,80,0 at 200 mag.

2 *a*) Set ISOLINES to 12
   b) In the top left viewport, alter the viewpoint with VPOINT-ROTATE with angles of 30 and −20.

3 Restore UCS FRONT and make the top right viewport active.

4 Refer to Fig. 29.5 and draw a **closed** polyline outline using the sizes given as a reference – or design your own.

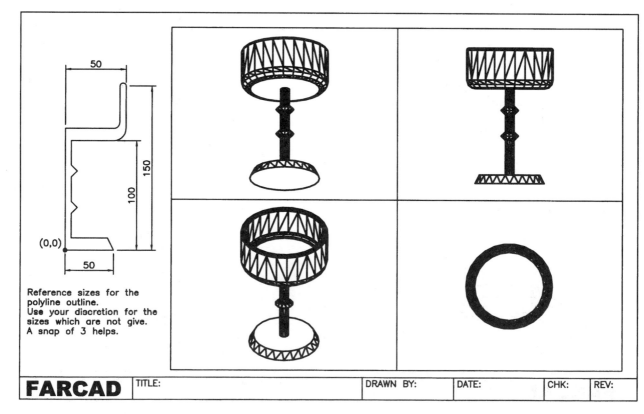

Figure 29.5 Resolved example 1 – a flagon.

5 Menu bar with **Draw-Solids-Revolve** and:
- *prompt*   Select objects
- *respond* **pick the polyline then right-click**
- *prompt*   Specify start point for axis of revolution or define axis by [Object/X (axis)/Y (axis)]
- *enter*   **Y <R>** – the Y axis option
- *prompt*   Specify angle of revolution
- *respond* **right-click** to accept the 360 (full circle) default.

6 The polyline outline will be revolved into a swept revolved solid.

7 Shade one of the 3D viewports and 3D orbit.

8 Save the completed model.

Revolved example 2: a shaft

1 Open the A3SOL template file, UCS BASE. Layer MODEL and the lower right viewport active

2 In each viewport zoom centre about 50,0,0 at 200 magnification

3 Refer to Fig. 29.6 and draw a **closed** polyline outline using the sizes given. Use the (0,−30) start point. Note that I have only displayed the 3D viewport with this exercise. This was for convenience purposes only.

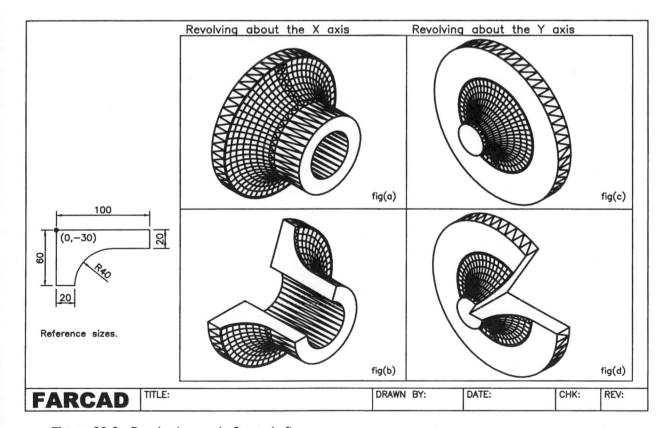

Figure 29.6   Resolved example 2 – a shaft.

4   Menu bar with **Draw-Solids-Revolve** and:

    prompt   Select objects

    respond **pick the polyline then right-click**

    prompt   Specify start point of axis of revolution or define axis
               by [Object/X (axis)/Y (axis)]

    enter   **X <R>** – the X axis option

    prompt   Specify angle of revolution

    enter   **360 <R>**.

5   The polyline outline will be revolved about the X axis as fig(a).

6   Observe the effect then undo the revolved effect to restore the original polyline outline.

7   Select the revolve icon from the solids toolbar and:
    a) objects: select the polyline outline then right-click
    b) axis of revolution: X axis
    c) angle of revolution: 250
    d) the revolved effect will be as fig(b). Observe then undo.

8   At the command line enter **REVOLVE <R>** and:
    a) objects: select polyline then right-click
    b) axis of revolution: enter Y <R>
    c) angle of revolution: 360
    d) the result will be as fig(c) – pan needed?
    e) observe and undo the revolved effect.

9   Finally revolve the polyline:
    a) about the Y axis
    b) with a 300 angle of revolution – fig(d).

10   Shade, 3D orbit, etc. then save if required.

11   This completes the swept primitive exercises.

Summary

1   Swept solids are obtained with the extrude and revolve commands.

2   The two commands can be activated:
    a) by icon selection from the Solids toolbar
    b) from the command line with Draw-Solids
    c) by entering EXTRUDE and REVOLVE at the command line.

3   Very complex models can be obtained from simple shapes

4   Only certain 'shapes' can be extruded/revolved. These are closed polylines, circles, ellipses, polygons, closed splines and regions (more on this in a later chapter).

5   Objects can be extruded:
    a) to a specified height
    b) with/without a taper angle
    c) along a path curve.

6   The extruded height is in the Z direction and can be positive or negative.

7   The taper angle can be positive or negative.

8   Objects can be revolved:
    a) about the X and Y axes
    b) about an object
    c) by specifying two points on the axis of revolution.

9   The angle of revolution can be full (360) or partial.

Assignment

During the excavation of the ancient city of CADOPOLIS, the intrepid diggers uncovered two artefacts, both of which they attributed to our master builder MACFARAMUS. They decided (how we will never know), that the artefacts were scale models of a pyramid and the partial wheel from a chariot. It is these that you have to create as solid models from swept primitives.

Activity 19: Two swept primitive models designed by MACFARAMUS

These two models have to be created from closed polylines. The dimensions taken by the site engineers were not complete and only the basic sizes have been given. You have to use your own discretion when drawing the two outlines. The procedure for both models is:

1 Open your template file.

2 Draw the outline of the model as a closed polyline, both with UCS BASE, layer MODEL and with the lower right viewport active.

3 Extrude the pyramid outline for a height of 150 and a taper angle of 10.

4 Revolve the wheel outline about the X or Y axis dependent on how the original outline was drawn. The partial angle of revolution is to be 270 degrees.

5 Centre the models in the viewports.

6 *Note.*
I have displayed both models on the one sheet of paper with:
a) pyramid: 3D and front views
b) wheel: two 3D views, from above and from below.

Chapter 30

Boolean operations and composite solids

The basic and swept solids which have been created are called **primitives** and are the 'basic tools' for solid modelling. With these primitives the user can create **composite solids**, so called because they are 'composed' of two or more solid primitives, i.e.

a) primitive: a box, wedge, cylinder, extrusion, etc.

b) composite: a solid made from two or more primitives.

Composite solids are created from primitives using the three **Boolean** operations of union, subtraction and intersection. Figure 30.1 demonstrates these operations with two primitives:

a) a box

b) a cylinder 'penetrating' the box.

Union

1 This operation involves 'joining' two or more primitives to form a single composite, the user selecting *all objects to be unioned*.

2 The operation can be considered similar to welding two or more components together.

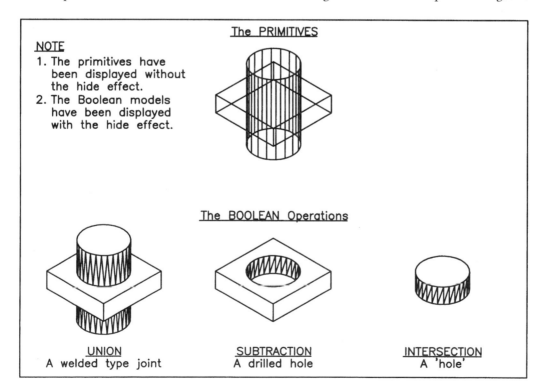

Figure 30.1 The three Boolean operations.

Subtraction

1 This involves removing one or more solids from another solid thereby creating the composite. The user selects:
   a) *the source solid*
   b) *the solids to be subtracted from the source solid.*

2 The result of a subtraction operation can be likened to a drilled hole, i.e. if the cylinder is subtracted from the box, a hole will obtained in the box.

3 *Note.*
   The source solid is generally 'the larger solid', i.e. you cannot normally take a large solid from a small solid.

Intersection

1 This operation gives a composite solid from other solids which have a common volume, the user selecting *all objects which have to be intersected*.

2 The box/cylinder illustration of the intersection operation gives a 'disc shape' or 'hole', i.e. if the box and cylinder are intersected, the common volume is the disc shape.

Creating a composite solid from primitives

There is no 'correct or ideal' method of creating a composite, i.e. the Boolean operations selected by one user may be different from those selected by another user, but the final composite may be the same. To demonstrate this, we will create an L-shaped component by three different methods, so:

1 Open your A3SOL template file refer to Fig. 30.2 and:
   a) enter paper space
   b) erase any text and the four viewports
   c) with layer VP current create a single viewport with:
      i) first point: pick to suit in lower left corner area
      ii) other corner: enter @360,220
   d) return to model space, UCS BASE, layer MODEL
   e) set a SE Isometric viewpoint.

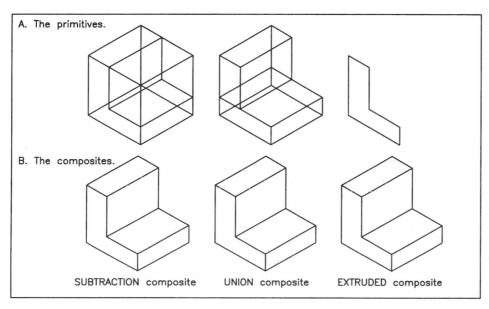

A. The primitives.

B. The composites.

SUBTRACTION composite   UNION composite   EXTRUDED composite

Figure 30.2

2 Create two box primitives:
   a) corner: 0,0,0   *b*) corner: 100,100,100
      cube option   length: −60
      length: 100   width: −100
      colour: red   height: −70
                                     colour: blue.

3 Create another two box primitives:
   a) corner: 125,125,0   *b*) corner: 125,125,30
      length: 100   length: 40
      width: 100   width: 100
      height: 30   height: 70
      colour: red   colour: blue.

4 Restore UCS FRONT and draw a 2D polyline shape:
   start pt: 500,250   next pt: @100,0   next pt: @0,30   next pt: @−60,0
   next pt: @0,70   next pt: @−40,0   next pt: close.

5 Restore UCS BASE and zoom centre about 100,250,0 at 400 mag.

6 From the menu bar select **Modify-Solids Editing-Subtract** and:
   prompt   Select solids and regions to subtract from..
              Select objects
   respond   **pick the left red box then right-click**
   prompt   Select solids and regions to subtract..
              Select objects
   respond   **pick the left blue box then right-click**
   and   the blue box is subtracted from the red box.

7 Menu bar with **Modify-Solids Editing-Union** and:
   prompt   Select objects
   respond   **pick the middle red and blue boxes then right-click**
   and   the two boxes will be unioned.

8 Restore UCS FRONT and:
   a) select the EXTRUDE icon from the Solids toolbar
   b) pick the L shaped polyline then right-click
   c) enter an extruded height of -100 with 0 taper
   d) the L-shape polyline is extruded into a composite.

9 *Task*.
   a) Hide the models − all the same.
   b) Gouraud shade the models and note colour effect between the union and subtraction composites − any comment?
   c) Return to 2D wireframe representation
   d) Menu bar with **Tools-Inquiry-Mass Properties** and:
       prompt   Select objects
       respond   **pick left composite then right-click**
       and   AutoCAD Text Window with:
                   Mass: 580000.00
                   Volume: 580000.00
                   Bounding box, Centroid, etc.
       enter **N <R>** in response to 'Write analysis to file' prompt
   d) Repeat the MASSPROP command and select the middle and right composites − same mass and volume?

10 *Question*.
   a) Why are the mass and volume the same?
      Answer: R2000 assumes a density value of 1 and does not support a materials library
   b) Is the volume of 580000 correct for the L shape?
   c) What are the volume units?

11 Now that we have investigated the Boolean operations, we will create some composite solid models which (I hole) will be interesting.

Summary

1 There are three Boolean operations – union, subtraction and intersection.

2 The three operations can be activated:
   a) from the menu bar with Modify-Solids Editing
   b) in icon form from the Solids Editing toolbar
   c) By entering the command from the keyboard.

3 The Boolean operations are derived from Boolean Algebra (set theory) and are essential for the creation of solid composites from primitives.

Chapter 31

Composite model 1 – a machine support

In this exercise we will create a composite solid from the box, wedge and cylinder primitives using the three Boolean operations. Once created, we will dimension the model using viewport specific layers.

The exercise is quite simple and you should have no difficulty in following the various steps in the model construction. Try and work out why the various entries are given – do not just accept them.

1 Open your A3SOL template file with UCS BASE, layer MODEL and with the lower left viewport active. Display the Solids, Solids Editing and other toolbars to suit.

2 Refer to Fig. 31.1 which displays only the 3D viewport of the model at various stages of its construction.

3 Zoom centre about 50,75,75 at 225 magnification in all viewports.

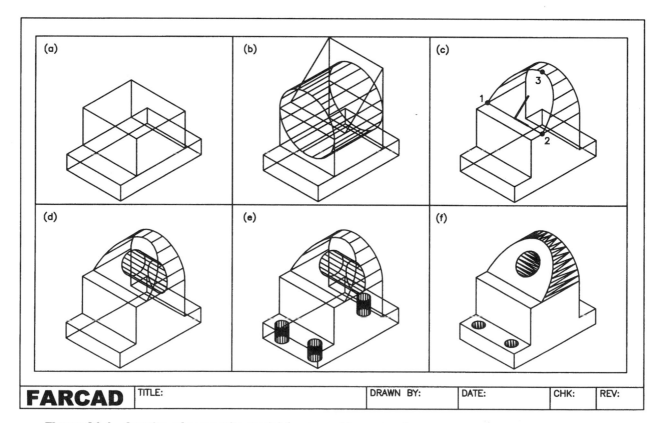

Figure 31.1 Creation of composite model 1 – a machine support.

4   Use the BOX icon to create two primitives as fig(a) with:
    a) corner: 0,0,0   *b*) corner: 100,120,25
        length: 100   length: −100
        width: 150   width: −90
        height: 25   height: 60
        colour: red   colour: blue.

5   Create a cylinder on top of the blue box with:
    a) centre: 50,30,85
    b) radius: 50
    c) height/other end: enter **C <R>** then **@0,90,0 <R>**
    d) colour: green.

6   Create a wedge with:
    a) corner: 0,120,85
    b) length: 70; width: 100; height: 70
    c) colour: magenta.

7   Rotate the magenta wedge:
    a) about the point: 0,120,85
    b) by: −90 degrees to give fig(b).

8   Select the INTERSECTION icon from the Solids Editing toolbar and:
    prompt   Select objects
    respond   **pick the green cylinder and magenta wedge then right-click**.

9   Select the UNION icon from the Solids Editing toolbar and:
    prompt   Select objects
    respond   **pick the red and blue boxes and the intersected wedge/cylinder then right-click**.

10 The model now appears as fig(c).

11 Refer to fig(c) and menu bar with **Tools-New UCS-3 Point** and set a new UCS with:
    a) origin: MIDpoint icon and pick line 12
    b) X axis: ENDpoint icon and pick pt2
    c) Y axis: QUADrant icon and pick pt3 on curve.

12 The UCS icon will move and align itself on the sloped surface.

    Note.
    If icon does not move, menu bar with View-Display-UCS Icon and ensure that On and Origin are ticked.

13 Save this UCS position as SLOPE.

14 Create a cylinder with:
    a) centre: 0,35,0
    b) radius: 18
    c) height: −100
    d) colour: number 54 – use the CHPROP command.

15 Select the SUBTRACT icon from the Solids Editing toolbar and:
    prompt   Select solids and regions to subtract from..
                Select objects
    respond   **pick the composite model then right-click**
    prompt   Select solids or regions to subtract
                Select objects
    respond   **pick the cylinder then right-click** – fig(d).

16 Restore UCS BASE.

17 Create a cylinder with:
centre: 20,15,0
radius: 9
height: 25
colour: number 174.

18 Multiple copy the cylinder:
a) from: 20,15
b) by: @60,0 and by: @30,120.

20 Using the SUBTRACT icon:
a) select the original composite then right-click
b) pick the three cylinders then right-click.

21 The model is now complete and is displayed in fig(e) without hide and in fig(f) with hide.

22 Gouraud shade the model, use 3D orbit in the 3D viewport, then restore the model to 2D wireframe representation.

23 At this stage save the composite as MODR2000\MACHSUPP.

Making the viewport specific layers

The screen displays the model in a four viewport configuration and we now want to add some dimensions. These dimensions must be added on viewport specific layers and these layers must now be created.

1 At the command line enter **VPLAYER <R>** and:
prompt   Enter an option [?/Freeze/Thaw/Reset/Newfrz/Vpvisdflt]
enter   **N <R>** – the Newfrz (new viewport freeze) option
prompt   Enter name(s) of new layers frozen in all viewports
enter   **DIMTL,DIMTR,DIMBR <R>**
prompt   Enter an option [?/Freeze/Thaw/..
respond **right-click** – as finished with command.

2 The command line entry VPLAYER is to activate viewport layer.

3 Make the top left viewport active and menu bar with **Format-Layer** and:
prompt   Layer Properties Manager dialogue box.

note: Three new layers – DIMBR, DIMTL, DIMTR with:
           i) Frozen in active viewport – blue icon
           ii) Frozen in new viewport – blue icon
respond 1. activate Show Details
           2. **pick DIMTL** (highlights) and note the details – Freeze in active viewport is on (tick)
           3. **pick blue icon Freeze in active viewport** to Thaw the layer and the tick is removed from Freeze in active viewport details list
           4. pick OK.

4 With the top right viewport active, Format-Layer and:
a) pick layer **DIMTR**
b) toggle the blue Freeze in active viewport icon to yellow to Thaw layer DIMTR in the top right viewport
c) pick OK.

5 With lower right viewport active, Format-Layer and:
   a) pick layer **DIMBR**
   b) toggle Freeze icon in active viewport from blue to yellow, i.e. from Frozen to Thaw to Thaw layer DIMBR in the lower right viewport
   c) pick OK.

6 What has been achieved in this section?
   a) three new viewport specific layers have been made
   b) these layers have been named DIMTL for the top left viewport, DIMTR for the top right viewport and DIMBR for the bottom left viewport
   c) the three layers were originally created:
      i) frozen in new viewports
      ii) currently frozen in all viewports
   d) each layer was currently thawed in a specific viewport, e.g. layer DIMTL is currently thawed in the top left viewport but is currently frozen in the other three viewports. Layers DIMTR and DIMBR are currently frozen in the top left viewport.

7 Before adding the dimensions, change the colour of the three new layers (DIMTL, DIMTR, DIMBR) to magenta with Format-Layer.

Adding the dimensions

1 Before the dimensions are added to the model, menu bar with **Dimension-Style** and using the Dimension Style Manager dialogue box:
   a) 3DSTD the current (and only) style?
   b) pick Modify
   c) pick the Fit tab
   d) Alter Scale for Features: Use overall scale of 2
   e) pick OK to return to Dimension Style Manager dialogue box
   f) pick Close.

2 This will scale all the dimension parameters by 2.

3 Make the lower right viewport active and:
   a) restore UCS BASE
   b) make layer DIMBR current
   c) refer to Fig. 31.2.

4 With Dimension-Linear from the menu bar, or with the LINEAR dimension icon from the Dimensions toolbar, add:
   a) the horizontal dimension
   b) the four vertical dimensions using the baseline option.

5 With the top right viewport active:
   a) restore UCS FRONT
   b) make layer DIMTR current
   c) add the two linear dimensions.

6 Make the top left viewport active and:
   a) restore UCS RIGHT
   b) make layer DIMTL current
   c) add the six dimensions.

7 The composite model is now complete with dimensions added and can be plotted with the layer VP frozen for effect – Fig. 31.2.

8 These dimension additions do not need to be saved.

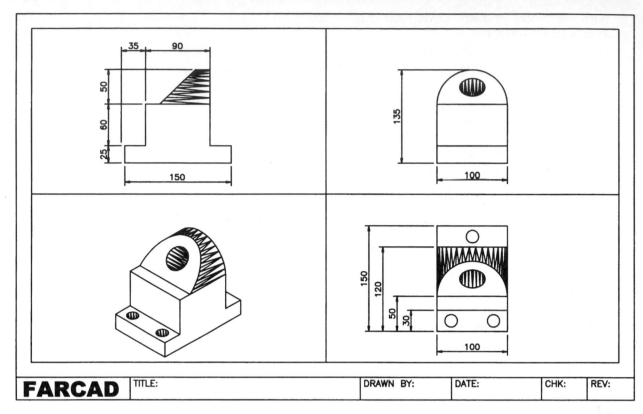

Figure 31.2 Completed solid model MACHINE SUPPORT with dimensions added.

Summary

1 Primitives and the Boolean operations can be used to create composite solid models.

2 Viewport specific layers are essential when adding dimensions to a multi-view model.

Chapter 32

Composite model 2 – a backing plate

In this exercise we will create a solid from an extruded swept primitive and then subtract various 'holes' to complete the composite. The exercise will also involve altering the viewport layout of the A3SOL template file which is an interesting exercise in itself. As with all the exercises, do not just accept the entries – work out why the various values are being used.

The model

Refer to Fig. 32.1 which details the model to be created and gives the relevant sizes. As an aside draw the three orthogonal views as given and then add the isometric (the arc 'hole' is interesting to complete in an isometric view). Time how long it takes to complete this 2D drawing. I spent about an hour to complete the four views with dimensions.

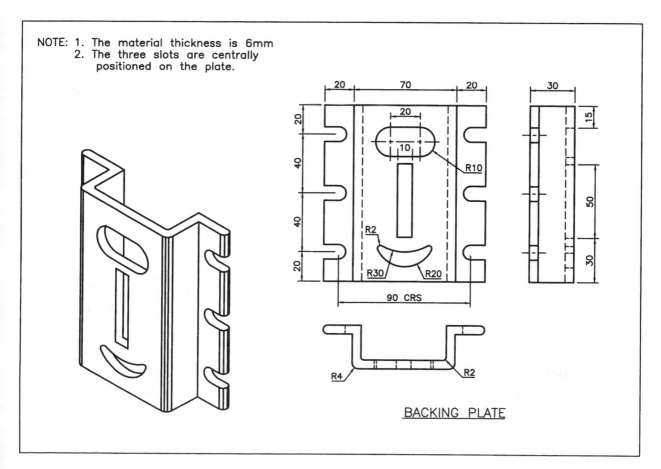

Figure 32.1 Backing plate drawn as orthogonal views and an isometric.

Setting the viewports

1   Open your A3SOL template file and:
    a) enter paper space
    b) erase the four viewports
    c) make layer VP current
    d) refer to Fig. 32.2.

2   Menu bar with **View-Floating Viewports-1 Viewport** and:
    prompt   Specify first corner and enter: **10,25 <R>**
    prompt   Specify other corner and enter: **@155,175 <R>**.

3   Create another three single viewports using the following coordinate entries:
    a) first corner: 165,25
        other corner: @160,70
    b) first corner: 175,95
        other corner: @160,155
    c) first corner: 325,95
        other corner: @70,155.

4   In model space:
    a) make layer MODEL current
    b) set UCSVP to 0 in each viewport
    c) set the 3D viewpoints in the viewports as fig(a)
    d) restore UCS BASE
    e) zoom centre about 0,10,60 at **1XP** – yes enter 1XP
    f) in paper space zoom in on viewport B then model space with viewport B active.

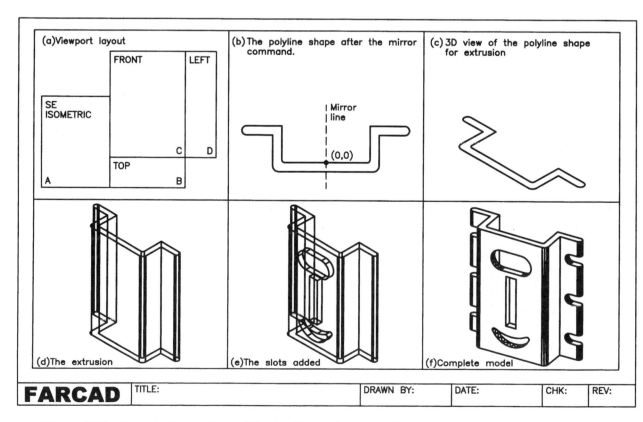

Figure 32.2   Steps in the creation of the backing plate composite.

Creating the extrusion

1 Using the polyline icon from the Draw toolbar, create a single polyline from line and arc segments with the following entries
   Start point   0,0
   Next point   @27,0
   Next point   Arc option, with endpoint of arc @2,2
   Next point   Line option, to @0,22
   Next point   @23,0
   Next point   Arc option, with endpoint of arc @0,–6
   Next point   Line option, to @–17,0
   Next point   @0, –20
   Next point   Arc option, with endpoint of arc @–4, –4
   Next point   Line option, to @–31,0
   Next point   right-click/enter.

2 Mirror the polyline shape about the points 0,0 and 0,50 and do not delete source objects

3 Use the menu bar sequence **Modify-Polyline** and:
   a) pick any point on the right-hand polyline
   b) enter **J <R>** – the join option
   c) pick the two polyline shapes then right-click
   d) enter **X <R>** to end the command.

4 The two 'halves' of the polyline have been joined into a single polyline as fig(b) in plan view and fig(c) in 3D.

5 At the command line enter **ISOLINES <R>** and:
   prompt   Enter new value for ISOLINES<24>
   enter   **3 <R>**.

   Note.
   The ISOLINES system variable has been reduced from 18 to 3 due to the 'corners' of the model. With a value of 18, the extrusion would result in these corners being 'very dense'.

6 Select the EXTRUDE icon from the Solids toolbar and:
   prompt   Select objects
   respond   **pick any point on the polyline then right-click**
   prompt   Specify height of extrusion or [Path] and enter: **120 <R>**
   prompt   Specify angle of taper for extrusion and enter: **0 <R>**.

7 The polyline shape will be extruded as fig(d).

8 Paper zoom-previous then return to model space.

Creating the 'holes'

1 Restore UCS FRONT with viewport C active

2 Create a box primitive with:
   a) corner: –5,30,0
   b) length: 10; width: 50; height: 6
   c) colour: blue.

3 Create the following three primitives:

box	*cylinder*	*cylinder*
corner: −10,85,0	centre: −10,95,0	centre: 10,95,0
length: 20	radius: 10	radius: 10
width: 20	height: 6	height: 6
height: 6	colour: green	colour: green.
colour: green		

4 Union the three green primitives.

5 Draw two circles:
   a) centre: 0,30 with radius: 20
   b) centre: 0,50 with radius: 30
   c) both circles colour green.

6 Trim the circles 'to each other' and fillet the 'corners' with a radius of 2.

7 Convert the four arcs into a single polyline with the menu bar sequence **Modify-Polyline** using the **J**oin option.

8 Extrude the arced polyline for a height of 6 with 0 taper, then change the colour of the extrusion to green.

9 Subtract the green and blue 'holes' from the red extrusion to display the model as fig(e).

10 Create the following two primitives:

cylinder	*box*
centre: 45,20,−24	corner: 45,15,−24
radius: 5	length: 30
height: 6	width: 10
colour: magenta	height: 6
	colour: magenta.

11 Union these two magenta primitives.

12 Rectangular array the magenta cylinder/box composite:
   a) for 3 rows and 1 column
   b) row distance: 40.

13 Mirror the three arrayed magenta composites about the points 0,0 and 0,50 and do not delete the source objects.

14 Subtract the six magenta composites from the red extrusion.

15 The model is now complete – fig(f) and the four viewport layout should be displayed as Fig. 32.3.

16 Save the model layout as MODR2000\BACKPLT.

17 Shade and use the 3D orbit command in the 3D viewport, then return the model to wireframe representation.

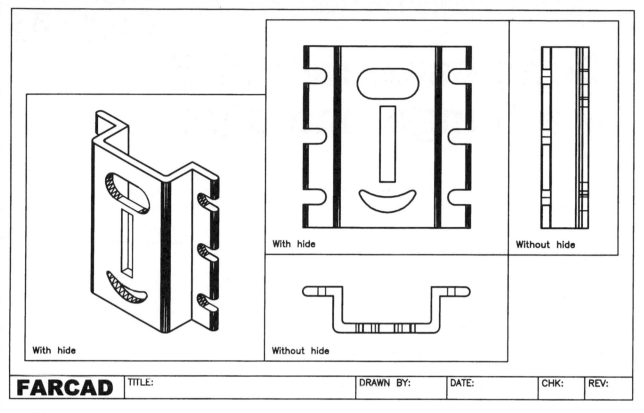

With hide

Without hide

With hide

Without hide

FARCAD | TITLE: | | DRAWN BY: | DATE: | CHK: | REV:

Figure 32.3 Complete solid model composite of backing plate.

Investigating the model

Display the Inquiry toolbar and make the 3D viewport active.

1 Select the LIST icon from the Inquiry toolbar and:
   prompt Select objects
   respond **pick the composite then right-click**
   and AutoCAD Text Window
   with details of the selected model
   respond view the details then cancel the text window.

2 Select the AREA icon from the Inquiry toolbar and:
   prompt Specify first corner or [Object..
   enter **0 <R>** – the object option
   prompt Select objects
   respond **pick the composite**
   and Area = 38171.70, Perimeter = 0.00
   This is the surface area of the model.

3 Select the MASS PROPERTIES icon and:
   prompt Select objects
   respond **pick the composite then right-click**
   prompt AutoCAD Text Window
   with Mass = 98283.83 and other 'technical' information about the model
   enter **N <R>**, i.e. do not write to file. More on this later.

4 This completes the exercise on the extruded model.

Chapter 33

Composite model 3 – a flange and pipe

This exercise will involve creating a composite mainly as a revolved swept primitive. Cylinder primitives will be subtracted from the revolved primitive to complete the composite.

1 Open A3SOL template file with layer MODEL and UCS BASE. Display the Solids toolbar

2 Zoom centre about −100, −30,0 at 300 magnification in all viewports.

3 With the lower left viewport active, restore UCS RIGHT and draw:
   a) circle: centre at 0,0 with radius: 30
   b) circle: centre at 0,0 with radius: 40
   c) line: start point at −200,0 and next point at @0,100.

4 Select the REVOLVE icon from the Solids toolbar and:
   prompt   Select objects
   respond **pick the smaller circle then right-click**
   prompt   Specify start point for axis of revolution or define axis
              [Object..
   enter   **O <R>** – the object option
   prompt   Select an object
   respond **pick the lower end of the vertical line**
   prompt   Specify angle of revolution
   enter   **70 <R>**.

5 Change the colour of the revolved pipe to green.

6 Revolve the larger circle using the same entries as step 4 and change the colour of the pipe to blue.

7 Erase the line then subtract the green pipe from the blue pipe. You may need a paper space zoom for this operation?

8 Make the lower right viewport active and restore UCS BASE.

9 With the POLYLINE icon from the Draw toolbar, draw a continuous closed polyline with the following entries:
   Start point   0, −30
   Next point   @0, −10
   Next point   Arc option with endpoint: @10, −10
   Next point   Line option with endpoint: @0, −50
   Next point   @30, 0
   Next point   @0, 70
   Next point   close option.

10 Using the REVOLVE icon from the Solids toolbar:
    a) pick a point on the polyline then right-click
    b) enter **X <R>** as the axis of revolution
    c) enter **360 <R>** as the angle.

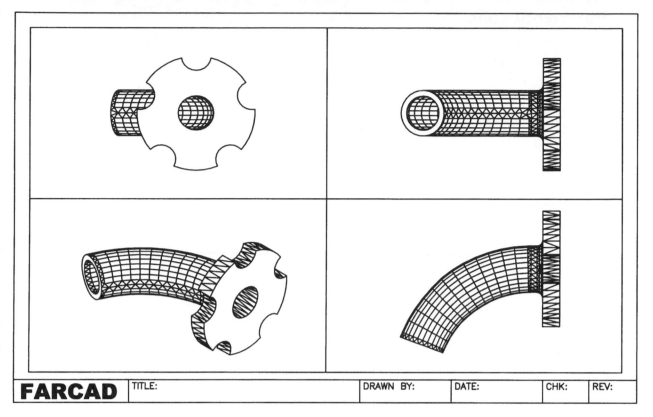

Figure 33.1 Creation of composite model 3 – pipe/flange.

11 Change the colour of the revolved solid to magenta.

12 With the top left viewport active, restore USC RIGHT.

13 Create a cylinder with:
   a) centre: 0, 100, 20
   b) radius: 25
   c) height: 30
   d) colour: number 222.

14 Polar array this cylinder about the point 0,0 for five items with 360 angle.

15 *a*) Subtract the five cylinders from the magenta flange
   b) union the flange and pipe.

16 The model is complete and can be saved as MODR2000\FLPIPE.

17 In paper space zoom the 3D viewport, then in model space use the 3D orbit command with a Gouraud shading effect. The result is very impressive.

18 *Note.*
   The three composite models MACHSUPP, BACKPLT and FLPIP will be used in later chapters to demonstrate other commands.

The layout tabs

AutoCAD R2000 allows the user to create different layouts for plotting using the layout tabs below the drawing screen. By default, AutoCAD has three layout tabs, these being Model, Layout1 and Layout2. Your screen should display a fourth layout tab (A3SOL or MV3DSTD) depending on how you created the solid model standard sheet/template file from Chapter 27. In this section, we will investigate the layout tabs, renaming the existing ones and creating a new layout.

1 The flange/pipe drawing should still be displayed in a four viewport configuration, and layout tab A3SOL should be active.

2 Move the pointer arrow onto the Model tab and left-click. The drawing screen should display a partial plan view of the component.

3 Zoom-all to give Fig. 33.2.

4 Move the pointer arrow onto the Layout1 tab and left-click to display a new layout as Fig. 33.3. This is a 'plot' layout, with:
  a) the white area: the drawing paper
  b) the dashed lines: the printable area
  c) the component displayed in plan view in a viewport.

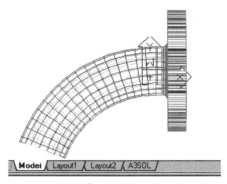

Figure 33.2 Model tab layout after zoom-all.

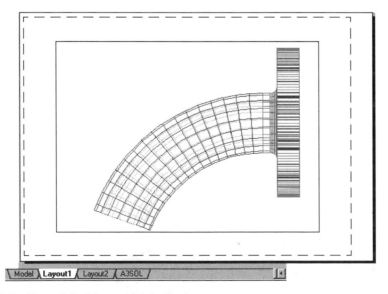

Figure 33.3 The original Layout1 tab display.

5   Erase the viewport and make layer VP current.

6   Menu bar with **View-Viewports-2 Viewports** and:
    prompt   Enter viewport arrangement
    enter   **V <R>** – vertical option
    prompt   Specify first corner and enter: **5,5 <R>**
    prompt   Specify opposite corner
    respond   drag out and pick the opposite corner at the top right within the dashed area.

7   Enter model space with **MS <R>** and with the menu bar sequence **View-3D Views** set the following viewpoints:
    a) left viewport: SW Isometric
    b) right viewport: NE Isometric.

8   In each viewport zoom at 1.5 then pan to suit and hide.

9   Enter paper space, position pointer arrow over the Layout1 tab, left-click and:
    prompt   Shortcut menu
    respond   pick Rename
    prompt   Rename layout dialogue box with Layout1
    respond   alter name to MINE1 then pick OK.

10 The drawing screen will be similar to Fig. 33.4.

11 Pick (left-click) the Model tab to display the plan view as Fig. 33.2.

12 Left-click on the Layout2 tab to display a blank screen with the dashed printable area. Where is the model? Think back a few steps.

13 With layer VP current, menu bar with **View-Viewports-3 Viewports** and:
    prompt   Enter viewport arrangement and enter: **L <R>**
    prompt   Specify first corner and enter: **5,5 <R>**
    prompt   Specify opposite corner
    respond   drag out and pick within the dashed area
    and   3 plan views of model displayed.

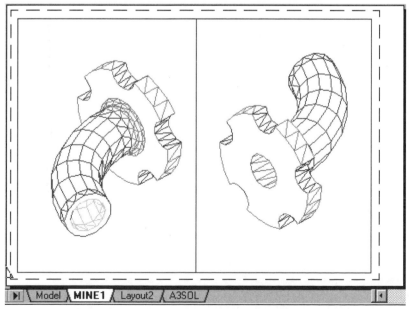

Figure 33.4   Screen display for layout1 tab, renamed MINE1.

14 In model space (MS <R>) set UCSVP to 0 in each new viewport then set the following viewpoints:
    a) left: SE Isometric
    b) top right: Right
    c) lower right: Front.

15 In each viewport zoom 1 and pan to suit then hide.

16 At the command line enter **LAYOUT <R>** and:
    prompt   Enter layout option and enter: **R <R>** – rename option
    prompt   Enter layout to rename and enter: **Layout2 <R>**
    prompt   Enter new layout name and enter: **MINE2 <R>**.

17 The resultant screen display should be Fig. 33.5.

18 Menu bar with **Insert-Layout-New Layout** and:
    prompt   Enter new Layout name
    enter   **MYNEW <R>**
    and   tab MYNEW added to tab list below drawing area
    respond   1. left-click on tab MYNEW to display the plan view of the model – Fig. 33.2
                2. erase this viewport.

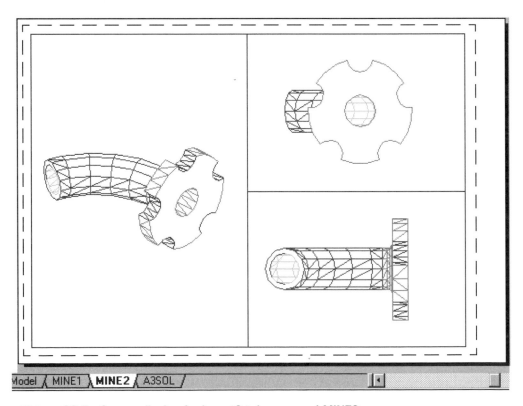

Figure 33.5   Screen display for layout2 tab, renamed MINE2.

19 With layer VP current, menu bar with **View-Viewports-Polygonal Viewport** and:
   prompt   Specify start point and enter: **50,50 <R>**
   prompt   Specify next point and enter: **50<0 <R>**
   prompt   Specify next point and enter: **50<60 <R>**
   prompt   Specify next point and enter: **50<120 <R>**
   prompt   Specify next point and enter: **50<180 <R>**
   prompt   Specify next point and enter: **50<-120 <R>**
   prompt   Specify start point and enter: **C <R>** – the close option.

20 A hexagonal viewport with a plan view of the model has been created.

21 Repeat the polygonal viewport selection and:
   prompt   Specify start point and enter: **150,100 <R>**
   prompt   Specify next point and enter: **A <R>** – the arc option
   prompt   Enter an arc boundary option and enter: **@100<0 <R>**
   prompt   Enter an arc boundary option and enter: **200,170 <R>**
   prompt   Enter an arc boundary option and enter: **CL <R>** – the close option.

22 Task.
   a) Create another two polygonal viewports of your own design
   b) Set your own viewpoints in the four viewports
   c) Save the drawing (with the layouts).

23 This completes the layout exercise.

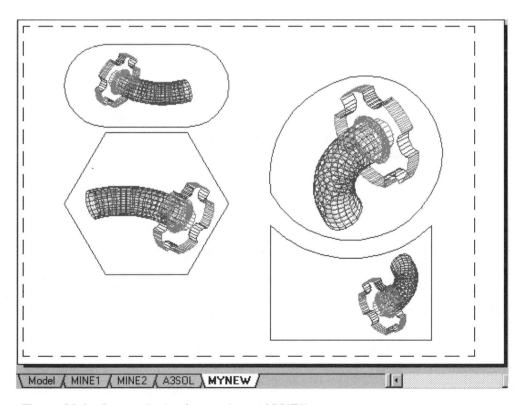

Figure 33.6   Screen display for new layout MYNEW.

Chapter 34

The edge primitives

Models can be modified to include a chamfer and fillet effect. These are the edge primitives – the third type of primitive which can be created. In this chapter we will investigate how solids can be constructed with these edge primitives.

Note.
The term 'edge primitive' is not now generally used, the models being considered to have been modified or edited. I personally still prefer this terminology.

Example 1 – a box solid

1 Open the A3SOL template file with the lower left viewport active, UCS BASE and layer MODEL. Display the Solids toolbar.

2 Refer to Fig. 34.1(a).

3 Use the BOX icon and create a primitive with:
   a) corner 0,0,0
   b) cube option with length: 100.

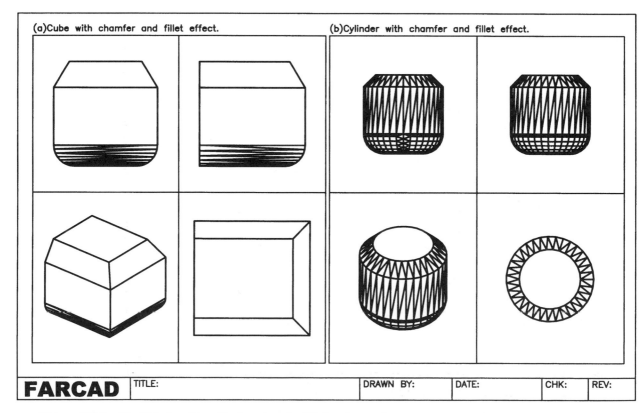

Figure 34.1 Modifying solids with the chamfer/fillet commands.

4 Zoom centre about 50,50,50 at 225 magnification.

5 Select the CHAMFER icon from the Modify toolbar and:
   prompt Select first line or [Polyline/Distance..
   respond **pick any line on top surface**
   prompt Base surface selection
   and *a*) one face of the cube will be highlighted
      b) it will be a 'side' or the 'top'
   prompt Enter surface selection option [Next/OK (current)]
   respond *a*) right-click/enter if top face is highlighted
      b) enter N<R> if side face is highlighted to highlight the top face then right-click/enter
   prompt Specify base surface chamfer distance and enter: **15 <R>**
   prompt Specify other surface chamfer distance and enter: **25 <R>**
   prompt Select an edge or [Loop]
   respond *a*) pick any three sides on top surface
      b) right-click/enter.

6 The top surface will be chamfered at the selected three edges.

7 *Note.*
   Entering **L** for loop will allow all edges to be chamfered with a single pick.

8 Select the FILLET icon from the Modify toolbar and:
   prompt Select first object or [Polyline/Radius/Trim]
   respond **pick any line on the base surface of the cube**
   prompt Enter fillet radius and enter: **20 <R>**
   prompt Select edge or [Chain/Radius]
   respond **pick any three edges of the base then right-click.**

9 The base of the cube will be filleted at the three selected edges and displayed as fig(a).

Example 2 – a cylinder solid

1 Erase the cube and at the command line enter **ISOLINES <R>** and check the value is 18.

2 Use the CYLINDER icon to create a cylinder with:
   a) centre: 0,0,0
   b) radius: 50
   c) height: 100.

3 Zoom centre about 0,0,50 at 200 magnification.

4 In paper space zoom-in on the 3D viewport then return to model space.

5 Select the CHAMFER icon and:
   prompt Select first line or..
   respond **pick the top surface circle edge**
   prompt Base surface selection
   then Enter surface selection option
   respond **<RETURN>** as the required surface is highlighted
   prompt Specify base surface chamfer distance and enter: **15 <R>**
   prompt Specify other surface chamfer distance and enter: **15 <R>**
   prompt Select an edge or..
   respond **pick top circle edge then right-click/enter.**

6 The top of the cylinder is chamfered with the entered values.

7 Select the FILLET icon and:
  prompt　　Select first object..
  respond　**pick bottom circle of cylinder**
  prompt　　Enter fillet radius and enter: **25 <R>**
  prompt　　Select an edge..
  respond　**right-click** as bottom edge already selected.

8 The cylinder is filleted at the base.

9 In paper space zoom-previous then return to model space.

10 The chamfer/fillet effect of the cylinder is displayed as fig(b).

A composite edge primitive solid

1 Erase the cylinder model and with UCS BASE, layer MODEL and the lower left viewport active, create four primitives with:

box	*cylinder*	*box*	*cylinder*
corner: 0,0,0	centre: 75,60,0	corner: 50,0,40	centre: 150,0,0
length: 150	radius: 40	length: 60	radius: 30
width: 120	height: 100	width: 120	height: 100
height: 100	colour: green	height: 40	colour: magenta
colour: red		colour: blue.	

2 In all viewports, zoom centre about 75,60,50 at 200 mag in the 3D viewport and 200 mag in the other viewports.

3 Subtract the green, blue and magenta primitives from the red box and note the 'interpenetration' effect.

4 Select the FILLET icon and:
  a) pick the top circle of the green object
  b) enter a radius of 15
  c) select an edge and right-click/enter.

5 The top edge of the cylinder is filleted 'outwards' and is red. Why is the fillet red and not green?

6 Select the CHAMFER icon and:
  a) pick the top long front edge of the red box
  b) press <RETURN> if the front vertical face is highlighted or N <R> until front vertical face is highlighted then right-click/enter
  c) enter base surface distance of 10
  d) enter other surface distance of 5
  e) pick the four front edges of the blue primitive then right-click/enter.

7 The blue box primitive is chamfered in red – not blue?

8 Now fillet the top curve of the magenta cylinder with a radius of 15.

9 The completed model is displayed as Fig. 34.2 and can be shaded and the 3D orbit command used.

10 The model can be saved if required, but will not be used again.

A practical use for fillet/chamfer with solids

Before leaving this chapter, we will investigate a practical use of the fillet and chamfer commands with solids so:

1 Erase the composite on the screen and ensure UCS BASE, layer MODEL and lower left viewport active. Refer to Fig. 34.3.

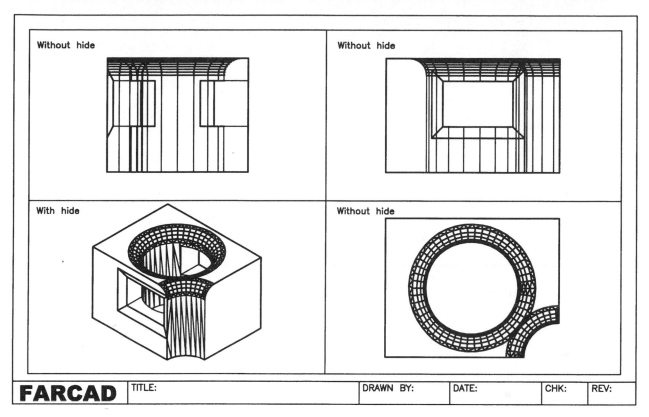

Figure 34.2 Chamfered and filleted composite.

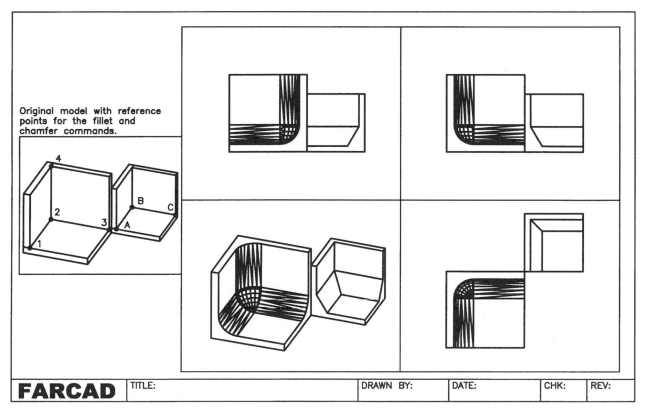

Figure 34.3 Fillet and chamfer effect at three corners.

2 Create the following three box primitives:

	box1	box2	box3
corner	0,0,0	0,0,100	10,100,10
length	100	10	90
width	100	100	−10
height	10	90	90.

3 Union the three boxes and copy the unioned composite from: 0,0,0 to 100,100,0.

4 Scale the copied composite about the point 100,100 by 0.75.

5 Change the viewpoint in the 3D viewport with VPOINT-ROTATE and angles of 300 and 30.

6 Zoom-centre in each viewport about the point 80,80,50 for 225 mag.

7 In paper space zoom in on the 3D viewport then model space.

8 Select the FILLET icon and:
prompt   `Select first object`
respond   **pick edge 12**
prompt   `Enter fillet radius` and enter: **25 <R>**
prompt   `Select an edge`
respond   **pick edges 12,23 and 24 then right-click/enter.**

9 Select the CHAMFER icon and:
prompt   `Select first line`
respond   **pick edge AB**
prompt   `Enter surface selection option`
respond   *a*) enter N <R> until horizontal surface is highlighted
           b) right-click/enter
prompt   `Specify base surface chamfer distance` and enter: **15 <R>**
prompt   `Specify other surface chamfer distance` and enter: **25 <R>**
prompt   `Select an edge`
respond   **pick edges AB and BC then right-click/enter.**

10 The model will be filleted and chamfered at the selected edges.

11 *Questions.*
    a) Is it possible to fillet more that three edges at the one time?
    b) Can a chamfer be added to three adjacent surfaces?

12 This completes the edge primitive exercise.

Summary

1 Primitives and solids can be chamfered and filleted with the 'normal' CHAMFER and FILLET commands.

2 Solids and primitives can be chamfered/filleted:
   a) inwards if a primitive
   b) outwards if a 'hole'.

3 Individual edges can be chamfered and filleted.

4 The chamfer command has a LOOP option allowing a complete surface to be chamfered.

5 The fillet command has a CHAIN option allowing a complete surface to be filleted.

6 Error messages will be displayed if the chamfer distances or the fillet radius are too large for the model being modified, and the command line will display:
   a) Failed to perform blend
   b) Failure while chamfering/Filleting.

Assignment

This activity requires a cube to be chamfered to give a 'truncated pyramid'. The model will be used in a later activity.

Activity 20: Penetrated pyramid of MACFARAMUS.

One of MACFARAMUS's model pyramids was unearthed from the desert and basically consisted if three primitives:
a) a cube of side 200
b) a cylinder with radius 25 with the centre 100 from the base
c) a square box of side 80 with the lower edge 30 from the base.

You have to create this model and the suggested approach is:

1 Position the cube (red) with corner at 0,0,0.

2 Chamfer the cube to give a square topped pyramid, the top having a side length along the top surface 100.

3 Position the square (blue) sided box.

4 Position the cylinder (green) – use other end option.

5 Subtract the box and cylinder from the pyramid.

6 Chamfer the blue square box 'front', distances: 10.

7 Fillet the green cylinder 'right side' with radius 10.

8 Save the composite as MODR2000\MODCOMP.

Chapter 35

Solids editing

Release 2000 allows solid primitives and composites to be edited, the commands being activated from the:
a) menu bar with Modify-Solids Editing
b) Solids Editing toolbar.

The editing facilities available are:

1 Boolean: union, subtraction, intersection.

2 Faces: extrude, move, offset, delete, rotate, taper, color, copy.

3 Edges: color, copy.

4 Body: imprint, clean, separate, shell, check.

The Boolean editing features have been used in the creation of the previous composites, and in this chapter we will investigate some of the other editing features.

Solids editing example 1

1 Open your SOLA3 template file and refer to Fig. 35.1 which only displays the 3D viewport for this example. Display the Solids, Solids Editing and Object Snap toolbars.

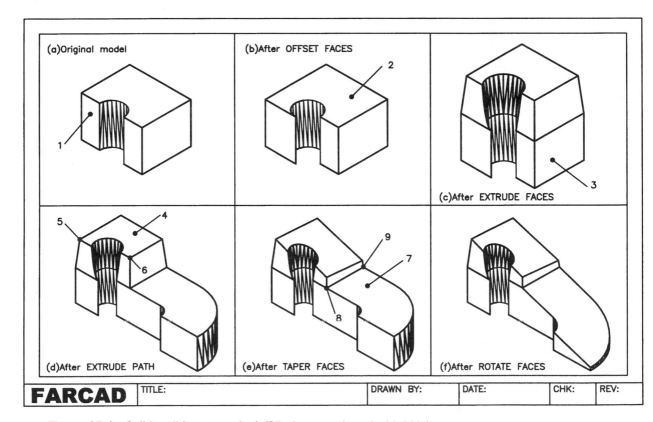

Figure 35.1 Solids editing example 1 (3D viewport plotted with hide).

2 With layer MODEL current, UCS BASE and the lower left viewport active, create the
following:
a) Box: corner at 0,0,0 with L: 150, W: 120, H: 100, colour: red
b) Cylinder: centre at 75,0,0, R: 30, H: 100, colour: blue
c) Subtract the blue cylinder from the red box
d) Zoom-centre about 75,60,50 at 250 mag – fig(a).

3 Select the OFFSET FACES icon from the Solids Editing toolbar and:
prompt   Select faces or [Undo/Remove]
respond **pick any pt1 on side surface then right-click/enter**
prompt   Specify the offset distance
enter   **30 <R>**
prompt   Enter a face editing option and enter: **X <R>**
prompt   Enter a solids editing option and enter: **X <R>**
and   selected face is offset as fig(b).

4 Select the EXTRUDE FACES icon from the Solids Editing toolbar and:
prompt   Select faces or [Undo/Remove]
respond **pick any pt2 on the top surface then right-click/enter**
prompt   Specify height of extrusion or [Path]
enter   **80 <R>**
prompt   Specify angle of taper
enter   **5 <R>**
and   top surface of model is extruded as fig(c).

5 Draw a polyline using:
Start point   150,120
Next point   @100,0
arc option with arc endpoint   @150,–150
arc endpoint   right-click/enter.

6 Menu bar with **Modify-Solids Editing-Extrude Faces** and:
prompt   Select faces or [Undo/Remove]
respond **pick any pt3 on right face then right-click/enter**
prompt   Specify height of extrusion or [Path]
enter   **P <R>** – the path option
prompt   Select extrusion path
respond **pick any point on polyline**
prompt   Enter a face editing option and enter: **X <R>**
prompt   Enter a solid editing option and enter: **X <R>**.

6 The selected face is extruded along the polyline path as fig(d).

7 Re-centre about the point 200,50,90 at 350 magnification.

8 Select the TAPER FACES icon from the Solids Editing toolbar and:
prompt   Select faces or [Undo/Remove]
respond **pick any pt4 on top surface then right-click/enter**
prompt   Specify the base point
respond **Endpoint icon and pick pt5**
prompt   Specify another point along the axis of tapering
respond **Endpoint icon and pick pt6**
prompt   Specify angle of taper and enter: **20 <R>**
prompt   Enter a face editing option and enter: **X <R> and X <R>**.

9 The selected top surface will be tapered as fig(e).

10 Menu bar with **Modify-Solid Editing-Rotate Faces** and:

prompt   Select faces or [Undo/Remove]
respond **pick any pt7 on face indicated then right-click/enter**
prompt   Specify an axis point
respond **Endpoint icon and pick pt8**
prompt   Specify the second point on the rotation axis
respond **Endpoint icon and pick pt9**
prompt   Specify a rotation angle
enter   **20 <R>**
prompt   Enter a face editing option and enter: **X <R> and X <R>**.

11 The selected face is rotated about the selected side as fig(f).

12 Shade and 3D orbit the model then save if required.

13 This exercise is now complete.

Solids editing example 2

1 Open your SOLA3 template file and refer to Fig. 35.2 which only displays the 3D viewport for this example. Display the Solids, Solids Editing and Object Snap toolbars.

2 With layer MODEL current, UCS BASE and the lower left viewport active, create the following:
   a) Box: corner at 0,0,0 with cube of length 200 and colour red
   b) Cone: centre at 0,100,100; radius: 80; Apex at @300,0 and colour: green
   c) Subtract the green cone from the red box
   d) Zoom-centre about 200,100,100 at 400 mag – fig(a).

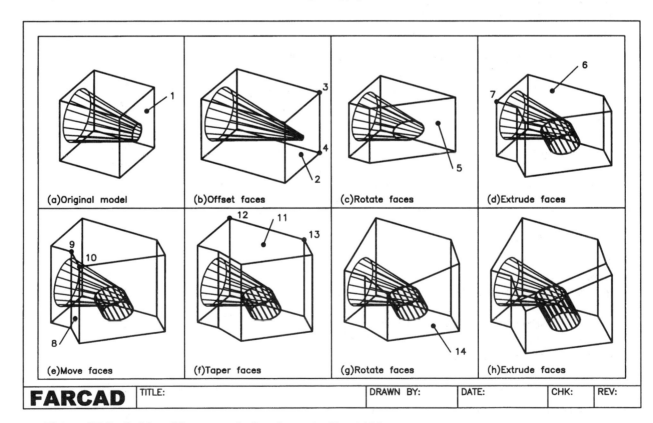

Figure 35.2 Solids editing example 2 – viewport without hide.

3 The options for this example are given as a series of simple steps which you should be able to follow:

Offset faces
a) pick face 1
b) distance: 75 – fig(b)

Rotate faces
a) pick face 2
b) axis with points 3 and 4
c) angle 45 – fig(c)

Extrude faces
a) pick face 5
b) height: 100 with taper: 0 – fig(d)

Move faces
a) pick face 6
b) base point at point 7
c) second point: @0,0,85 – fig(e)

Taper faces
a) pick face 8
b) axes points 9 and 10
c) taper angle: 25 – fig(f)

Extrude faces
a) pick face 14
b) height of extrusion: 75 with taper: 0 – fig(h).

4 This completes the second example.

Note

1 The two examples have concentrated on the faces editing options.

2 It is sometimes difficult to select a face for the solids editing options, and it is sometimes easier to select an edge. As an edge 'belongs' to two adjacent faces, the unwanted face can easily be removed from the 'selection' with the 'R' entry.

3 The solids editing command allows the user repetitive options, i.e. when one option has been completed, the command is still active. The UNDO option is very useful.

4 The solids editing command is exited with two X <R> or ESC.

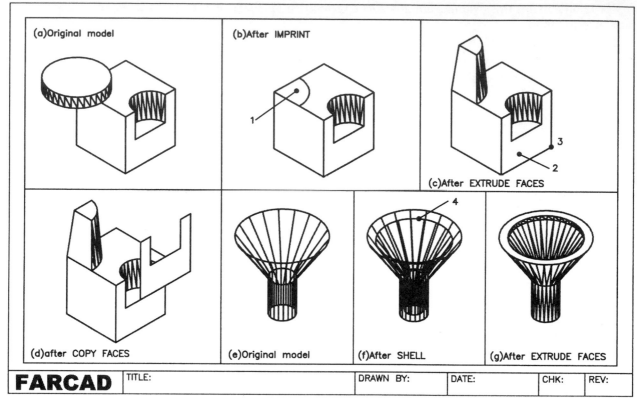

Figure 35.3 Solids editing example 3.

Solids editing example 3

1 Open your SOLA3 template file and refer to Fig. 35.3 which again only displays the 3D viewport. Display suitable toolbars.

2 With layer MODEL current, UCS BASE and the lower left viewport active, create the following:
   a) Box: corner at 0,0,0 with cube of length 100 and colour red
   b) Cylinder: centre at 0,0,100; radius: 50; height 80
   c) Cylinder: centre at 100,50,100; radius: 30; height: −50
   d) Subtract the second cylinder from the box
   e) Zoom-centre about 50,50,50 at 250 mag – fig(a).

3 Select the IMPRINT icon from the Solids Editing toolbar and:
   prompt   Select a 3D solid
   respond **pick the cube**
   prompt   Select an object to imprint
   respond **pick the R50 cylinder**
   prompt   Delete the source object <N>
   enter   **Y <R>** then X <R> and X <R>.

4 The cylinder outline is imprinted on the cube – fig(b).

5 With the EXTRUDE FACES option:
   a) pick face 1
   b) enter an extrusion height of 80 with 0 taper – fig(c).

6 Select the COPY FACES icon from the Solids Editing toolbar and:
   prompt   Select faces
   respond **pick face 2 then right-click/enter**
   prompt   Specify a base point or displacement
   respond **Endpoint icon and pick pt3**
   prompt   Specify a second point of displacement
   enter   **@50,0,100 <R>** then exit the command.

7 The selected face is copied as fig(d).

8 Erase the composite and create two primitives:
   a) cylinder: centre 0,0,0; radius: 30; height: 100
   b) cone: centre: 0,0,200; radius: 100; height: -150
   c) union the cone and cylinder – fig(e).

9 Select the SHELL icon from the Solids Editing toolbar and:
   prompt   Select a 3D solid
   respond **pick and point on cylinder/cone then right-click/enter**
   prompt   Enter the shell offset distance
   enter   **10<R>** then X <R> and X <R>.

10 The cylinder/cone is offset by 10 in 'all directions' – fig(f).

11 With the EXTRUDE FACES icon:
    a) pick face 4
    b) extrusion height: −10 with 0 taper.

12 The result is fig(g).

13 This completes the third solids editing example.

Other solids editing options

Not all of the solids editing options have been used in the worked examples. The following is a brief description of those not considered:

Clean: removes all redundant edges and vertices, e.g. imprinted edges.

Separate: separates 3D solid objects with disjointed volumes into independent 3D objects. It **DOES NOT** separate composites created by Boolean operations into the original primitives.

Check: confirms that a selected object is a valid ACIS solid.

Color Edges/Faces: a very useful option as it allows individual edges and faces to be coloured, i.e. a cube could be created on layer MODEL (red) and the six faces of the cube assigned different colours.

Copy Edges/Faces: should be obvious.

Delete faces: allows faces of a model to be deleted, but the option has obvious limitations. Useful with fillet/chamfer edges.

Solids editing errors

When a solids editing option is activated and completed, the command line will display:
a) Solid validation started
b) Solid validation completed.

Solids editing will not always work due to the model selected or the option which has been activated. Errors which are displayed include:

1 No solution for an edge.

2 No solution for a vertex.

3 No loop through new edges and vertices.

4 Could not taper surface as requested.

5 Improper edge/edge intersection.

6 Gap cannot be filled.

If and error message is obtained, then the active option cannot be performed on the selected object. Try again.

Summary

1 Solids editing with R2000 allows the user several options.

2 These options can result in very interesting and complex models which may be difficult to achieve from basic primitives.

3 The solids editing options are divided into four categories:
a) Boolean operations
b) face options
c) edge options
d) body options.

4 Solid editing options which cannot be performed result in an error message being displayed.

5 The solids editing command allows repetitive entries and has an undo option.

Chapter 36

Regions

A region is a *closed* 2D shape created from lines, circles, arcs, polylines, splines, etc. and can be used with the extrude and revolve command to create solid composites. When created, a region has certain characteristics:

- it is a solid of zero thickness
- it is coplanar, i.e. must be created on the one plane
- it consists of **loops** – outer and inner
- the loops must be continuous closed shapes
- every region has one outer loop
- there may be several inner loops
- inner loops must be in the same plane as the outer loop
- regions can be created with the *BOUNDARY* command
- regions can be used with EXTRUDE or REVOLVE.

With the exception of the boundary option, using regions does not allow the user any new ability to create solid models – it is another variation to be considered. We will investigate regions with several worked examples.

Example 1 – a splined shaft

1 Open your A3SOL template file with layer MODEL, UCS BASE and the lower right viewport active. Refer to Fig. 36.1 which only displays the 3D viewport of the exercise. Display suitable toolbars.

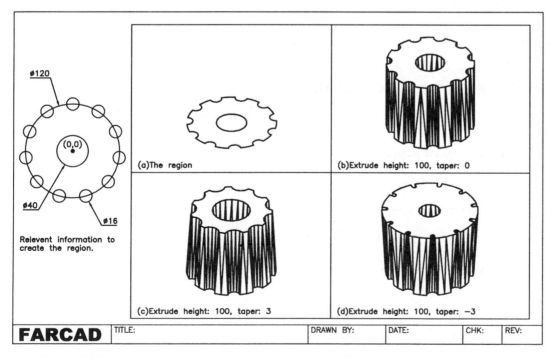

Figure 36.1 Region example 1 – an extruded component.

2 Refer to Fig. 36.1 and create the layout from three circles of diameters 120, 40 and 16. The actual layout is your design.

3 Zoom centre about 0,0,40 at 200 magnification – all viewports.

4 Select the SUBTRACTION icon from the Solids Editing toolbar and pick the largest circle then right-click and:
   prompt No solids or regions selected.

5 Select the REGION icon from the Draw toolbar and:
   prompt Select objects
   respond **pick all circles then right-click**
   prompt 13 loops extracted
            13 Regions created.

6 Menu bar with **Modify-Solids Editing-Subtract** and:
   prompt Select solids or regions to subtract from
            Select objects
   respond **pick the largest circle then right-click**
   prompt Select solids or regions to subtract
            Select objects
   respond **pick the 12 smaller circles then right-click**
   and the region is created as fig(a).

7 At this stage save as MODR2000\REGEX for the next exercise.

8 With the lower left viewport active select the EXTRUDE icon from the Solids toolbar and:
   a) objects: pick the region
   b) height: 100
   c) taper angle: 0 – fig(b).

9 Undo the extrusion effect, then use the EXTRUDE icon with the following entries:
   i) height: 100, taper angle: 3 – fig(c). Then undo.
   ii) height: 100, taper angle: −3 – fig(d).

10 This exercise does not need to be saved.

Example 2 – a revolved component

1 Open drawing file MODR2000\REGEX saved from the previous exercise with UCS BASE – Fig. 36.2(a).

2 Menu bar with **Tools-New UCS-Origin** and:
   prompt Origin point<0,0,0>
   enter −100,−100,0 <R>.

3 Zoom centre about 150,0,0 at 250 magnification.

4 Select the REVOLVE icon from the Solids toolbar and:
   prompt Select objects
   respond pick the region **then right-click**
   prompt Specify start point for axis of revolution or define axis
            by..
   enter **X <R>** – the X axis option
   prompt Specify angle of revolution
   enter **−90 <R>**
   and pan model to suit then hide – fig(b).

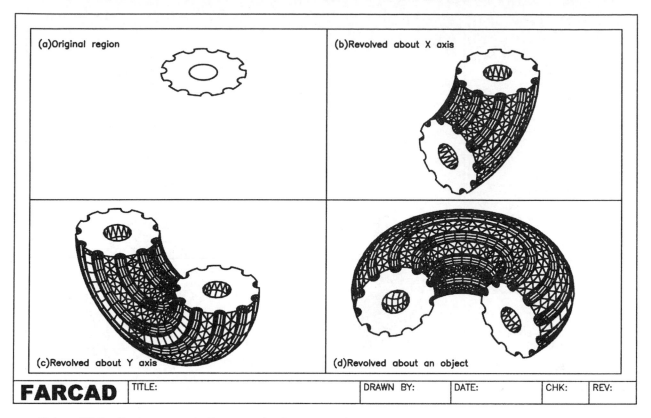

FARCAD	TITLE:		DRAWN BY:	DATE:	CHK:	REV:

Figure 36.2   Region example 2 – a revolved component.

5   Undo the hide and revolve effect to leave the original region.

6   Using the REVOLVE icon:
   a) pick the region then right-click
   b) enter Y as the axis if revolution
   c) enter 180 as the angle
   d) pan and hide – fig(c)
   e) undo the hide and revolve effect.

7   Draw a line from: 0,0,0 to: @0,0,100.

8   Menu bar with **Modify-3D Operation-Rotate 3D** and:
   a) pick the region then right-click
   b) enter X <R> as the axis
   c) enter 100,100,0 as a point on the axis
   d) enter 90 as the rotation angle.

9   With the REVOLVE icon:
   a) pick the rotated region the right-click
   b) enter **O <R>** – object option
   c) pick lower end of vertical line
   d) enter 240 as the angle of revolution
   e) pan to suit then hide – fig(d).

10   This completes the second exercise. Save if required.

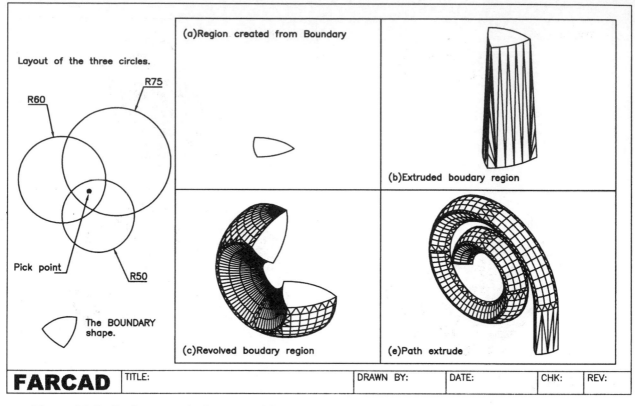

Figure 36.3 Region example 3 – created from a boundary.

Example 3 – using a boundary

1 Open your A3SOL template file with UCS BASE, layer MODEL and the lower right viewport active. Refer to Fig. 36.3.

2 Draw three circles:
   a) centre: 50,0, radius: 50
   b) centre: 0,50, radius: 60
   c) centre: 75,75, radius: 75.

3 Make a new layer: BND, colour blue and current.

4 Zoom centre about 50,50,50 at 200 magnification.

5 Menu bar with **Draw-Boundary** and:
   prompt   Boundary Creation dialogue box – Fig. 36.4
   respond   1. pick Object type: Region
              2. pick Pick Points
   prompt   Select internal point
   respond   **pick a point indicated in Fig. 36.3**
   prompt   Selecting everything..
              Selecting everything visible..
              Analyzing the selected data
              Analyzing internal islands
   then   Select internal point
   respond   **right-click**
   prompt   1 loop extracted
              1 Region created
              BOUNDARY created 1 region.

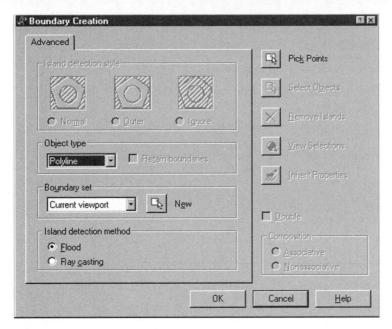

Figure 36.4 Boundary Creation dialogue box.

6 Erase the three circles to leave the blue region – fig(a).

7 Using the EXTRUDE icon:
   a) pick the blue boundary region then right-click
   b) enter a height of 125
   c) enter a taper angle of 2
   d)hide the model – fig(b).

8 Undo the hide and extrude effects to leave the blue region.

9 With the REVOLVE icon:
   a) select the blue region then right-click
   b) enter Y as the axis of revolution
   c) enter 270 as the angle of revolution
   d) hide – fig(c).

10 Undo the hide and revolve effect.

11 Restore UCS FRONT, and with layer MODEL current draw a polyline:
   Start point   0,0
   Next point   @0,100
   Next point   arc option with endpoint: @–200,0
   Next point   arc endpoint: @120,0
   Next point   arc endpoint: @–60,0 then right-click.

12 Restore UCS BASE and make layer BND current.

13 With the EXTRUDE icon:
   a) select the blue region
   b) enter **P <R>** for the path option
   c) pick the red polyline
   d) pan to suit
   e) hide to give fig(d).

14 The exercise is complete, save?

Summary

1 A region is created from closed shapes, e.g. polylines, arcs, circles, ellipses, etc.

2 Regions can be created using the BOUNDARY command.

3 Regions consist of loops and all regions must have an outer loop. There can be several inner loops.

4 Regions can be extruded and revolved.

5 All parts of a region are extruded/revolved to the same height or angle.

6 Regions are extruded along the Z-axis of the current UCS. The height of the extrusion can be positive or negative.

7 Regions can be extruded along a path.

Assignment

This activity requires a region to be created from circles, copied, scaled and then extruded to different heights.

Activity 21: Ratchet mechanism of Macfaramus

While digging in a water bed outside the city of CADOPOLIS, a device was discovered which was thought to be a ratchet mechanism for a primitive type of waterwheel. This mechanism has three distinct 'parts' to it, each having the same shape.

Using the reference sizes given, create the outline from circles, convert these circles into regions, then subtract the smaller circles from the larger. The other parts of the mechanism are scaled by 0.85 and 0.55 from the original. When the three parts have been created, they have to be extruded as follows:

a) lower part: height of −50 with −5 taper

b) middle part: height of 50 with 0 taper

c) top part: height of 50 with −2 taper.

Notes.

1. Use a 0,0 centre point for the large circle and for copying and scaling purposes.

2. Each scaled part is positioned on top of the previous part.

3. Use your discretion for sizes not given.

Chapter 37

Inquiring into models

In this chapter we will create two new composites and then use the AutoCAD inquiry commands to determine the properties of these solids. We will also investigate how the material properties file is created.

Composite model 4 – a slip block

1 Open the A3SOL template file with UCS BASE, layer MODEL and the lower left viewport active.

2 Display the Inquiry toolbar and refer to Fig. 37.1.

3 Create the following primitives:

Box	*Wedge*
corner: 0,0,0	corner: 120,0,0
length: 120	length: 50
width: 100	width: 100
height: 100	height: 70
colour: red	colour: blue.

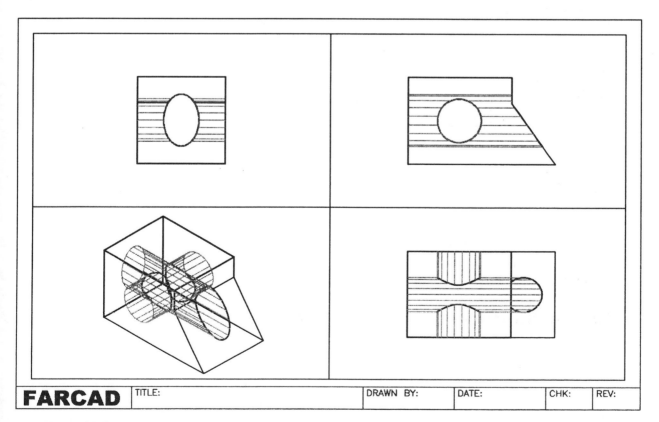

Figure 37.1 Composite model 4 – a slip block (plotted without hide).

4 Centre the model about 80,50,50 at 200 magnification.

5 Create two green cylindrical primitives with:
   a) centre: 60,0,50
      radius: 25
      centre of other end: @0,100
   b) elliptical option
      centre of ellipse: 0,50,50
      axis endpoint: @20,0
      length of other axis: @0,0,30
      centre of other end: @180,0.

6 *a*) union the red box and blue wedge
   b) subtract the two green cylinders from the composite
   c) note the 'curves of interpenetration'
   d) shade and note the colour effect
   e) use the 3D orbit command with the model, then restore the original wireframe representation.

7 At this stage save the composite as MODR2000\SLIPBL.

8 Select the AREA icon from the Inquiry toolbar and:
   prompt Specify first corner point or [Object/Add/Subtract]
   enter   **O <R>** – the object option
   prompt Select objects
   respond **pick the composite**
   prompt Area = 98062.84, Perimeter = 0.00.

9 This is the surface area of the composite in square units (mm?). A solid composite has no perimeter, hence the 0 value.

10 Select the MASS PROPERTY icon from the Inquiry toolbar and:
   prompt Select objects
   respond **pick the composite then right-click**
   prompt AutoCAD Text Window
   with   details on the composite including:
             Mass = 995882.69
             Volume = 995882.69
   prompt Write to a file?<N>
   enter   **Y <R>**
   prompt Create Mass and Area Properties File dialogue box
   respond 1. check – Save in A: drive or named folder
             2. check – Save as type ***.mpr** – materials properties
             3. enter File name: **SLIPBL**
             4. pick Save – more on this file later.

11 Note that the mass and volume values are the same as AutoCAD R2000 assumes a density of 1. R2000 does not support a materials library.

Composite model 5 – a casting block

1 A3SOL template file, UCS BASE, layer MODEL, lower left viewport active and:
   a) refer to Fig. 37.2
   b) zoom centre about 37,50,18 at 150 magnification.

2 Create a red box primitive with:
   corner: 0,0,0
   length: 75, width: 100, height: 36

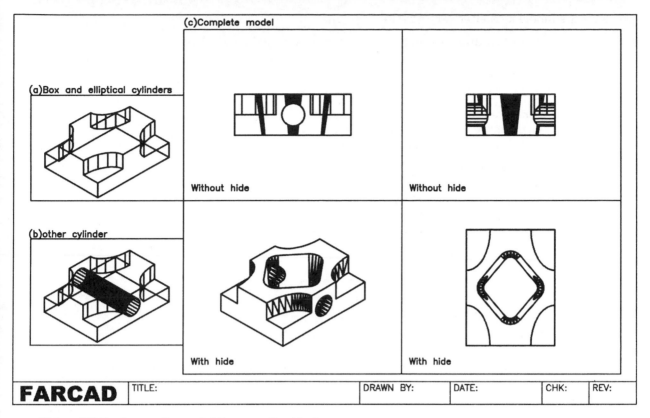

Figure 37.2 Composite model 5 – a casting block.

3 Create a red elliptical cylinder with:
   centre: 0,0,36
   axis endpoint: @20,0
   length of other axis: @0,35
   height: −18.

4 Rectangular array the elliptical cylinder:
   a) 2 rows and 2 columns
   b) row distance: 100, column distance: 75.

5 Subtract the four cylinders from the box – fig(a).

6 Create another red cylinder with:
   centre: 0,50,18
   radius: 10
   centre of other end: @75,0,0.

7 Subtract the cylinder from the composite – fig(b).

8 *a*) Draw a polyline:
      start: 0,0 next: 25,30 next: 0,60 next: −25,30 to: close
   b) fillet the polyline with a radius of 6
   c) move the polyline from: 0,0 by: @37.5,20
   d) extrude the polyline for a height of 36 with −8 taper.

9 Complete the model by subtracting the extruded polyline from the box composite
   – fig(c).

10 Save the model as MODR2000\CASTBL.

11 Menu bar with **Format-Units** and using the Units Control dialogue box:
   a) Units: Engineering
   b) Precision: 0'–0.00"
   c) Insert units: inches.

12 Select the AREA icon from the Inquiry toolbar and:
   a) use the object option and pick the composite
   b) Area = 29416.67 square in (204.2824 square ft).

13 Select the MASS PROPERTIES icon, pick the composite and:

prompt	AutoCAD Text Window	
with	Mass	155027.84 lb
	Volume	155027.84 cu in
respond	<RETURN> to the prompt	
prompt	Write Analysis to a file?<N>	
enter	**Y <R>**	
prompt	Create Mass and Area Properties File dialogue box	
with	SLIPBL listed from previous exercise	
respond	1. enter file name: CASTBL	
	2. pick Save.	

15 *Investigate..*
   a) The area and mass properties have been 'calculated' with the UCS BASE. There are two other UCS saved positions, FRONT and RIGHT. Using these saved UCS's, determine the area and mass/volume values with engineering units. My values were:

UCS	Area(sq in)	Mass (lb)/Volume (cu in)
BASE	30824.09	155027.84
FRONT	30824.09	155029.90
RIGHT	30824.09	155027.59

   These slight variations in mass/volume are due to the way in which R2000 performs the calculations.
   b) Using the relevant commands, find the area and mass for the composite models created in previous chapters. My values with UCS BASE and decimal units were:

	Model/chap	Area	Mass
Machine support	31	81270.75	1022333.68
Backing plate	32	38171.70	98283.83
Pipe/flange	33	190938.19	1305275.35.

Mass properties file

When the mass properties command is used with a solid model, the AutoCAD Text Window will display 'technical' information about the model including the mass and volume.

The user has the option of saving this information to a Mass Property file with the extension **.mpr**. As the mass property file is a 'text file' it can be opened in any 'text editor' type package. To demonstrate this:

1 Select the Windows Start icon from the Windows bar at the bottom of the screen.

2 Select **Programs-Accessories-Notepad** and:

prompt	Untitled Notepad screen
respond	1. menu bar with **File-Open**
	2. activate the A: drive or named folder
	3. alter file name to *.mpr
	4. pick SLIPBL
	5. pick Open.

```
(a)Material Properties File: SLIPBL

--------------- SOLIDS ---------------

Mass:                     995882.69
Volume:                   995882.69
Bounding box:       X: 0.00  --  170.00
                    Y: 0.00  --  100.00
                    Z: 0.00  --  100.00
Centroid:           X: 71.51
                    Y: 50.00
                    Z: 45.60
Moments of inertia: X: 6600251050.50
                    Y: 10169084802.67
                    Z: 10478010529.73
Products of inertia: XY: 3560930335.79
                     YZ: 2270747372.92
                     ZX: 2944997049.96
Radii of gyration:  X: 81.41
                    Y: 101.05
                    Z: 102.57
Principal moments and X-Y-Z directions about centroid:
                    I: 1943214694.71 along [0.95 0.00 -0.30]
                    J: 3004980586.96 along [0.00 1.00 0.00]
                    K: 2991529207.67 along [0.30 0.00 0.95]


(b)Materials Properties File: CASTBL

--------------- SOLIDS ---------------

Mass:                     155027.84 lb
Volume:                   155027.84 cu in
Bounding box:       X: 0.00  --  75.00 in
                    Y: 0.00  --  100.00 in
                    Z: 0.00  --  36.00 in
Centroid:           X: 37.50 in
                    Y: 50.00 in
                    Z: 15.15 in
Moments of inertia: X: 599835677.34 lb sq in
                    Y: 344913627.59 lb sq in
                    Z: 841241799.96 lb sq in
Products of inertia: XY: 290677192.05 lb sq in
                     YZ: 117437118.81 lb sq in
                     ZX: 88077839.11 lb sq in
Radii of gyration:  X: 62.20 in
                    Y: 47.17 in
                    Z: 73.66 in
Principal moments (lb sq in) and X-Y-Z directions about centroid:
                    I: 176681563.73 along [1.00 0.00 0.00]
                    J: 91321212.53 along [0.00 1.00 0.00]
                    K: 235664305.14 along [0.00 0.00 1.00]
```

Figure 37.3 Materials properties files from Notepad.

3 The screen will display the saved material property file for the slip block composite – Fig. 37.3(a).

4 This file can then be printed if required.

5 Figure 37.3 also displays the material property file for the casting block.

6 Exit Notepad to return to AutoCAD.

7 The exercise is now complete.

Summary

1 Mass properties can be obtained from solid models.

2 The mass properties include mass, volume, centroid, radius of gyration, etc.

3 The mass properties can be saved to a .mpr text file.

4 R2000 does not support a materials library and hence mass and volume are always the same, as density is assumed to be 1.

Chapter 38

Slicing and sectioning solid models

Solid models can be sliced (cut) and sectioned relative to:
a) the three coordinate planes
b) three points defined by the user
c) the viewing plane of the current viewpoint
d) user-defined objects.

The two commands are very similar in operation and when used:
a) the slice command results in a new composite model. This model retains the layer and colour properties of the original solid
b) the section command adds a 2D region to the model. The region is displayed on the current layer **BUT NO HATCHING IS ADDED TO THE REGION**.

The two commands will be demonstrated using previously created composite models.

Slice example 1 – using the three coordinate planes

1   Open the composite model MODR2000\SLIPBL with UCS BASE, layer MODEL and the lower left viewport active. This model was created in Chapter 37.

2   Refer to Fig. 38.1 which only displays the 3D viewport for the exercise.

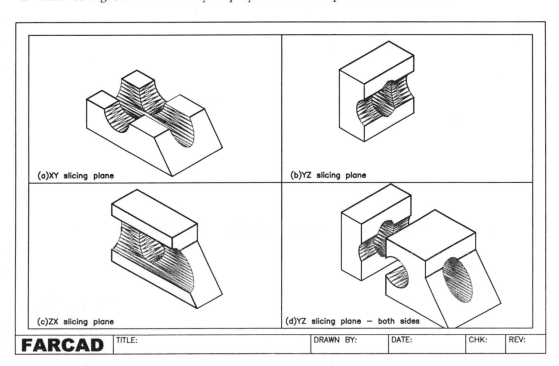

Figure 38.1   Slice example 1 – using the slicing planes with model SLIPL.

3. Select the SLICE icon from the Solids toolbar and:
   prompt   Select objects
   respond **pick the composite then right-click**
   prompt   Specify first point on slicing plane by [Object/Zaxis/
              View/XY/YZ/ZX/3 point]
   enter   **XY <R>** – the XY plane option
   prompt   Specify a point on the XY plane<0,0,0>
   enter   **0,0,50 <R>** – why these coordinates?
   prompt   Specify a point on desired side of plane or [keep Both
              sides]
   enter   **@0,0,-10 <R>**, i.e. keep part 'below' slicing plane
   and   a new model is created – fig(a).

4. Undo the slice effect with **U <R>.**

5. Menu bar with **Draw-Solids-Slice** and:
   a) pick the composite then right-click
   b) enter YZ <R> as the slicing plane
   c) enter 50,0,0 <R> as a point on the plane
   d) enter @−10,0,0 <R> to keep part 'to left' of slice plane
   e) the new composite is created as fig(b).

6. Undo the slice effect.

7. At the command line enter **SLICE <R>** and:
   a) pick the composite then right-click
   b) enter ZX as the slicing plane
   c) enter 0,50,0 as a point on the plane
   d) enter @0,10,0 to keep part 'to right' of the slice plane
   e) new composite as fig(c).

8. Undo the slice effect, activate the slice command and:
   a) pick the composite then right-click
   b) select the YZ plane
   c) enter 40,0,0 as a point on the plane
   d) enter **B <R>** to keep both sides
   e) model is now 'sliced' into two new composites.

9. With the MOVE command:
   a) pick the blue wedge then right-click
   b) base point: enter 170,0
   c) second point of displacement: enter @50,0
   d) the two new composites are separated – fig(d).

10. This completes the first exercise which does not need to be saved.

Slice example 2 – using user-defined slicing planes

1. Open the drawing file MODR2000\MACHSUPP – the first composite solid created in Chapter 31. Ensure USC BASE, layer MODEL and the lower left viewport active. Refer to Fig. 38.2 which displays the 3D viewport for the exercise.

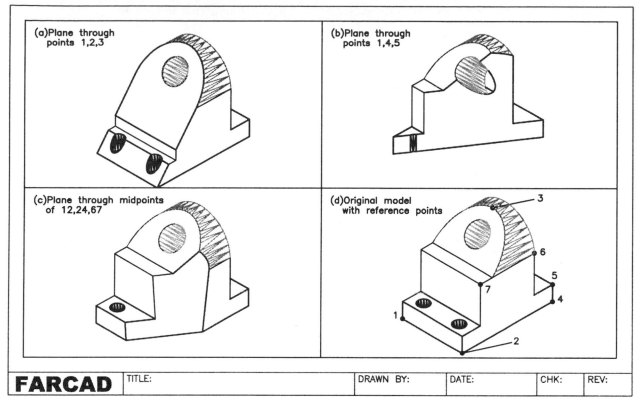

Figure 38.2 Slice example 2 – machine support using three-defined points.

2 Activate the SLICE command and:
   prompt   Select objects
   respond   **pick the composite then right-click**
   prompt   Specify first point on slicing plane ..
   respond   **right-click/enter** – accepting the 3 point default
   prompt   Specify first point on plane and: **ENDpoint icon and pick pt1**
   prompt   Specify second point on plane and: **ENDpoint icon and pick pt2**
   prompt   Specify third point on plane and: **QUAdrant icon and pick pt3**
   prompt   Specify a point on desired side of plane..
   enter   **@0,0,–10 <R>** – why this entry?

3 A new composite will be created as fig(a). This has been 'sliced' through an inclined plane.

4 Hide and shade the model.

5 Undo the shade, hide and slice commands to leave the original composite – or re-open MACHSUPP.

6 With the SLICE command:
   a) pick the composite then right-click
   b) enter <R> to activate the 3 point option
   c) first point on plane: ENDpoint and pick pt1
   d) second point on plane: ENDpoint and pick pt4
   e) third point on plane: ENDpoint and pick pt5
   f) point on plane: enter @0,10,0
   g) hide the new composite – fig(b).

7 This new composite has been sliced through a vertical plane from corner to corner.

8 Undo the hide and slice effects.

9 Use the SLICE command on the composite, activate the 3 point option and:
   a) first point on plane: MIDpoint of line 12
   b) second point on plane: MIDpoint of line 24
   c) third point on plane: MIDpoint of line 67
   d) point on plane: enter: @–10,0,0
   e) new composite displayed as fig(c)
   f) hide and shade.

10 Exercise is now complete.

Slice example 3 – view and object options

1 Open the drawing file MODR2000\FLPIPE of the flange-pipe composite from Chapter 33, UCS BASE and layer MODEL.

2 Refer to Fig. 38.3 and set the following 3D viewpoints:
   viewport   *viewpoint*
   top left   NW Isometric
   top right   NE Isometric
   bottom right   SW Isometric
   bottom left   SE Isometric – should be set to this.

3 Re-centre about –100,–30,0 at 300 mag and pan to suit.

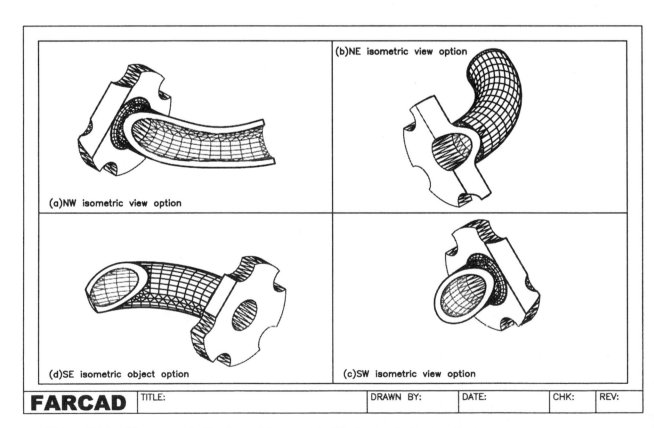

Figure 38.3 Slice example 3 – flange/pipe model with view and object options.

4 With the top left viewport active, select the SLICE icon and:
   prompt   `Select objects`
   respond   **pick the composite then right-click**
   prompt   `Specify first point on slicing plane or..`
   enter   **V <R>** – the view option
   prompt   `Specify a point on the current view plane<0,0,0>`
   enter   **0,50,0 <R>**
   prompt   `Specify a point on desired side of plane..`
   enter   **0,-10,0 <R>**, i.e. keep part 'behind' the plane
   and   new composite displayed as fig(a)
   then   hide the model.

5 *Note.*
The view option assumes a 'line of sight' which is perpendicular to the view plane.

6 Undo the hide and slice effects to restore the original model.

7 With the top right viewport active, SLICE and:
  a) pick the composite then right-click
  b) enter V <R> for the view option
  c) enter 0,50,0 <R> as a point on the view plane
  d) enter 0,–10,0 <R> as a point on the desired side on the plane
  e) new composite created
  f) hide the model – fig(b).

8 Undo the hide and slice effects.

9 Make the lower right viewport active and slice with:
  a) the composite
  b) the view option
  c) 0,–50,0 as a point on the plane
  d) 0,10,0 as a point on the desired side of the plane
  e) new composite as fig(c)
  f) hide then undo both the hide and slice effects.

10 Finally with the lower left viewport active:
  a) draw a circle with centre: 0,–100 and radius: 100
  b) rotate 3D this circle:
    i) about the X axis
    ii) with the circle centre as a point on the axis
    iii) for a reference angle of 45 degrees
  c) with the SLICE command:
    i) pick the composite then right click
    ii) enter **O <R>** for the object option
    iii) pick the circle as the object
    iv) enter 0,10,0 as a point on desired side
    v) erase the circle then hide and composite as fig(d).

11 The slice examples are now complete.

Section example – three point option

The section command is very similar in operation to the slice command, and only one example will be demonstrated.

1 Open the drawing file MODR2000\SLIPBL from Chapter 37, UCS BASE, layer MODEL and the lower left viewport active. Refer to Fig. 38.4.

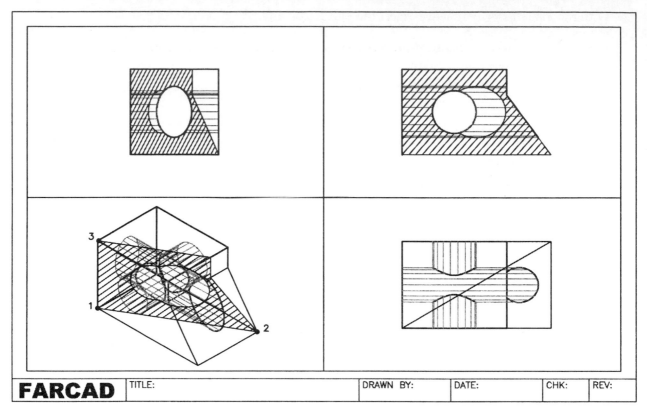

FARCAD | TITLE: | | DRAWN BY: | DATE: | CHK: | REV:

Figure 38.4 Section example with model SLIPBL plotted without hide.

2 Make layer SECT current – or make a new section layer.

3 Select the SECTION icon from the Solids toolbar and:
   prompt   Select objects
   respond **pick the composite then right-click**
   prompt   Specify first point on section plane by..
   respond **<R>** – to activate the three point option
   prompt   Specify first point on plane and pick ENDpoint of pt1
   prompt   Specify second point on plane and pick ENDpoint of pt2
   prompt   Specify third point on plane and pick ENDpoint of pt3.

4 A region is added to the model – the section plane.

5 *Note.*
   a) Hatching is not automatically added to the region.
   b) Hatching must be added to the section region by the user.
   c) The section region is displayed in all viewports, and the viewport specific layer concept is used to 'currently freeze' the section in specific viewports.
   d) If hatching is to be added to the section region (as it should?), remember to alter the UCS position.
   e) My section region in Fig. 38.4 has hatching added using the following system variable values: – HPNAME: ANSI31, HPSCALE: 2 and HPANG: 0.
   f) Hide the model in each viewport with interesting results.
   g) In a later chapter we will section models 'more realistically'.

Using the slice and section commands

If a 'true section' has to be obtained from a solid composite, then the slice and section commands can both be used. To demonstrate this concept:

1 Open drawing file MODR2000\CASTBL from Chapter 37 with UCS BASE, layer MODEL and the lower left viewport active.

2 The original model is displayed in Fig. 38.5(a).

3 With the SLICE command:
   a) pick the composite then right-click
   b) use the three points on slicing plane option and pick the ENDpoints of points 1,2 and 3
   c) enter 0,100,0 as the point on the desired side on the plane
   d) a new composite will be displayed.

4 With layer SECT current, use the SECTION command and:
   a) pick the new composite then right-click
   b) use the three point options with the same selection as step 3
   c) region added to composite.

5 Hatch the region with correct UCS setting.

6 Figure 38.5(b) displays the result of the SLICE and SECTION commands.

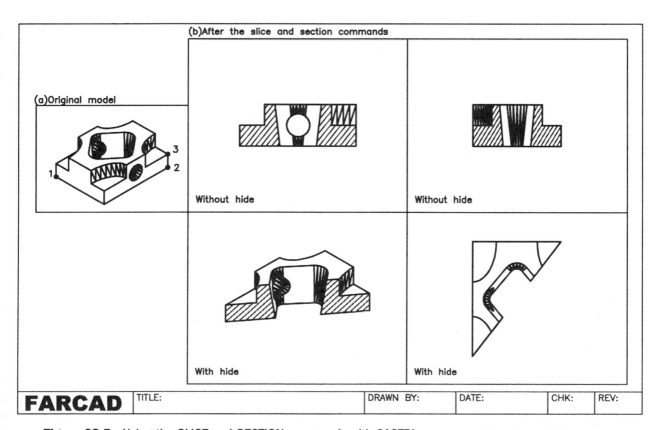

Figure 38.5 Using the SLICE and SECTION commands with CASTBL.

Summary

1 The SLICE command produces a new composite on the same layer as the original model.

2 The SECTION command adds a region to the section plane of the model, but does not add any hatching to this region. Hatching must be added by the user and is UCS dependent.

3 Both commands are very similar with the following options:
   a) the XY, YZ and ZX slicing/sectioning planes
   b) defining any three points on the slice/section plane
   c) relative to an object
   d) relative to the viewing plane in the current viewpoint.

4 The SLICE command requires:
   a) a point on the slicing plane
   b) a point on the desired side of the plane which is to 'be kept'.

5 The SECTION command only requires a point on the sectioning plane.

6 The orientation of the UCS will affect the XY,YZ and ZX planes.

7 The two commands can be activated:
   a) by icons from the Solids toolbar
   b) from the menu bar with Draw-Solids
   c) by entering SLICE or SECTION from the keyboard.

Chapter 39

Profiles and true shapes

When the HIDE command is used with a solid composite, the model is displayed with hidden line removal – as expected. From an 'engineering viewpoint' this is not what is wanted, as the front, top and end views should have lines which represent hidden detail. AutoCAD R2000 allows this hidden detail to be 'added' to a solid model with the PROFILE command and when used, new layers are automatically added to the existing drawing.

A profile is defined as: an image which displays the edges of solid surfaces in the current view.

The command will be demonstrated with previously created models.

Example 1 – slip block

1 Open drawing MODR2000\SLIPBL from Chapter 37.

2 In paper space, use the LIST command and pick the top right viewport border. The AutoCAD Text Window will display information about the viewport including the **HANDLE** number. Take a note of this handle number, then repeat the LIST command selecting the other three viewport borders. In each case note the handle as it will be referred to in the exercise. My handle numbers for the four viewports were:
    top right: 70   top left: 72
    lower right: 76   lower left: 74.

3 *Note.*
    a) all objects created in AutoCAD are given a handle number and this number increases every time a new object is added to the drawing
    b) the handle numbers are in hexadecimal format – don't worry about this if you have never heard of it. It is not important at this level of AutoCAD
    c) the handles are for assisting with the AutoCAD database
    d) your four viewport handle numbers may differ from mine. This is perfectly normal. Simply note them.

4 After the viewport border handle numbers have been noted, return to paper space with UCS BASE.

5 Make layer 0 current and the top left viewport active.

6 Refer to Fig. 39.1.

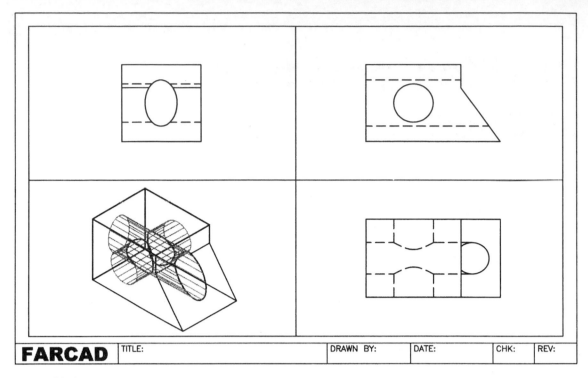

Figure 39.1

7 Select the SETUP PROFILE icon from the Solids toolbar and:
   prompt   Select objects
   respond   **pick the composite then right-click**
   prompt   Display hidden profile lines on a separate layer?[Yes/No]<Y>
   enter   **Y <R>**
   prompt   Project profile lines onto a plane?[Yes/No]<Y>
   enter   **Y <R>**
   prompt   Delete tangential edges?{Yes/No]<Y>
   enter   **Y <R>**
   and   the model in the top left viewport will be displayed with black lines over the
               model lines.

8 Menu bar with **Format-Layer** and:
   prompt   Layer Properties Manager dialogue box
   with   two new layers:
               a) **PH-72** for hidden profile lines – Hidden linetype?
               b) **PV-72** for visible profile lines – Continuous
   respond   1. check the linetype for layer PH-72
               2. if it is not Hidden, then LOAD the HIDDEN linetype and set it to layer PH-72
               3. freeze layer MODEL in the active viewport
               4. pick OK.

   Note.
   These two new layers will have the same handle number as top left viewport, in my
   case 72.

9 The top left viewport will only display the profile visible and hidden lines for the
   composite as layer MODEL has been currently frozen in the active viewport. Do you
   understand why the linetype for layer PH-72 was set to HIDDEN?

10 Make the top right viewport active and from the menu bar select **Draw-Solids-Setup-Profile** and:
     prompt   Select objects
     respond   **pick the composite then right-click**
     prompt   Display hidden profile lines.. and <R>
     prompt   Project profile lines.. and <R>
     prompt   Delete tangential edges.. <R>.

11 The model will be displayed with black visible and hidden lines.

12 Menu bar with **Format-Layer** and:
     prompt   Layer Properties Manager dialogue box
     with   Two new layers:
                    a) PH-70 with HIDDEN linetype
                    b) PV-70 with CONTINUOUS linetype
     respond   1. freeze layer MODEL in active viewport
                  2. pick OK.

     Note.
     a) remember that PH-70 and PV-70 are the visible and hidden layers for my viewport handles. You may have different PH and PV handle numbers
     b) layer PH-70 has HIDDEN linetype as this linetype was loaded in step 8.

13 The top right viewport will display visible and hidden lines for the model.

14 Make the lower right viewport active, still with layer 0 current.

15 At the command line enter **SOLPROF <R>** and:
     a) pick the model then right-click
     b) enter Y <R> to the display hidden profile lines prompt
     c) enter Y <R> to the project profile lines prompt
     d) enter Y <R> to the delete tangential edges prompt
     e) layer properties manager dialogue box and:
          i)   two new layers: PH-76 and PV-76
          ii) currently freeze layer MODEL
          iii) pick OK.

16 The viewport will display the visible and hidden detail lines for the model in the viewport.

17 At this stage the layout should resemble Fig. 39.1 and can now be saved if required. This exercise is now complete.

18 *Explanation*.
     The PROFILE command is **viewport specific** and when activated:
     a) two viewport specific layers are automatically created, these being **PH-??** and **PV-??**
     b) the PH layer is for hidden detail
     c) the PV layer is for visible detail
     d) the ?? with the layer name is the current viewport handle number and is not controlled by the user
     e) the PV linetype is continuous
     f) the PH linetype is hidden, but **MAY HAVE TO BE LOADED**
     g) the command must be used in each viewport in which profile detail has to be extracted
     h) the command is generally used in viewports which display top, front and side views of the model
     i) the command is generally not used in a viewport which displays a 3D view of the model
     j) the hidden and visible detail added are blocks, i.e. there is a hidden detail block and a visible detail block. These blocks can be exploded if required.

Example 2 – the pipe and flange

1 Open the pipe/flange model created in Chapter 33 with UCS BASE, layer MODEL, lower left viewport active and refer to Fig. 39.2.

2 In the top left viewport, activate the PROFILE command and:
   a) pick the model then right-click
   b) enter Y <R> to the three prompts
   c) activate the Layer Properties Manager dialogue box and:
      1. load the HIDDEN linetype and set to the new PH layer
      2. freeze layer MODEL in the active viewport.

3 Repeat step 2 in the top right and lower right viewports, but do not load the HIDDEN linetype – it is already loaded.

4 Extracting profiles is as simple as this!

5 Profile drawings can be dimensioned using viewport specific layers using the same procedure as Chapter 25. I will let you try and add the dimensions for yourself, but remember to:
   a) create a new layer for each viewport
   b) set the correct UCS – dimensioning is a 2D concept.

6 Save the layout when complete.

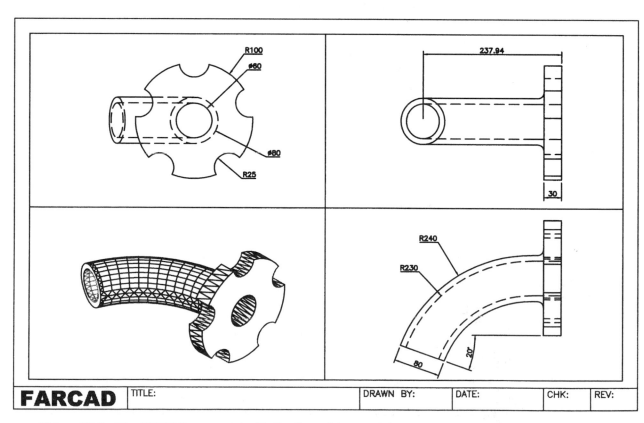

Figure 39.2 The PROFILE command with the flange/pipe model.

Profile explanation

When the profile command is used with a solid model, three prompts are displayed and it is usual to enter Y to these prompts.

a) *Display hidden profile lines on separate layers* This creates two blocks, one for visible lines and one for hidden lines. Two new viewport specific layers are created for this block information PH-?? and PV-??. The actual ?? number is the handle of the current viewport, i.e. it is unique The PV (visible detail) has a continuous linetype, while the PH (hidden detail) has a hidden linetype. The hidden linetype must be loaded before it can be 'assigned' to the PH layer.

b) *Project profile lines onto a plane* The profile detail is displayed as 2D objects and is projected onto a plane perpendicular to the viewing direction and passing through the UCS origin.

c) *Delete tangential edges* A tangential edge is an imaginary edge where two faces meet at a tangent. Tangential edges are not shown for most drawing applications.

True shapes

A true shape is obtained when a surface (face) is viewed at right angles. In AutoCAD R2000 this can be obtained with the PLAN and Solids Editing commands. We will use a model from a previous chapter to demonstrate how a true shape can be obtained.

1 Open the machine support model from Chapter 31 and refer to Fig. 39.3.

2 In the top two viewports, use the PROFILE command and:
   a) accept the three Y prompts
   b) freeze layer MODEL in these two active viewports
   c) load linetype HIDDEN and set to the two new PH layers.

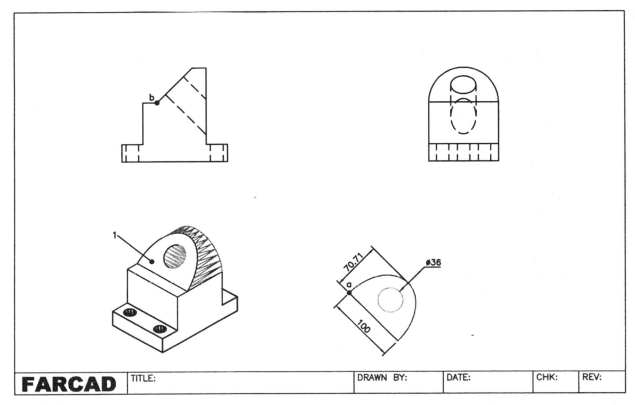

Figure 39.3 True shape extraction using composite model 1.

3   Create a new layer TS, colour to suit and current.

4   With the lower right viewport active, restore UCS SLOPE which should have been saved with the model during the Chapter 31 exercise.

5   Menu bar with **View-2D Views-Plan View-Current UCS** to display the sloped surface of the model as a 'true shape'.

6   Menu bar with **Modify-Solids Editing-Copy faces** and:
    prompt   Select objects
    respond   **pick any pt 1 within the sloped face then right-click and enter**
    prompt   Specify a base point and enter: **0,0 <R>**
    prompt   Specify a second point of displacement and enter: **@0,0,10 <R>**.

7   *a*) Freeze layer MODEL in the active (lower right) viewport to display the true shape of the sloped surface
    b) making each of the other viewports active, freeze layer TS in the other three active viewports
    c) make the lower right viewport active, still with UCS SLOPE.

8   Menu bar with **Modify-Rotate** and:
    prompt   Select objects
    respond   **pick any point on the true shape**
    prompt   Specify base point and enter: **0,0 <R>**
    prompt   Specify rotation angle and enter: **–45 <R>**.

9   The true shape is rotated and now has to be positioned relative to the sloped surface 'from which it was copied'.

10 In the lower right viewport, zoom centre about 0,0,0 at 240 mag to 'scale' the true shape to the same 'value' as the model.

11 In paper space, activate the MOVE command and:
    prompt   Select objects
    respond   **pick any point on the lower right viewport border then right-click**
    prompt   Specify base point or displacement
    respond   **Endpoint icon and pick pt a**
    prompt   Specify second point of displacement
    respond   **Endpoint icon and pick pt b**.

12 Repeat the MOVE command with:
    a) objects: pick the moved viewport border
    b) base point: endpoint icon and pick pt b
    c) second point: enter @180<–45.

13 The true shape is moved to another part of the screen.

14 *Task*.
    a) dimension the true shape with the correct UCS and layer. This layer will need to be currently frozen in the other viewports
    b) freeze the layer VP to give the layout as Fig. 39.3.

15 The exercise is now complete and can be saved.

Summary

1 Profiles can be extracted from models.

2 Profiles display views of solid models with visible and hidden details.

3 New layers are created with the PROFILE command, PV for visible objects and PH for hidden objects.

4 The PH and PV layers are not controlled by the user and are assigned handle numbers. These handle numbers are those of the viewport in which the profile was extracted.

5 True shapes can be extracted from models with the copy faces solids editing command.

Chapter 40

A detailed drawing

In this example a new composite will be created and used to display the model as a detailed drawing. The model to be created is a desk tidy, so open your A3SOL template file with UCS BASE, layer MODEL, lower left viewport active and refer to Fig. 40.1.

Altering the viewports

1 In paper space select the STRETCH icon from the Modify toolbar and
   prompt   Select objects
   enter   **C <R>** – the crossing option
   prompt   Specify first corner and enter: **160,100 <R>**
   prompt   Specify opposite corner and enter: **260,200 <R>**
   prompt   4. found, Select objects
   respond **right-click**
   prompt   Specify base point or displacement and enter: **200,135 <R>**
   prompt   Specify second point of displacement and enter: **@–25,25 <R>**.

2 The viewport configuration will be altered.

3 Return to model space with UCS BASE.

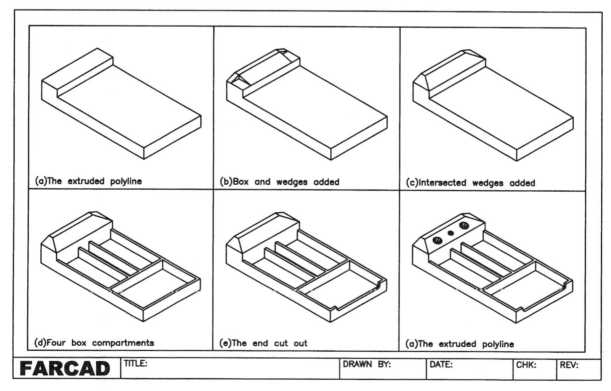

(a)The extruded polyline   (b)Box and wedges added   (c)Intersected wedges added

(d)Four box compartments   (e)The end cut out   (a)The extruded polyline

FARCAD | TITLE: | | DRAWN BY: | DATE: | CHK: | REV:

Figure 40.1   Steps in the construction of the desk tidy (3D view only with hide).

The basic shape

1 With the lower left viewport active restore UCS FRONT.

2 Draw a polyline using the following entries:
Start point @ 0,0   *Next point* @156,0   *Next point* @0,15   *Next point* @−132,0
Next point @0,10   *Next point* @−24,0   *Next point* close.

3 With the EXTRUDE icon from the Solids toolbar, extrude the red polyline with:
a) height: **−85**
b) taper: **0**.

4 Restore UCS BASE and zoom centre about the point 78,42,8 at **0.9XP** in the 3D viewport and **1XP** in the other three viewports. The XP entry is to allow for the different viewport sizes, i.e. the model is being zoomed about a centre point relative to the size of the viewport.

5 The extruded polyline will be displayed as fig(a).

The top

1 Create a box primitive with:
a) corner: 0,12,25
b) length: 6; width: 61; height: 5.

2 Create three wedges using the following information:
a) corner: 6,12,25; length: 18; width: 61; height: 5
b) corner: 6,12,25; length: 12; width: −6; height: 5
c) corner: 6,73,25; length: 12; width: 6; height: 5.

3 With the ROTATE icon, rotate the following wedges:
i) wedge (b) about the point 6,12,25 by **−90**
ii) wedge (c) about the point 6,73,25 by **90**.

4 Union the box and the three wedges with the red extrusion.

5 The model at this stage resembles fig(b).

6 Create another two wedges with:
a) corner: 6,0,25; length: 18; width: 12; height: 5
b) corner: 24,12,25; length: 12; width: −18; height: 5.

7 Rotate the second wedge (b) about the point 24,12,25 by **−90**.

8 Menu bar with **Modify-Solids Editing-Intersect** and:
prompt   Select objects
respond   **pick the two wedges then right-click**.

9 Menu bar with Modify-3D Operation-Mirror 3D and:
prompt   Select objects
respond   **pick the intersected wedges then right-click**
prompt   Specify first point of mirror plane or..
enter   **ZX <R>** – the ZX plane option
prompt   Specify point on ZX plane
enter   **0,42.5,25 <R>**
prompt   Delete source objects?<N> and enter: **N <R>**.

10 Union the two sets of intersected wedges with the composite.

11 The model should be displayed as fig(c).

The compartments

The desk tidy compartments will be created from boxes subtracted from the composite.

1 With lower left viewport active and UCS BASE, create the following four box primitives:

	box1	*box2*	*box3*	*box4*
corner	153,3,3	100,3,3	100,36,3	100,52,3
length	−50	−76	−76	−76
width	79	30	13	30
height	20	20	20	20
colour	magenta	blue	green	blue.

2 Subtract the four boxes from the red composite – fig(d).

3 Shade the model in the 3D viewport then return to wireframe representation.

The end cut-out

1 Lower left viewport with UCS BASE.

2 Set a new UCS position with the 3 point option using:
a) origin: 156,0,0
b) x-axis position: 156,85,0
c) y-axis position: 156,0,15
d) save UCS position as NEWEND.

3 Draw a polyline with the following keyboard entries:
Start point 10,15
Next point @0,−3
Next point arc option with arc endpoint: @3,−3
Next point line option with line endpoint: @59,0
Next point arc option with arc endpoint: @3,3
Next point line option with line endpoint: @0,3
Next point close.

4 Set ISOLINES to 6 and FACETRES to 0.5.

5 Extrude the polyline for a height of **−3** with **0** taper.

6 Subtract the extruded polyline from the composite – fig(e).

7 Restore UCS BASE.

The holes on the slope

1 In paper space zoom in on the 3D sloped area then model space.

2 Set a new UCS position with the 3 point option using:
a) origin: 24,42.5,25
b) x-axis position: 24,85,25
c) y-axis position: 6,42.5,30
d) save UCS position as SLOPE.

3 Create three cylinders, colour magenta with:

	cylinder 1	*cylinder 2*	*cylinder 3*
centre	0,9.34077,0	20,9.34077,0	−20,9.34077,0
radius	3	5	5
height	−12	−20	−20.

4 Subtract the three cylinders from the red composite – fig(f).

5 In paper space, zoom previous and return to model space.

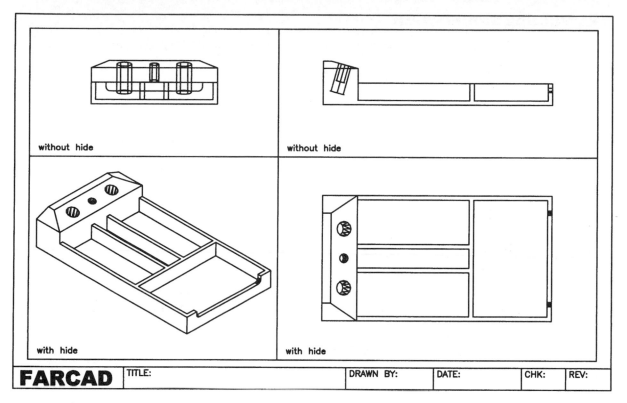

Figure 40.2 Complete desk tidy model.

The complete model

1 Restore UCS BASE.

2 The model is now complete and your screen display should be similar to Fig. 40.2.

3 Save the model at this stage as MODR2000\DESKTIDY.

4 In the 3D viewport use the 3D orbit command with Gouraud shading then return the original view as wireframe.

Extracting a profile

1 Refer to Fig. 40.3 and with the top left viewport active, select the SETUP PROFILE icon from the Solids toolbar and:
   prompt Select objects
   respond **pick the composite then right-click**
   prompt Display hidden profile lines.. and enter: **Y <R>**
   prompt Project profile line.. and enter: **Y <R>**
   prompt Delete tangential edges and enter: **Y <R>**.

2 The model will be displayed with black lines.

3 Using the Layer Properties Manager dialogue box:
   a) note new layers PH?? and PV??
   b) load the linetype HIDDEN (if required) and set the new PH?? layer with this linetype
   c) freeze layer MODEL in this active viewport.

Extracting the section

1 With the top right viewport active, ensure UCS BASE and make layer SECT current.

2 With the SECTION icon from the Solids toolbar:
   a) pick the composite then right-click
   b) enter ZX as the section plane
   c) enter 0,42,5,0 as a point on the plane
   d) a region will be displayed in all viewports.

3 *a*) Actively freeze layer MODEL in the top right viewport
   b) actively freeze layer SECT in the other three viewports.

4 With an appropriate UCS setting, add hatching to the region using:
   pattern name: ANSI32; scale: 1; angle: 0.

Extracting the true shape

1 The layout on your screen at present will differ from Fig. 40.3 so in paper space use the MOVE command to interchange the viewports, i.e. the two lower viewports to the top of the paper sheet and the two top viewports to the bottom of the sheet. Use the endpoint icon and pick a viewport border corner.

2 Make a new layer named TS, colour to suit and current.

3 In the top left and the two lower viewports, freeze the new layer TS in these active viewports.

4 With the top right viewport active, restore UCS SLOPE.

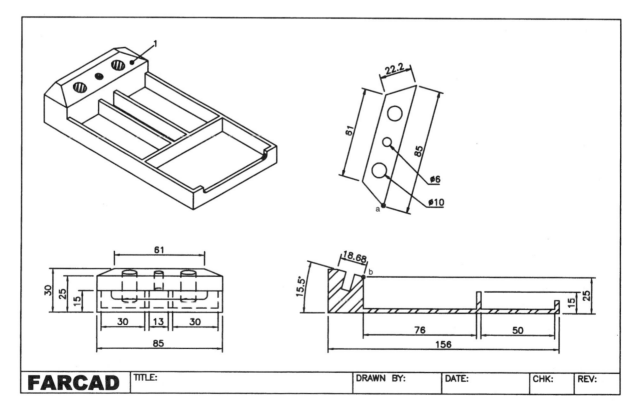

Figure 40.3 Extracting details for the desk tidy model.

5 Menu bar with **Modify-Solids Editing-Copy faces** and:
   prompt   Select faces
   respond **pick any point within the sloped face indicated by pt 1 in the top left viewport then right-click/enter**
   prompt   Specify a base point and enter: **0,0,0 <R>**
   prompt   Specify a second point and enter: **@0,0,1 <R>**
   prompt   Enter a face editing option and enter: **X <R> and X <R>**

6 Now actively freeze layer MODEL in the top right viewport to display the coloured true shape of the sloped surface.

7 With the ROTATE icon:
   a) pick the shape and <R>
   b) enter 0,0 as the base point
   c) enter −15.5 as the rotation angle – this angle should be obvious once the dimensions have been added to the model.

8 In paper space activate the MOVE command and:
   a) objects: pick the top right viewport border then right-click
   b) base point: endpoint icon and pick pt a
   c) second point: endpoint icon and pick pt b.

9 Repeat the MOVE command and:
   a) objects: pick the same viewport border then right-click
   b) base point: endpoint icon and pick pt b
   c) second point: enter @50<74.5 <R>.

10 The true shape is now positioned relative to the slope from which it was copied

Task

1 Inquire into the model and:
   a) Area: 47433.58
   b) Mass: 106339.71 – my figures.

2 Using viewport specific layers and with the correct UCS, add the dimensions as Fig. 40.3.

3 The detail exercise is now complete and the VP layer can be frozen.

4 The exercise can now be saved.

Chapter 41

Blocks, wblocks and external references

Blocks can be created and inserted with solid models as with any other 2D or 3D object. In this chapter we will create two interesting (I hope) solid model assembly drawings from blocks and then investigate solid model external references. We will also investigate the 'interference' between solids.

Example 1 – a desk tray assembly

1 Open your A3SOL template file with UCS BASE, layer MODEL and the lower left viewport active. Refer to Fig. 41.1.

2 Zoom centre about 55,40,20 at 0.75XP in all viewports.

3 Set the ISOLINES system variable to 8.

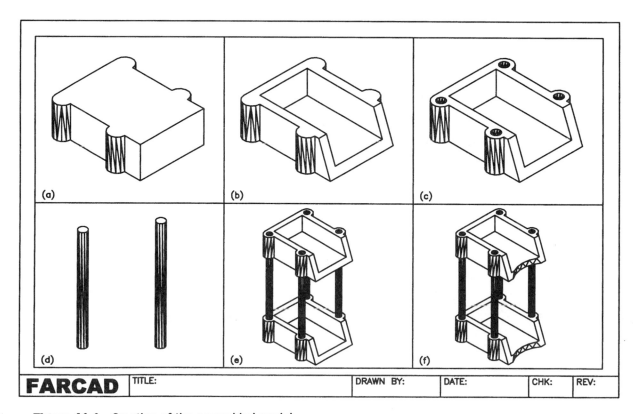

(a) (b) (c) (d) (e) (f)

FARCAD   TITLE: DRAWN BY: DATE: CHK: REV:

Figure 41.1 Creation of the assembled model.

The tray

1 Make a new layer TRAY, colour blue and current.

2 Create two primitives from:

Box	*Cylinder*
corner: 0,0,0	centre: 10,0,0
length: 110	radius: 10
width: 80	height: 40
height: 40.	

3 Rectangular array the cylinder:
  a) for 2 rows and 2 columns
  b) row distance: 80 and column distance: 70.

4 Union the box and the four cylinders – fig(a).

5 Create another two primitives from:

Box	*Wedge*
corner: 10,10,10	corner: 110,0,40
length: 110	length: –15
width: 60	width: 80
height: 40	height: –40.

6 Subtract the box and wedge from the composite – fig(b).

7 Create a cylinder with centre: 10,0,0; radius: 5 and height: 10.

8 Menu bar with **Modify-3D Operation-3D Array** and:

prompt	Select objects
enter	**L <R><R>** – two returns for the cylinder (last object)
prompt	Enter the type of array and enter: **R <R>**
prompt	Enter the number of rows and enter: **2 <R>**
prompt	Enter the number of columns and enter: **2 <R>**
prompt	Enter the number of levels and enter: **2 <R>**
prompt	Specify the distance between rows and enter: **80 <R>**
prompt	Specify the distance between columns and enter: **70 <R>**
prompt	Specify the distance between levels and enter: **30 <R>**.

9 Subtract the eight cylinders from the composite – fig(c). A paper space zoom may be needed to help with this?

Making the tray block

1 At the command line enter **-BLOCK <R>** and:

prompt	Enter block name and enter: **TRAY <R>**
prompt	Specify insertion base point and enter: **0,0,0 <R>**
prompt	Select objects
respond	**pick the composite then right-click**.

2 The -BLOCK entry allows the insertion prompts to be entered from the keyboard and not from the dialogue box.

The support

1 Make a new layer SUPPORT, colour magenta and current.

2 Create two cylinders from:

Cylinder 1	*Cylinder 2*
centre: 0,0,0	centre: 50,50,0
radius: 5	radius: 5
height: 130	height: 140.

3 Change the colour of the 140 high cylinder to green.

4 The two cylinders are displayed as fig(d).

5 Make two blocks of these cylinders with:
   a) Name: SUP1
      Insertion base point: 0,0,0
      Objects: pick the magenta cylinder and right-click
   b) Name: SUP2
      Insertion base point: 50,50,0
      Objects: pick the green cylinder and right-click.

Inserting the blocks

1 Zoom centre about 55,40,90 at 0.5XP in all viewports.

2 Make layer TRAY current.

3 Menu bar with **Insert-Block** and:
   prompt   Insert dialogue box
   respond   1. At Name scroll and pick TRAY
               2. ensure the on-screen prompts are active (tick)
               3. pick OK
   prompt   Specify insertion point and enter: **0,0,0 <R>**
   prompt   Enter X scale factor and enter: **1 <R>**
   prompt   Enter Y scale factor and enter: **1 <R>**
   prompt   Specify rotation angle and enter: **0 <R>**.

4 Repeat the INSERT command and insert block TRAY:
   a) at the point 0,0,150
   b) full size (i.e. X=Y=1) with 0 rotation.

5 At the command line enter **-INSERT <R>** and:
   prompt   Enter block name and enter: **SUP2 <R>**
   prompt   Specify insertion point and enter: **10,0,30 <R>**
   prompt   Enter X scale factor and enter: 1 <R>
   prompt   Enter Y scale factor and enter: 1 <R>
   prompt   Specify rotation angle and enter: 0 <R>.

6 Menu bar with **Modify-Solids Editing-Union** and:
   prompt   Select objects
   respond   **pick the three inserted blocks then right-click**
   prompt   At least 2 solids or coplanar regions must be selected.

7 What does this prompt mean? The union operation has not been successful with the three inserted blocks. This is because blocks must be exploded before they can be used with Boolean operations.

8 Using the EXPLODE icon from the Modify toolbar, select the three inserted blocks.

Checking for interference

1 Make layer 0 current.

2 Select the INTERFERE icon from the Solids toolbar and:
   prompt Select the first set of solids, Select objects
   respond **pick the top blue tray then right-click**
   prompt Select the second set of solids, Select objects
   respond **pick the green support then right-click**
   prompt Comparing 1 solid against 1 solid
            Interfering solids (first set) : 1
                             (second set) : 1
            Interfering pairs   : 1
            Create interference solids>[Yes/No]<N>
   enter **Y <R>**.

3 The model will be displayed with a black cylinder (layer 0) where interference occurs between the tray and the support leg. This interference is due to the support leg (SUP2) being too long, or the TRAY being inserted into the drawing at the wrong insertion point. We deliberately created the support leg (SUP2) with a height of 140 to obtain interference.

4 Erase the green support leg and the black interference cylinder will still be displayed. Erase this interference cylinder.

Inserting the correct support

1 Still with the two (exploded) inserted trays displayed?

2 UCS BASE, lower left viewport active and layer SUPPORT current.

3 INSERT the magenta block SUP1 with:
   a) insertion point: 10,0,30
   b) full size with 0 rotation
   c) explode this inserted block.

4 Rectangular array the magenta support:
   a) for 2 rows and 2 columns
   b) row distance: 80 and column distance: 70.

5 Make layer MODEL current.

6 Menu bar with **Modify-Solids Editing-Union** and pick the six exploded blocks then right-click – fig(e).

7 The composite will be displayed blue or magenta. Why is this when layer MODEL (red) is current? The colour of the composite depends on the order you selected for the union operation. If a tray was the first object selected, then the composite will be blue, and if a support was first selected, then the composite will be magenta.

8 Using the CHANGE command, pick the composite and change the layer to MODEL. The composite will be displayed in red.

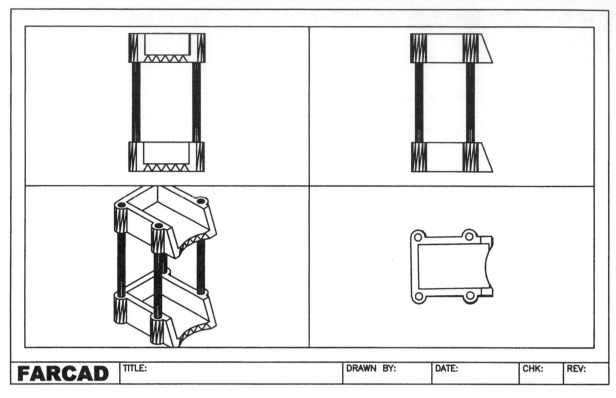

| FARCAD | TITLE: | | DRAWN BY: | DATE: | CHK: | REV: |

Figure 41.2 Complete desk tidy assembly.

Completing the model

1 Create a cylinder with:
centre: 150,40,0
radius: 50 and height: 200.

2 Subtract this cylinder from the composite – fig(f).

3 The model is now complete and can be saved as MOD\DESKTRAY.

4 Figure 41.2 displays the four viewport configuration of the model.

Example 2 – a wall clock

In this example, seven different coloured blocks will be created and used for an assembly drawing. The assembly will then be used for a profile and section extraction.

1 Open your A3SOL template file with layer MODEL and the lower left viewport active. Refer to Fig. 41.3 which displays the blocks as created.

2 Restore UCS FRONT, layer MODEL and zoom centre about 100,75,0 at 250 mag in all viewports.

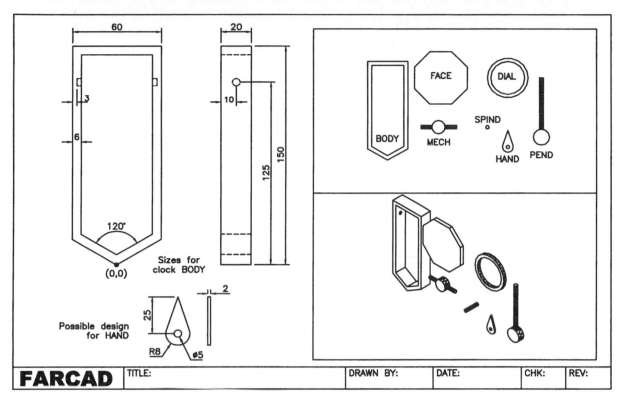

Figure 41.3 Wall clock solids for block creation.

Creating the blocks

Body (red).

1 Create the clock body from two polylines using the sizes given. The start point should be at 0,0 and your discretion is needed for any sizes not given. Hint: I created the body from lines then used the polyline edit command to join them into one polyline. I then offset the polyline by 6.

2 Solid extrude the two polylines for a height of −20 with 0 taper.

3 Subtract the inside extrusion from the outside extrusion.

4 Set ISOLINES to 6 and FACETRES to 0.5.

5 Create a cylinder with:
   a) centre: −27,125,−10 and diameter: 5
   b) centre of other end option: @54,0,0..

6 Subtract the cylinder from the extruded composite

7 Make a block of the composite body with:
   a) block name: BODY
   b) insertion base point: 0,0,0.

Face (blue).

1 Draw a blue octagon with:
   a) centre: 80,0,125
   b) circumscribed in a circle of radius: 40.

2 Solid extrude the octagon for a height of 6 with 0 taper.

3 Make a block of the extruded octagon with:
   a) block name: FACE
   b) insertion base point: 80,125,0.

   Dial (green).
1 Create two green cylinders:
   a) centre: 180,125,0; diameter: 60; height: 5
   b) centre: 180,125,0; diameter: 50; height: 5.

2 Subtract the smaller cylinder from the larger cylinder.

3 Block the composite as DIAL with insertion base point: 180,125,0.

   Mechanism (magenta).
1 Create two magenta cylinders:
   a) centre: 50,50,0; diameter: 5; centre of other end: @54,0,0
   b) centre: 77,50,−5; diameter: 20; height: 10.

2 Union the two cylinders.

3 Block the composite as MECH, insertion base point: 77,50,0.

   Pendulum (cyan).
1 Create two cyan cylinders:
   a) centre: 230,125,0; diameter: 6; centre other end: @0,−90,0
   b) centre: 230,35,−5; diameter: 24; height: 10.

2 Union the two cylinders.

3 Block the composite as PEND with insertion base point: 230,125,0.

   Spindle (colour number 124).
1 Create a cylinder (colour number 20) with:
   a) centre: 150,50,0
   b) diameter: 5 and height: 25.

2 Block as SPIND with insertion base point: 150,50,0.

   Hand (colour number 124).
1 Create a cylinder with centre: 180,20,0, diameter: 5 and height: 2.

2 Create a polyline outline using sizes as a guide – own design.

3 Solid extrude the polyline for a height of 2 with 0 taper.

4 Subtract the cylinder from the extrusion.

5 Block as HAND with insertion base point: 120,20,0.

Inserting the blocks

1 Still with UCS FRONT, layer MODEL and lower left viewport.

2 Zoom centre about 0,75,0 at 200 magnification – all viewports.

3 At the command line enter **-INSERT <R>** and:
   prompt   Enter block name and enter: **BODY**
   prompt   Specify insertion point and enter: 0,0,0
   prompt   Enter X scale factor and enter: 1
   prompt   Enter Y scale factor and enter: 1
   prompt   Specify rotation angle and enter: 0.

4 Insert the other blocks using the following information:

name	insertion pt	scale	rot
FACE	0,125,0	X=Y=1	0
DIAL	0,125,6	X=Y=1	0
MECH	0,125,−10	X=Y=1	0
PEND	0,125,−10	X=Y=1	0
SPIND	0,125,−5	X=Y=1	0
HAND	0,125,15	X=Y=1	0
HAND	0,125,18	X=Y=0.75	−150.

5 Shade the 3D viewport (Gouraud) the use the 3D orbit command. The result is very impressive.

6 **DO NOT** union the inserted blocks but save as MODR2000\CLOCK for rendering.

Tasks.

1 Union the eight inserted blocks – explode needed? The model will be displayed with the block inserted colours. Why is this different from the desk tidy example when the union command resulted in the model being displayed in one colour? Think layers!

2 In the lower right viewport extract a profile of the model to display hidden detail and remember:
   a) hidden linetype must be loaded and set to the pH layer
   b) currently freeze layer MODEL in the viewport
   c) optimize the LTSCALE variable.

3 In the top left viewport extract a vertical section through the model and remember:
   a) use the layer SECT with the required section plane
   b) add hatching to the region – UCS is important
   c) currently freeze layer MODEL in this viewport
   d) currently freeze layer SECT in other viewports.

4 Add an additional viewport to display the assembled model from below.

5 The final layout should be as Fig. 41.4 and can be saved.

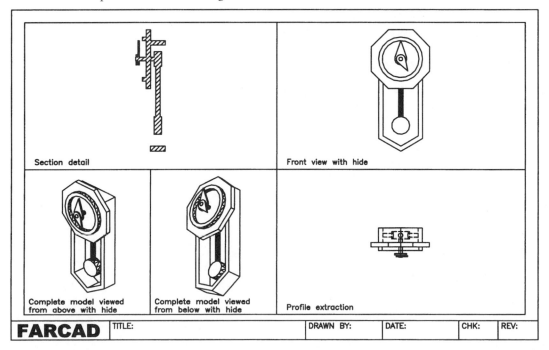

Figure 41.4 Assembled wall clock with profile and section extraction.

External references with solid models

To demonstrate how solid models can be used as external references, a relatively simple layout will be created to represent a workshop, the machines being large machining centres. Solid model composite will be used for these machining centres.

1 Open your A3SOL template file with UCS BASE, layer MODEL and the lower left viewport active.

2 Restore the WCS with the command line entry **UCS <R>** then **W <R>**.

3 Create the following primitives:

	box	wedge	wedge
corner:	0,0,0	100,0,70	100,80,70
length:	100	−50	−50
width:	80	15	−25
height:	70	−50	−50
colour:	red	blue	green.

4 Create a cylinder, centre at 20,0,70 and radius 20 with centre of other end at @0,80,0. This cylinder is to be magenta.

5 Union the box and cylinder and subtract the two wedges from the composite. This model represents the machining centre.

6 At the command line enter WBLOCK <R> and:
    prompt   Write Block dialogue box
    respond   1. Source: objects
              2. Base point with X: 0, Y: 0, Z: 0
              3. Objects: pick Select objects and:
    prompt   `Select objects`
    respond   pick the composite then right-click
    prompt   Write Block dialogue box
    respond   1. File name: MACH1
              2. Location: c:\MODR2000 or named folder
              3. Insert units: Millimeters
              4. pick OK
    prompt   Write block preview displayed at top left of screen.

7 Erase the composite then create another box and cylinder with:
box: corner at 0,0,0 with cube option of length 40
cylinder: centre at 40,20,20, radius 15 with centre of other end at @40,0.

8 Change the colour of the box and cylinder to colour number 24 then union the two primitives. This model represents the robot feeder for the machining centres.

9 Make a second wblock with:
    a) source: objects
    b) base point: X 0, Y 0, Z 0
    c) objects: select objects, pick composite, right-click
    d) file name: MACH2
    e) location: C:\MODR2000 or named folder
    f) insert units: millimeters
    g) pick OK.

10 Close the A3SOL file (no save) then re-open it again.

11 Restore the WCS (UCS-W) then zoom centre about 0,100,50 at 300 magnification in all viewports.

12 With the 3D viewport active, menu bar with **Insert-External Reference** and:
    prompt   Select Reference File dialogue box
    respond   1. scroll and pick C:\MODR2000 or named folder
                2. scroll and pick MACH1
                3. pick Open
    prompt   External Reference dialogue box
    respond   1. ensure all on-screen prompts active (tick)
                2. reference type: Attachment
                3. pick Open
    prompt   Specify insertion point and enter: –200,–40,0 <R>
    prompt   Enter X scale factor and enter: 1 <R>
    prompt   Enter Y scale factor and enter: 1 <R>
    prompt   Specify rotation angle and enter: 0 <R>.

13 Polar array the insertion external reference about the point 0,0 for four items with rotation, the angle to fill being –180.

14 At the command line enter **XREF <R>** and:
    prompt   Xref Manager dialogue box
    with   MACH1 listed
    respond   **pick Attach**
    prompt   Select External Reference dialogue box
    respond   1. ensure MODR2000 active folder
                2. scroll and pick MACH2
                3. pick Open
    prompt   External Reference dialogue box
    respond   1. ensure all on-screen prompts active
                2. reference type: Attachment
                3. pick Open
    prompt   Specify insertion point and enter: **0,-20,0 <R>**
    prompt   Enter X scale factor and enter: **1 <R>**
    prompt   Enter Y scale factor and enter: **1 <R>**
    prompt   Specify rotation angle and enter: **0 <R>**.

15 Rotate this inserted xref about the point 0,0 by 120 degrees.

16 Now save as **MODR2000\SHOPLAY**.

17 Figure 41.5(a) displays this layout as a 3D and top view only.

18 Close this file then open drawing file MACH1. Plan view displayed?

19 Set a SE isometric viewpoint and ensure UCS World current.

20 Create the following primitives:
    a) box with corner: 40,30,70; L: 30, W: 20, H: 40, colour: red
    b) cylinder with centre: 100,0,70, radius: 20, centre of other end at @0,80, colour: magenta.

21 Union the box and subtract the cylinder from the composite.

22 Menu bar with **File-Save** to automatically update MACH1 then close the file and open MACH2.

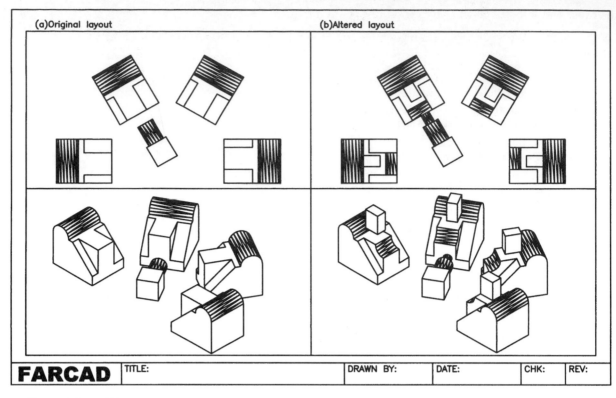

Figure 41.5 SHOPLAY created from external references.

23 Set a SE Isometric viewpoint with UCS World.

24 Create a red cylinder with centre at 80,20,20, radius: 8 and centre of other end: @20,0.

25 Menu bar with File-Save to automatically update MACH2 then close the drawing file.

26 Open the SHOPLAY drawing file and the prompt line will display:
```
Resolve Xref "MACH1": C:\modr2000\MACH1.dwg
"MACH1" loaded
Resolve Xref "MACH2": C:\modr2000\MACH2.dwg
"MACH2" loaded.
```

27 The SHOPLAY will be displayed with the modified solid composites. This completes the chapter.

Summary

Blocks, wblocks and eternal references can be used with solid modelling as with any other type of drawing.

Chapter 42

The setup commands

The setup commands (Drawing, View and Profile) allow drawing layouts to be created by the user. As the profile command has been discussed in a previous chapter, we will only consider the View and Drawing commands in this chapter. These two commands can be summarized as:

View: creates floating viewports using orthographic projection to lay-out multi and sectional views of 3D solid models.

*Draw*ing: generates profiles and sections in viewports which have been created with the setup VIEW command.

Basically the two commands allow the user to create multiple viewport configurations which will display top, front, end and auxiliary views as well as extracting profile and sections of the model. In other words the two commands will create the same type of layout that has been achieved with our A3SOL template file, the 3D viewpoint command and with the SECTION and PROFILE commands.

We will demonstrate the two commands with four examples, these being three previously created models and one completely new model.

Example 1 – the backing plate

1 Open the drawing file MODR2000\BACKPLT from Chapter 32 and:
  a) restore UCS BASE with layer MODEL current
  b) in paper space erase three viewports but leave the 3D view
  c) scale the 3D viewport about the point 10,25 by 0.3
  d) in model space, zoom centre about 0,10,60 at 0.3XP.

2 The original model will be centred in this modified viewport.

3 Refer to Fig. 42.1.

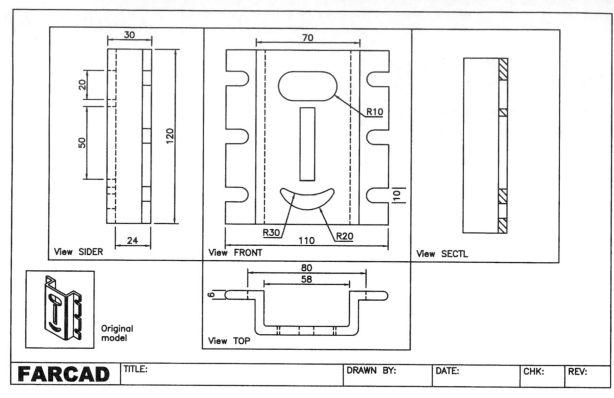

Figure 42.1 View and drawing example 1 – the backing plate.

The Setup View command

1 Select the SETUP VIEW icon from the Solids toolbar and:

prompt	Enter an option [Ucs/Ortho/Auxiliary/Section]
enter	**U <R>** – the Ucs option
prompt	Enter an option [Named/World/?/Current]<Current>
enter	**N <R>** – the named option
prompt	Enter name of UCS to restore
enter	**BASE <R>**
prompt	Enter view scale<1>
enter	**1 <R>**
and	paper space entered – icon displayed
prompt	Specify view center
enter	**200,50 <R>**
and	UCS icon positioned at the entered point
prompt	Specify view center – reposition view center?
respond	**right-click** – accept entered value
prompt	Specify first corner of viewport
enter	**130,25 <R>**
prompt	Specify opposite corner of viewport
enter	**270,85 <R>**
prompt	Enter view name
enter	**TOP <R>**
prompt	Enter an option [Ucs/Ortho/Auxiliary/
enter	**X <R>** – to end the command
and	a top view of the model is displayed in a viewport.

2   Menu bar with Draw-Solids-Setup-View and:
   prompt   Enter an option [Ucs/Ortho/Auxiliary/
   enter   **O <R>** – the ortho option
   prompt   Specify side of viewport to project
   respond   pick bottom horizontal line of the new viewport and note the midpoint snap
            effect
   prompt   Specify view center and enter: **200,170 <R>**
   prompt   Specify view center and right-click
   prompt   Specify first corner of viewport and enter: **130,85 <R>**
   prompt   Specify opposite corner of viewport and enter: **270,245 <R>**
   prompt   Enter view name and enter: **FRONT <R>**
   prompt   Enter an option [Ucs/Ortho/Auxiliary/.. and enter: **X <R>**.

3   A front view of the model is displayed in a viewport

4   At the command line enter **SOLVIEW <R>** and:
   prompt   Enter an option [Ucs/Ortho/Auxiliary/ and enter: **O <R>**
   prompt   Specify side of viewport to project
   respond   pick right vertical line of the new (front) viewport
   prompt   Specify view center and enter: **80,165 <R>**
   prompt   Specify view center and right-click
   prompt   Specify first corner of viewport and enter: **130,85 <R>**
   prompt   Specify opposite corner of viewport and enter: **25,245 <R>**
   prompt   Enter view name and enter: **SIDER <R>**
   prompt   Enter an option [Ucs/Ortho/Auxiliary/ and enter: **X <R>**.

5   A right view of the model is displayed

6   Activate the setup View command and:
   prompt   Enter an option [Ucs/Ortho/Auxiliary/
   enter   **S <R>** – the section option
   prompt   Specify first point of cutting plane
   respond   1 pick the new 'front' viewport
            2 enter **0,0,0 <R>**
   prompt   Specify second point of cutting plane
   enter   **0,120 <R>**
   and   a dashed 'section' line is displayed
   prompt   Specify side to view from
   respond   **pick a point to left of section line**
   prompt   Enter view scale and enter: **1 <R>**
   prompt   Specify view center and enter: **320,165 <R>**
   prompt   View center and right-click
   prompt   Specify first corner of viewport and enter: **270,85 <R>**
   prompt   Specify opposite corner of viewport and enter: **370,245 <R>**
   prompt   Enter view name and enter: **SECTL <R>**
   prompt   Enter an option [Ucs/Ortho/Auxiliary/ and enter: **X <R>**.

7   A left view of the model is displayed.

8   *Note.*
   a) In the example I have given coordinates for the view centre point, the viewport
      corners, the section line, etc. It is usual to 'pick these points' on the screen rather than
      enter coordinates. The only reason for the coordinate entry was that this was our first
      example with the commands.
   b) The view names can be entered as V1, V2, etc. or as TOP, FRONT. This is dependent
      on the user. Just ensure that you know what view has been allocated to the name.

Investigating the layers

1 Menu bar with Format-Layer and note the new layer names:
   a) FRONT-DIM, FRONT-HID, FRONT-VIS
   b) SECTL-DIM, SECTL-HAT, SECTL-HID, SECTL-VIS
   c) SIDER-DIM, SIDER-HID, SECTR-VIS
   d) TOP-DIM, TOP-HID, TOP-VIS
   e) VPORTS.

2 Each new viewport has a dimension, hidden and visible layer and the section viewport has a hatch layer.

3 In model space make the TOP viewport active and activate the Layer Properties Manager dialogue box. The FRONT, SECTL and SIDER layers are all frozen in this active viewport.

4 Load the linetype HIDDEN and set the four -HID layers to this linetype.

5 The layers are automatically created with the SETUP VIEW command and are viewport specific as follows:
   a) -DIM: for dimensions
   b) -HID: for hidden detail
   c) -VIS: for visible lines
   d) -HAT: for hatching detail if the section option has been used.

6 Pick OK when the HIDDEN linetype has been loaded and set.

The Setup Draw command

1 In model space with any viewport active, set the following system variables from the command line:
command line	enter
HPNAME	ANSI31
HPANG	0
HPSCALE	1.

2 Select the SETUP DRAW icon from the Solids toolbar and:
   and   `paper space entered`
   prompt `Select viewports to draw`
   then   `Select objects`
   respond **pick the four new viewports then right-click**.

3 The four new viewports will display the model:
   a) with hidden line removal: top, front, right
   b) as a section: left – with no hidden detail.

4 Optimize the LTSCALE system variable for the hidden line detail.

5 *Note*.
   The three command line entries of HPNAME, HPANG and HPSCALE have set the hatch pattern name, angle and scale. This could have been achieved after the hatching was added to the section view with the Modify-Hatch command.

6 *Task*.
   Add dimensions to the new viewports remembering:
   a) the -DIM layers are viewport specific but need to be current in the appropriate viewport
   b) the correct UCS is needed
   c) Figure 42.1 displays the complete layout with dimensions
   d) save the model if required.

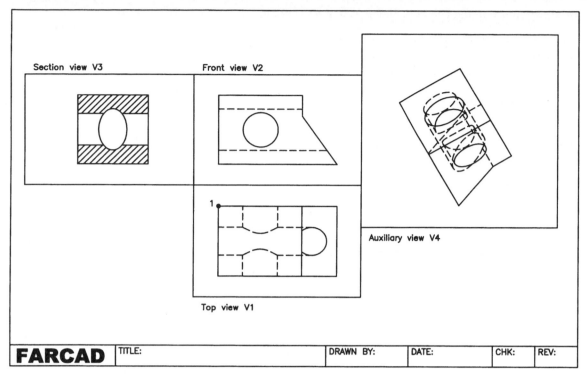

Section view V3   Front view V2

1

Auxiliary view V4

Top view V1

FARCAD	TITLE:		DRAWN BY:	DATE:	CHK:	REV:

Figure 42.2 Setup view and drawing example 2 – the slip block.

Example 2 – the slip block

1 Open model MODR2000\SLIPBL from Chapter 37 and:
   a) in paper space erase three viewports to leave the 3D view
   b) in model space restore UCS BASE and layer MODEL
   c) refer to Fig. 42.2.

2 Use the Setup View command with:
   a) options: U
   b) UCS options: N then BASE
   c) view scale: 0.5
   d) view center: 190,90
   e) first corner of viewport: 130,50
   f) opposite corner of viewport: 250,130
   g) view name: V1
   h) options: X.

3 In paper space erase the original 3D view then return to model space.

4 Use the SOLVIEW command with:
   a) options: U
   b) UCS options: N then FRONT
   c) view scale: 0.5
   d) view center: 190,170
   e) first corner of viewport: 250,130
   f) opposite corner of viewport: 130,210
   g) view name: V2
   h) options: X.

5   In model space make the new viewport active – should be.

6   With the SOLVIEW command use the following:
    a) options: S – section
    b) first point of cutting plane: 50,0
    c) second point of cutting plane: 50,100
    d) side to view from: pick to right of the section line
    e) view scale: 0.5
    f) view centre: 0,100 – note ortho effect
    g) first corner of viewport: 130,210
    h) opposite corner of viewport: 10,130
    i) view name: V3
    j) options: X.

7   Activate the Setup View command and:
    prompt   `Enter an option [Ucs/Ortho/Auxiliary/`
    enter   **A <R>** – the auxiliary option
    prompt   `Specify first point of inclined plane`
    respond **ENDpoint icon and pick pt1**
    prompt   `Specify second point of inclined plane`
    enter   **@100<-60 <R>**
    prompt   `Side to view from`
    respond **pick 'below' the inclined plane**
    prompt   `View centre`
    enter   **0,175 <R>**
    prompt   `Specify first corner of viewport` and enter: **250,100 <R>**
    prompt   `Specify opposite corner of viewport` and enter: **390,240 <R>**
    prompt   `View name` and enter: **V4 <R>**
    prompt   `Enter an option [Ucs/Ortho/Auxiliary/` and enter: **X <R>**.

8   Select the Setup Drawing icon and pick the four new viewport borders and the display will be:
    a) as a section: the left viewport
    b) with hidden line removal: the other three viewports after the HIDDEN linetype has been loaded and set to the -HID layers and the LTSCALE system variable has been optimized.

9   Note the hatch effect is the ANGLE hatch pattern. This is the default setting.

10 To alter the hatch pattern, enter model space and make the left (section) viewport active. Restore UCS RIGHT.

11 Menu bar with **Modify-Hatch** and:
    prompt   `Select associative hatch object`
    respond pick the hatching
    prompt   Hatch Edit dialogue box
    respond 1. Type: User-defined
               2. Angle: 45
               3. Spacing: 4
               4. pick OK.

12 The model layout is now as Fig. 42.2 and can be saved.

13 *Note.*
    The view centre entry with the section and auxiliary options is perpendicular to the paper space icon. This icon is orientated relative to the:
    a) section plane
    b) auxiliary inclined plane.

Example 3 – the pipe and flange model

1 Open the drawing file MODR2000\FLPIP created in Chapter 33 and:
   a) paper space to erase the viewports leaving the 3D view
   b) model space with UCS BASE and layer MODEL current
   c) load the linetype HIDDEN
   d) set the LTSCALE variable value
   e) set the following hatch variables:
      HPNAME: ANSI32; HPANG: 0; HPSCALE: 1
   f) refer to Fig. 42.3 for the viewport layouts.

2 Activate the setup View command and:
   a) UCS option with UCS BASE
   b) view scale: 0.25
   c) view centre: 200,200
   d) position viewport: pick to suit yourself
   e) name: MYVIEW1
   f) options: X.

3 Repeat the setup View command:
   prompt   Ucs/Ortho/Auxiliary/..
   enter   **O <R>** – the ortho option
   prompt   Specify side of viewport to project
   respond **pick lower horizontal line of viewport** (snap set?)
   prompt   Specify view center
   enter   **200,100 <R>**
   prompt   Specify corners of viewport
   respond **pick to suit your layout**
   prompt   Enter view name and enter: **MYVIEW2 <R>**
   prompt   Enter an option and continue with next part of exercise.

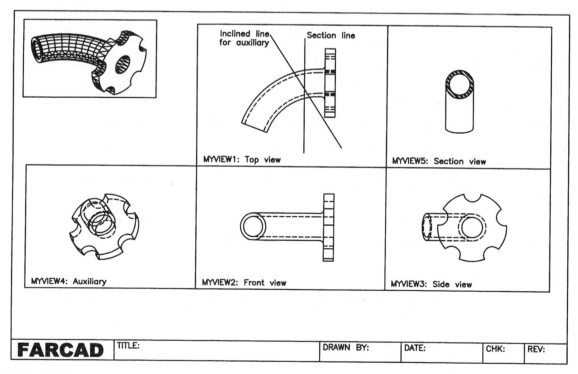

Figure 42.3   Setup view and drawing example 3 – the flange/pipe model.

4 Setup view options and:
   a) select the Ortho option
   b) pick right vertical line of front viewport
   c) view center: pick a point to right to suit
   d) viewport corners: pick points to suit
   e) view name: MYVIEW3
   f) options
   g) select the Auxiliary option
   h) Inclined plane points: pick to suit – see Fig. 42.3
   i) Side to view from: pick 'below' the inclined line
   j) view center: pick a point to suit
   k) viewport corners: position to suit
   l) view name: MYVIEW4
   m) options
   n) select the section option
   o) cutting plane points: pick points as indicated in Fig. 42.3
   p) side to view from: pick to right of the section line
   q) view scale: 0.25
   r) view center: pick to suit
   s) viewport corners: pick to suit the layout
   t) name: MYVIEW5.

5 Linetype HIDDEN and three HP variables set?

6 Activate the Setup Drawing command and pick the five viewports to display the layout with hidden line removal and section detail as Fig. 42.3.

7 Freeze layer VPORTS if required.

8 *Question*.
   In our three setup examples the type of layout has not been mentioned, i.e. first or third angle. I am sure that you are aware of the projections obtained, the first two examples being in first angle, and the third example being in third angle. This is the 'power' of the setup commands. First and third angle detail layouts can be obtained for models by simply picking the relevant view centre points.

9 Save the exercise as it is now complete.

Example 4 – a computer link as a detailed drawing

The three examples selected to demonstrate the View and Drawing commands have used previously created models. The fourth example will create a new model 'from scratch' the example being quite complex, but worth the time and effort spent in creating it.

1 Open your A3SOL template/drawing file with layer MODEL UCS BASE and the 3D viewport active. In paper space erase the other three viewports then return to model space.

2 Set ISOLINES to 6 and refer to Fig. 42.4.

3 The new model will be created from five primitives, each requiring a new UCS position.

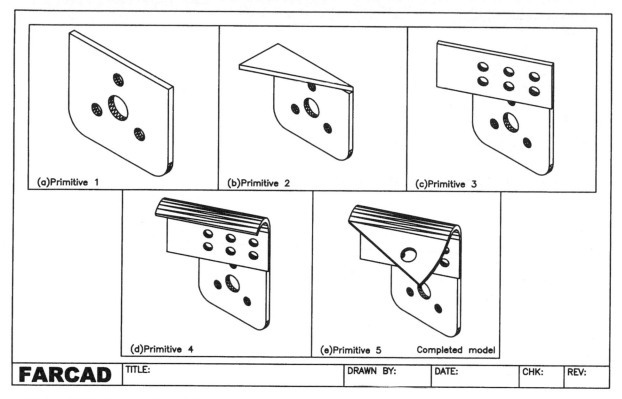

FARCAD	TITLE:		DRAWN BY:	DATE:	CHK:	REV:

Figure 42.4 Construction of the computer link model.

Primitive 1: the base

1 Rotate the UCS about the X axis by 90 and save as PRIM1.

2 Draw a polyline:
   start point 0,50   *Next point* @60,0   *Next point* @0,−40
   arc to   @−10,−10   *line to*   @−40,0   *arc to*   @−10,10   *line to*   close

3 Zoom all then solid extrude the polyline for a height of 3 with taper.

4 Create two cylinders:
   centre: 30,25,0   30,40,0
   diameter: 12   6
   height: 3   3.

5 Polar array the smaller cylinder about 30,25 for 3 items with full circle rotation.

6 Subtract the four cylinders from the extruded polyline – fig(a).

Primitive 2: wedge on top of first primitive

1 UCS PRIM1 current.

2 Set a new 3 point UCS position with:
   a) origin: 0,50,0
   b) x-axis: 60,50,0
   c) y-axis: 0,50,3
   d) save as: PRIM2.

3 Create a wedge with:
   a) corner: 0,0,0
   b) length: 60; width: −3; height: −30.

4 Rotate 3D this wedge:
   a) about the X axis
   b) with 0,0,0 as a point on the axis
   c) for 90 degrees.

5 Union the wedge and the extruded polyline – fig(b).

Primitive 3: box on top of wedge

1 UCS PRIM2 current.

2 Set a new 3 point UCS position with:
   a) origin: 60,0,0
   b) x-axis: 0,30,0
   c) y-axis: 60,0,−3
   d) save as: PRIM3.

3 Create a box with corner: 0,0,0 and:
   length: 67.08; width: 30; height: −3. Why 67.08?

4 Create a cylinder with centre: 10,10,0 and:
   diameter: 6; height: −3.

5 Rectangular array the cylinder:
   a) for 2 rows and 3 columns
   b) row distance: 10; column distance: 15.

6 *a*) subtract the six cylinders from the box
   b) union the box and the composite – fig(c).

Primitive 4: curved extension on top of box

1 UCS PRIM3 current.

2 Set a new 3 point UCS position with:
   a) origin: 0,30,−3
   b) x-axis: 67.08,30,−3
   c) y-axis: 0,30,0
   d) save as: PRIM4.

3 Zoom in on the 'free edge' of the box.

4 Draw two line segments with: *Start point*: 0,0; *Next point* @0,−15; *Next point* @50,0.

5 Draw a polyline about the 'top rim' of the box using the ENDpoint snap and the close option.

6 With the solid revolve command:
   a) objects: enter L <R><R> – to select the polyline
   b) options: enter O <R> – object option
   c) object: pick the left end of long construction line
   d) angle: enter 120.

7 Erase the two line segments.

8 Union the revolved component and the composite – fig(d).

Primitive 5: final curved component

1 UCS PRIM4 current.

2 Set a new 3 point UCS position with:
   a) origin: 67.08,–22.5,–12.99
   b) x-axis: 0,–22.5,–12.99
   c) y-axis: 67.08,–24,–15.59
   d) save as: PRIM5
   e) can you work out the three sets of coordinates?

3 In paper space, zoom-in on the 'free end' of the curved component then return to model space.

4 Draw a polyline about the free end of the curved component using the ENDpoint snap and the close option.

5 With the Solid revolve command:
   a) objects: enter L <R><R> – to select the polyline
   b) options: enter Y <R> – the Y axis
   c) angle: enter –30.

6 Create a cylinder with:
   a) centre: 45,0,15
   b) diameter: 10
   c) centre of other end: @0,10,0.

7 Subtract the cylinder from the revolved component, then union the revolved component with the cylinder – fig(e).

8 In paper space zoom the model then model space.

9 The model is now complete, so:
   a) restore UCS BASE
   b) save as MODR2000\COMPLINK.

Laying out the viewports

This part of the exercise will involve using all the options of the setup View command.

1 Model displayed with UCS BASE.

2 *a*) Load linetype HIDDEN
   b) set the following variables:
      HPNAME: ANSI31; HPANG: 0; HPSCALE: 1
   c) set the LTSCALE value to suit.

3 Activate the setup View command with:
   a) UCS BASE option
   b) view scale: 1
   c) view center: 200,75
   d) viewport corners: pick to suit
   e) view name: TOP
   f) options: X.

4 Using the SOLVIEW command:
   a) UCS option with PRIM1 as the named UCS
   b) view scale: 1
   c) view center: 200,200
   d) viewport corners: pick to suit
   e) view name: FRONT.

5 SOLVIEW command with:
   a) Ortho option
   b) side: pick right vertical side of the front viewport
   c) view center: 70,200
   d) viewport corners: pick to suit
   e) view name: RIGHT.

6 With the setup View command:
   a) activate the Section option
   b) pick any point in the FRONT viewport
   c) cutting plane points: 30,0 and 30,120
   d) side to view from: pick a point to left of section line
   e) view scale: 1
   f) view center: 0,−110
   g) viewport corners: pick to suit
   h) view name: SECTION.

7 The final SOLVIEW command is with:
   a) the Auxiliary option
   b) first point of inclined plane: ENDpoint of pt1 (see Fig. 42.5)
   c) second point of inclined plane: PERP to line 23
   d) side to view from: pick to left of inclined line
   e) view center: 0,200
   f) viewport corners: pick to suit
   g) view name: AUXILIARY.

8 Using the setup Drawing command, pick the five viewports to display hidden detail and a section view – linetype HIDDEN loaded?

9 *Tasks.*
   a) Interrogate the model:
      Area: 20196.01
      Mass: 26758.64.
   b) Using the viewport specific -DIM layers, add the dimensions displayed in Fig. 42.5. Remember you will need to restore the correct UCS for dimensioning. I'll let you Fig. these out for yourself – especially the auxiliary view dimensions.
   c) Freeze the VP and VPORTS layers.
   d) In paper space, optimize your drawing.
   e) Save the completed exercise – worth the effort?

Summary

1 The set View and Drawing commands allow the user to layout multi-view drawings without the need to create viewports and set viewpoints.

2 Both commands can be activated:
   a) by selecting the icon from the Solids toolbar
   b) from the menu bar with Draw-Solids-Setup
   c) from the command line with SOLVIEW and SOLDRAW.

3 The setup View command has options which allow views to be created:
   a) relative to a named UCS
   b) as an orthographic view relative to a selected viewport
   c) as an auxiliary view relative to an inclined plane
   d) as a section view relative to a cutting plane.

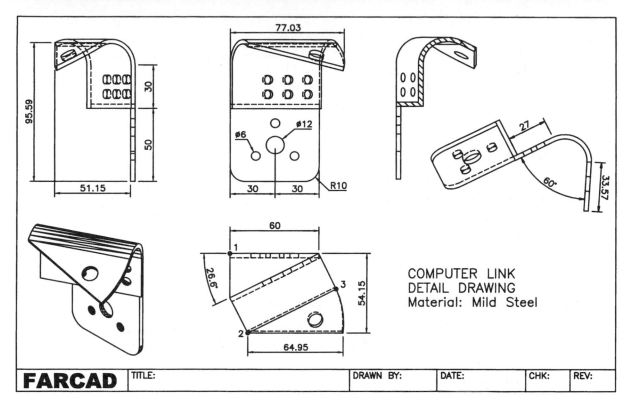

Figure 42.5 Computer link detail drawing using the setup commands.

4 When used, the View command creates viewport specific layers, these being relative to the viewport handle number with the following names:
-VIS   for visible lines
-HID   for hidden lines
-DIM   for dimensions
-HAT   for hatching – only created if the section option is used.

5 The View command requires the user to:
a) enter the view scale
b) position the viewport centre point
c) position the actual viewport corners.

6 With the Ortho option, both First and Third angle projections can be obtained dependent on which side the new viewport is to be placed.

7 The section option requires that the system variables HPNAME, HPANG and HPSCALE are set. It is usual to use the ANSI31 hatch pattern name, but this is not essential.

8 The Drawing command will display models which have been created with the View command:
a) with visible and hidden detail
b) as a section if the section option has been used.

9 It is recommended that the linetype HIDDEN be loaded before the Drawing command is used.

10 The hidden linetype appearance is controlled by the LTSCALE system variable.

11 *Note.*

The user now has two different methods for creating multi-view layouts of solid models:

a) using the A3SOL template file idea which sets the viewports and viewpoints prior to creating the model. Profiles can then be extracted to display hidden detail

b) using the VIEW and DRAWING commands with a solid composite to layout the drawing in First or Third angle projection with sections and auxiliary views as required.

c) it is now the user's preference!

Assignment

To give some additional practice with the View and Drawing commands I have included another new model. This model is to be created using the same procedure as example 4 and I would suggest:

1 Use your A3SOL template file.

2 Erase three viewports but keep the 3D viewport.

Activity 22: Dispenser of MACFARAMUS

One of the discoveries in the city of CADOPOLIS was a container which was thought to be a dispenser belonging to MACFARAMUS. It is this container which has to be created using the setup commands.

1 Make two new layers BODY blue and TOP green.

2 With UCS FRONT, draw two closed polylines using the reference sizes in Fig. 42.6. Use the start points given.

3 Solid revolve the two polylines for a full circle.

4 Create the holes in the top.

5 Use the VIEW and DRAWING commands to create a multi-view layout to display:
a) top and front views with hidden detail
b) two section views through the planes indicated
c) an auxiliary view through an inclined plane at 45 degrees
d) a 3D view.

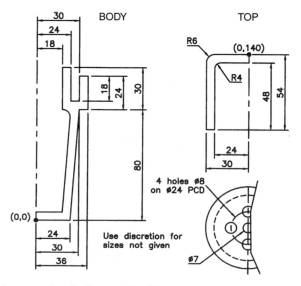

Figure 42.6 Reference details for activity 22.

Chapter 43

Rendering

Rendering is a topic with its own terminology and we will discuss this terminology by rendering previously created models.

What is render?

Rendering is a process which creates an image (usually in colour) of a 3D surface or solid model. This image is created from a scene using a view with lights.

How is render activated?

AutoCAD render is automatically loaded into memory when the RENDER command (or any render option) is selected. The RENDER command can be activated with:

a) the menu bar selection **View-Render-Render**

b) the RENDER icon from the Render toolbar

c) entering **RENDER <R>** at the command line

The three methods give the Render dialogue box as Fig. 43.1, which (at present) has three main areas:

1 the rendering types

2 the rendering destinations

3 the scene which is to be rendered.

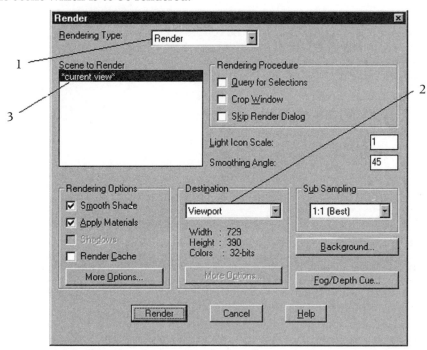

Figure 43.1 The Render dialogue box.

Rendering types

There are three 'types' of rendering, these being:

1 Render: the basic AutoCAD render option which allows models to be rendered without the need for scenes, lights or materials. This is the default 'setting'.

2 Photo Real: is a photo-realistic renderer which can display bitmapped and transparent materials. Volumetric and mapped shadows can also be generated.

3 Photo Raytrace: is a photo-realistic raytrace renderer which can generate reflections, refraction and precise shadows.

Rendering destination

The rendered image of the model can be:

1 displayed in the current viewport of a multi-screen layout

2 displayed in the render window

3 saved to a file for future recall.

Scene to render

Allows the user to select a named scene of the model to render. The user can 'make' several scenes using different views of the model with various lights and materials added – these will be discussed in later chapters. AutoCAD provides a 'default' scene for rendering purposes. This default scene uses a distant light which cannot be modified by the user. At all times it should be remembered that:

*** A scene is a view with lights added ***

R2000 lights

Adding lights to a model layout immediately improves the render appearance and lights can be used to illuminate a complete model or to highlight specific parts of the layout. AutoCAD R2000 has four 'types' of light available, these being:
• ambient light
• distant light
• point light
• spotlight.

Ambient light

1 Provides a constant illumination to all surfaces of a model.

2 It is always 'there' and does not originate from any particular source.

3 The user has control of the intensity of the ambient light.

4 Generally the ambient light intensity should be a low value or the model will be displayed 'too bright'.

5 The default ambient intensity value is 0.3.

6 Ambient light on its own does not produce good rendered images.

Distant light

1 Gives a parallel beam in a particular direction.

2 The user specifies the target point and the light source location.

3 Think of a torch shining at an object.

4 Distant light rays extend to infinity on either side of the light source.

5 The distant light intensity is **not** affected by the distance of the source from the target.

6 It is recommended that distant lights are positioned at the extents of the drawing.

7 Distant lights are used to give a 'uniform lighting' facility.

8 A single distant light simulates the sun.

Point light

1 A point light emits light in all directions from its position.

2 The user specifies the point light location.

3 Think of a light bulb.

4 The intensity of a point light is affected by the distance from the model.

5 Point lights are used for general lighting effects.

6 Point lights are used with spot lights for lighting effects.

Spot light

1 Gives a directional cone of light.

2 The user specifies the direction of the light and the size of the cone.

3 The intensity of a spot light diminishes with the distance from the model.

4 Spot lights have 'hot-spots' and 'fall-off angles' that determine how the light diminishes at the edge of the cone.

5 Spot lights can be used to highlight specific features on a model.

Point lights, distant lights and spot lights are represented in a drawing with symbols, the light name being displayed within the light symbol – Fig. 43.2.

POINT LIGHT   DISTANT LIGHT   SPOT LIGHT
SYMBOL   SYMBOL   SYMBOL

Figure 43.2 Light symbols with 'names' added.

Models to be rendered

In this chapter, two previously solid models will be used be demonstrate how lights, scenes, materials, shadows, etc. can be added to a layout and produce a rendered coloured image. The models selected are the extruded backing plate and the wall clock created from wblocks.

Render example 1 – the solid model backing plate

1 Open your saved drawing MODR2000\BACKPLT from Chapter 32.

2 In paper space, zoom the 3D viewport then return to model space with the 3D viewport active, UCS BASE and layer MODEL current. Display to render toolbar.

3 The first requirement with rendering is to save a view, position some lights and save a scene.

4 At the command line enter **-VIEW <R>** and:

prompt	`Enter an option [?/Orthographic/Delete/..`
enter	**S <R>** – the save option
prompt	`Enter view name to save`
enter	**V1 <R>**.

5 Select the LIGHTS icon from the render toolbar and:

prompt	Lights dialogue box
respond	1. set Ambient Light Intensity to 0.3
	2. scroll at New and pick Point Light
	3. pick New
prompt	New Point Light dialogue box
respond	1. Light name: enter P1
	2. Intensity: alter to 90
	3. pick Modify
prompt	`Drawing screen returned with rubber band effect to light position`
and	`Enter light location<current>`
enter	**0,0,200 <R>**
prompt	New Point Light dialogue box
respond	pick OK
prompt	Lights dialogue box with P1 listed
respond	1. scroll at New and pick Distant Light
	2. pick New
prompt	New Distant Light dialogue box
respond	1. Light name: enter D1
	2. Intensity: alter to 0.9
	3. pick Modify
prompt	`Drawing screen returned with rubber band effect to light position`
and	`Enter light direction TO`
enter	**35,15,30 <R>**
prompt	`Enter light direction FROM`
enter	**@50,–50,100 <R>**
prompt	New Distant Light dialogue box
respond	pick OK
prompt	Lights dialogue box with D1 and P1 listed
respond	1. scroll at New and pick Spotlight
	2. pick New

prompt   New Spotlight dialogue box
respond   1. Light name: enter S1
       2. Intensity: alter to 100
       3. Hotspot: alter to 20
       4. Falloff: alter to 30
       5. pick Modify
prompt   `Enter light target` and enter: **–10,–5,50 <R>**
prompt   `Enter light location` and enter: **@–50,–50,100 <R>**
prompt   New Spotlight dialogue box
respond   pick OK
prompt   Lights dialogue box with S1, D1 and P1 listed
respond   pick OK.

6 Select the SCENES icon from the render toolbar and:
   prompt   Scenes dialogue box
   respond   pick New
   prompt   New Scenes dialogue box
   respond   1. enter Scene name: SC1
          2. pick View: V1
          3. pick Lights: *ALL*
          4. pick OK
   prompt   Scenes dialogue box with SC1 listed
   respond   pick OK.

7 Select the RENDER icon from the render toolbar and:
   prompt   Render dialogue box
   respond   1. Rendering Type: scroll and pick Photo Real
          2. Scene to Render: pick SC1
          3. Destination: scroll and pick Render Window
          4. Rendering Options: ensure Smooth Shade and Apply Materials are both
             active (tick)
          5. pick Render
   prompt   Render window will be displayed with a coloured image of the backing plate.
         Note.
         a) the light effect and the white background
         b) the 'roundness' of the model
         c) impressive effect?
   respond   1. cancel the render window
          2. pick AutoCAD from the Windows taskbar to return to the drawing screen.

8 We now want to add a background to the display and a material to the model.

9 AutoCAD allows rendered images to be displayed with four 'types' of background, these
   being:
   a) the default white background
   b) a one coloured background
   c) a gradient background of three colours
   d) an 'picture' background of an already saved image.

10 Select the BACKGROUND icon from the Render toolbar and:
   prompt   Background dialogue box
   respond   1. Select Gradient
          2. Accept the RGB colour settings
          3. Alter Horizon: 0.7; Height: 0.8; Rotation: 20
          4. pick Preview then OK.

11 Render scene SC1 with Photo Real to the Render Window and the model image will be displayed with the set gradient background.

12 Cancel the render window then return to the AutoCAD screen.

13 Select the MATERIALS LIBRARY icon from the Render toolbar and:
   prompt   Materials Library dialogue box
   with   *a*) Materials in Current Drawing – Global
               b) Current Library list
   respond   1. scroll at Current Library list
               2. pick WOOD-WHITE ASH
               3. pick Preview-Cube
               4. pick <-Import
   and   WOOD-WHITE ASH added to Current Drawing list
   respond   pick OK.

14 *Note.*
   The current library list will display either a few material names or a large number of names. If only a few names are displayed then it will be necessary to open an **MLI** file. This is achieved by:
   a) picking Open from the Materials Library dialogue box
   b) scrolling and opening other render.mli files, usually in the Support sub-folder of the AutoCAD folder
   c) you can use any material name for this exercise.

15 Select the MATERIALS icon from the Render toolbar and:
   prompt   Materials dialogue box
   respond   1. pick WOOD-WHITE ASH
               2. pick Attach<
   prompt   Select objects to attach "WOOD-WHITE ASH" to
   respond   pick the composite and right-click
   prompt   Materials dialogue box
   respond   pick OK.

16 Now render scene SC1 to the render window to display the model with a material and a background. When you have viewed the display, cancel the render window and return to the AutoCAD screen.

17 Our model display is almost complete, but we now want a shadow effect from the three lights. To 'see' shadows it is necessary to have a surface on which to 'cast the shadows' and we will create two boxes to obtain this effect.

18 From the menu bar select **Draw-Solids-Box** and create two box primitives with:

	box 1	box 2
corner:	−70,−20,0	−70,78,0
length:	200	200
width:	100	2
height:	−2	100
colour:	number 40	number 40.

19 Union the two box primitives then zoom with a factor of 2.

20 Create a new view with the command line entry -VIEW and use the save option with the name NEWV1.

21 Menu bar with **View-Render-Light** and:
   prompt   Lights dialogue box
   respond   pick Light P1 then Modify

prompt   Modify Point Light dialogue box
respond   1. activate Shadow On
           2. pick Shadows Options and activate Shadow Volume/Ray Trace Shadows
              (tick) then pick OK
prompt   Modify Point Light dialogue box and pick OK
prompt   Lights dialogue box
respond   pick OK.

22 Using the same procedure as step 21, Modify lights D1 and S1 and set Shadows On with
    the Shadow Volume/Ray Trace option.

23 Menu bar with **View-Render-Scene** and:
    a) make a new scene SCNEW
    b) pick view NEWV1
    c) pick all lights
    d) pick OK then OK.

24 Menu bar with **View-Render-Render** and:
    prompt   Render dialogue box
    respond   1. pick scene SCNEW
               2. render type: photo real
               3. destination: render window
               4. rendering options active: Smooth Shade, Apply Materials, Shadows
               5. pick Render.

25 The render process may take some time, but when completed, the model will be displayed
    on a base with a shadow effect and must be considered quite impressive?

26 This model is a bit map image and can be saved from the render menu bar with File-Save.

27 The rendered image is displayed in Fig. 43.3.

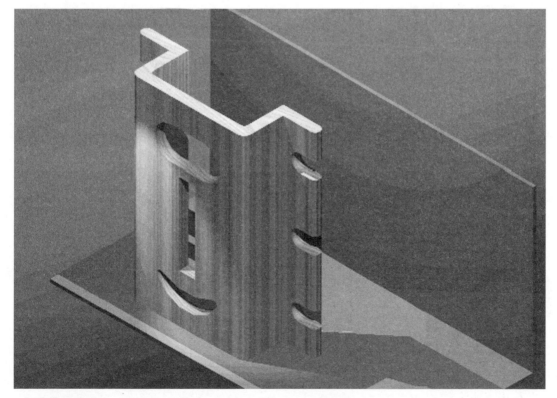

Figure 43.3   Rendered image of the backing plate model.

Render example 2 – the wall clock

Preparing a model for rendering follows the basic procedure used with example 1, i.e. save a view, position lights, create a scene, attach materials, render the scene. For our second example we will use the wall clock model and attach several materials to the various parts of the model.

1   Open model CLOCK of the wall clock creation from Chapter 41.

2   In paper space zoom in on the 3D viewport then return to model space with UCS BASE and layer MODEL.

3   Create a box primitive with:
corner: −90,40,−20
length: 180; width: 2; height: 240
colour: number 201.

4   At this point save the layout as a view with name V1.

5   Position the following lights:
    a) Point   name: P1   name: P2
                          int: 100   int: 50
                          location: 0,20,300   location: 0,-90,150
    b) Distant   name: D1
                          int: 0.75
                          direction TO: −50,−20,150
                          direction FROM: @−50,−50,50
    c) Spotlight name: S1
                          int: 100
                          hotspot: 30 falloff: 35
                          target: 50,−20,150
                          location: @50,−50,−5.

6   For distant light D1 and spotlight S1, set shadows on, both with the volumetric option.

7   Make a scene named SC1 with view V1 and all four lights.

8   Using the materials library icon, import the materials COPPER, MARBLE GREEN, PINK MARBLE, WOOD-MED ASH and BLUE PLASTIC.

9   With the Materials icon, attach the imported materials to the following parts of the model:
COPPER: pendulum
MARBLE GREEN: octagonal face
PINK MARBLE: circular dial
WOOD MED ASH: body
BLUE PLASTIC: hands.

10   Set a gradient background of your choice.

11   Render scene SC1 with:
    a) photo real
    b) render window
    c) shadow options on.

12   Save the rendered image to your named folder.

13   The rendered image of the clock is displayed in Fig. 43.4.

Figure 43.4 Rendered image of wall clock model.

This chapter has introduced the reader to how models can be rendered. Hopefully you will investigate the topic in more detail as rendering is a fascinating subject and the results really enhance the final appearance of models.

Final thoughts

Hopefully by this time you have a good knowledge of how to model with AutoCAD R2000.

The three basic types of model – wire-frame, surface and solid have been introduced with a series of exercises which I hope you have enjoyed creating. The introduction of rendering greatly improves the final image of a model. You should now have the ability and confidence to 'tackle' all modelling tasks.

ACTIVITY 1
The coloured pyramid of MACFARAMUS

Using the extruded elevation and thickness method with the data given, create the model as a 'plan' then view in 3D from above and from below.

VPOINT 'R' at 300° and 30°   VPOINT 'R' at 300° and −15°

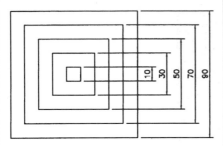

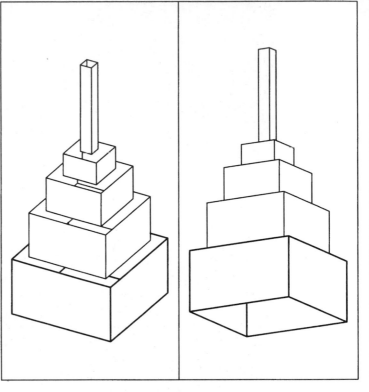

LEVEL	SIZE	ELEV	THICK	COLOUR
1	90sq	0	50	red
2	70sq	50	40	green
3	50sq	90	30	blue
4	30sq	120	20	magenta
5	10sq	140	80	own choice

ACTIVITY 2
Create the 3D wire-frame model using the sizes given, and save for future recall.

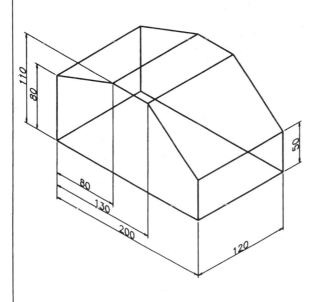

MACFARAMUS's SHAPED BLOCK No.1

ACTIVITY 3
Create the 3D wire-frame model of the given shaped block and save for future recall.

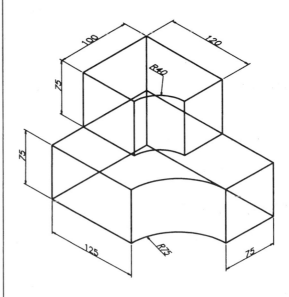

MACFARAMUS's SHAPED BLOCK No.2

ACTIVITY 4
(a) open the wire—frame model from activity 2
(b) set and save UCS positions
(c) add the given dimensions
(d) save for future recall

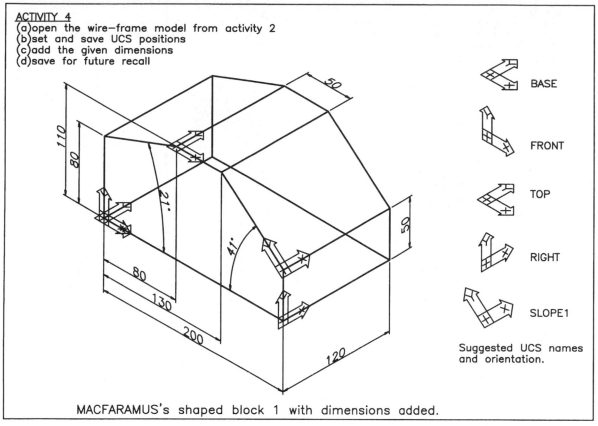

Suggested UCS names and orientation.

BASE
FRONT
TOP
RIGHT
SLOPE1

MACFARAMUS's shaped block 1 with dimensions added.

ACTIVITY 5
(a) Create the wire—frame model using the sizes given
(b) Set and save a UCS for each plane on the model. Four UCS names and orientations are suggested
(c) Dimension the model
(d) Save for future recal
(e) Answer MACFARAMUS's questions

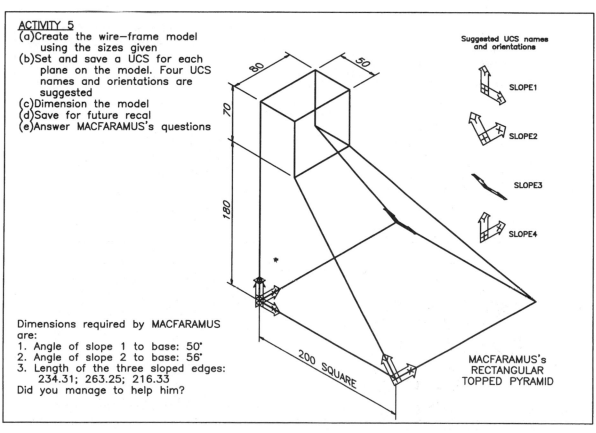

Suggested UCS names and orientations

SLOPE1
SLOPE2
SLOPE3
SLOPE4

MACFARAMUS's
RECTANGULAR
TOPPED PYRAMID

Dimensions required by MACFARAMUS are:
1. Angle of slope 1 to base: 50°
2. Angle of slope 2 to base: 56°
3. Length of the three sloped edges: 234.31; 263.25; 216.33
Did you manage to help him?

ACTIVITY 6
Using the saved UCS settings, add hatching to the five 'visible planes' using the hatch information given.

ACTIVITY 7
Using the slope and vertical saved UCSs, add hatching to the 'planes' using the hatch information given.

MACFARAMUS's SHAPED BLOCK
with hatching added

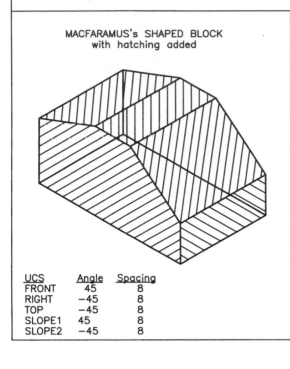

UCS	Angle	Spacing
FRONT	45	8
RIGHT	−45	8
TOP	−45	8
SLOPE1	45	8
SLOPE2	−45	8

MACFARAMUS's
HATCHED
PYRAMID

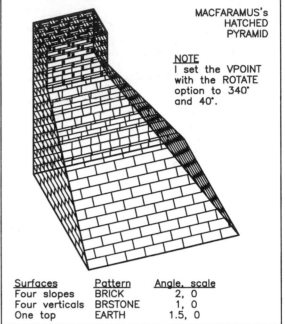

NOTE
I set the VPOINT with the ROTATE option to 340° and 40°.

Surfaces	Pattern	Angle, scale
Four slopes	BRICK	2, 0
Four verticals	BRSTONE	1, 0
One top	EARTH	1.5, 0

ACTIVITY 8   HATCHED SHAPE BLOCK of MACFARAMUS
1. Open the hatched shaped block model
2. Create a four viewport configuration
3. Set the viewpoint to display the model as shown
4. Centre the model in each viewport about the point 100,60,55 at 150 mag (225 in 3D viewport)

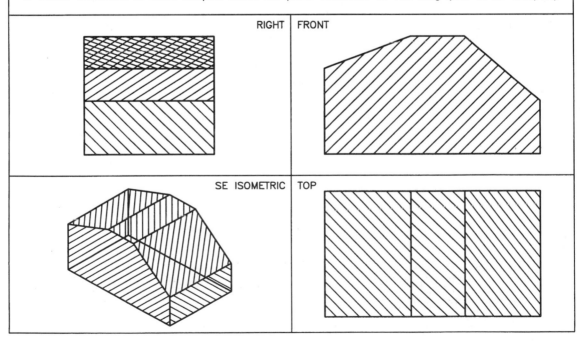

ACTIVITY 9   HATCHED PYRAMID of MACFARAMUS
1. Open the hatched pyramid model
2. Create a four viewport configuration to display the views stated
3. Centre the model in each viewport with:
   a)zoom—scale with a scale factor of 1 (3D value?)
   b)zoom—centre about the point 100,100,125 at 300 mag (3D value?)

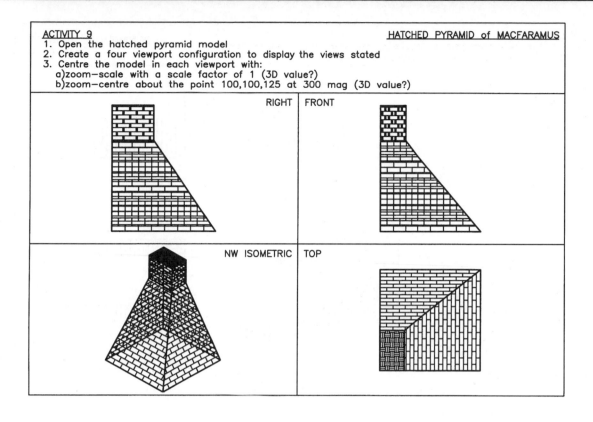

RIGHT | FRONT

NW ISOMETRIC | TOP

ACTIVITY 10   HEXAGONAL COLUMN of MACFARAMUS
1.Create a wire—frame model
  using the sizes given
2.Use the 3DFACE command to
  covert the wire—frame model
  into a surface model
3.Hide/shade etc.

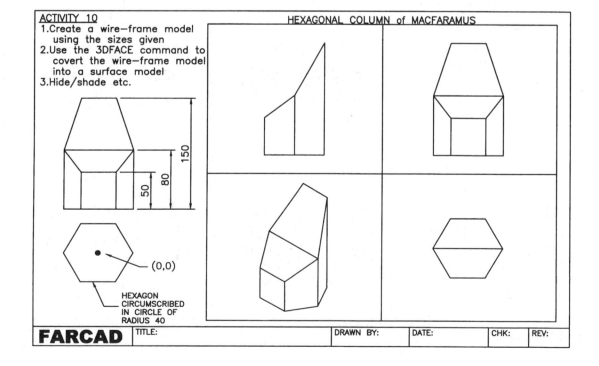

150
80
50

(0,0)

HEXAGON
CIRCUMSCRIBED
IN CIRCLE OF
RADIUS 40

FARCAD | TITLE: | DRAWN BY: | DATE: | CHK: | REV:

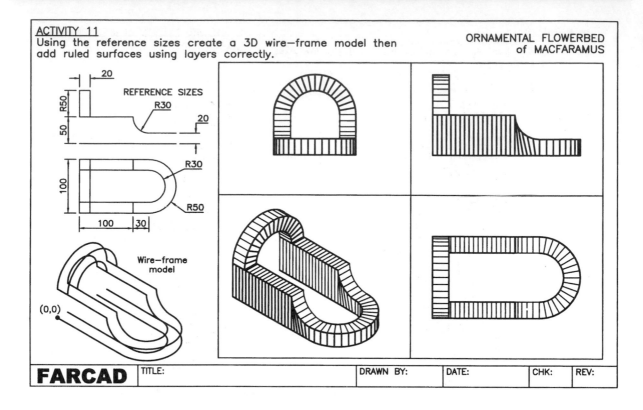

ACTIVITY 11
Using the reference sizes create a 3D wire-frame model then add ruled surfaces using layers correctly.

ORNAMENTAL FLOWERBED of MACFARAMUS

REFERENCE SIZES

Wire-frame model

(0,0)

FARCAD

TITLE:		DRAWN BY:	DATE:	CHK:	REV:

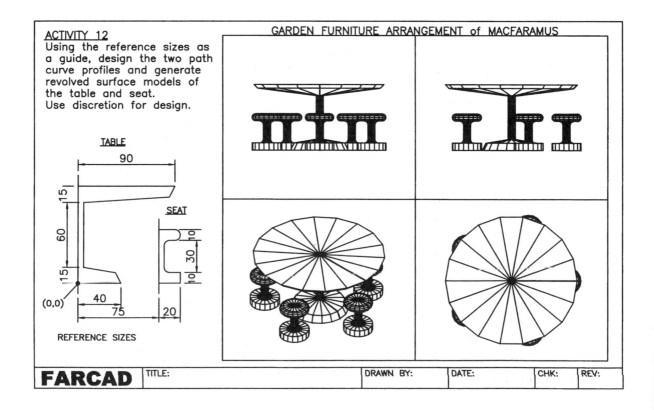

ACTIVITY 12
Using the reference sizes as a guide, design the two path curve profiles and generate revolved surface models of the table and seat.
Use discretion for design.

GARDEN FURNITURE ARRANGEMENT of MACFARAMUS

TABLE

SEAT

(0,0)

REFERENCE SIZES

FARCAD

TITLE:		DRAWN BY:	DATE:	CHK:	REV:

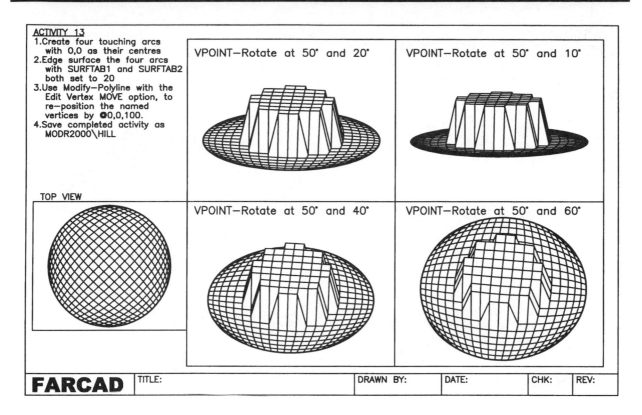

ACTIVITY 13
1. Create four touching arcs with 0,0 as their centres
2. Edge surface the four arcs with SURFTAB1 and SURFTAB2 both set to 20
3. Use Modify—Polyline with the Edit Vertex MOVE option, to re—position the named vertices by @0,0,100.
4. Save completed activity as MODR2000\HILL

TOP VIEW

VPOINT—Rotate at 50° and 20°

VPOINT—Rotate at 50° and 10°

VPOINT—Rotate at 50° and 40°

VPOINT—Rotate at 50° and 60°

FARCAD | TITLE: | | DRAWN BY: | DATE: | CHK: | REV:

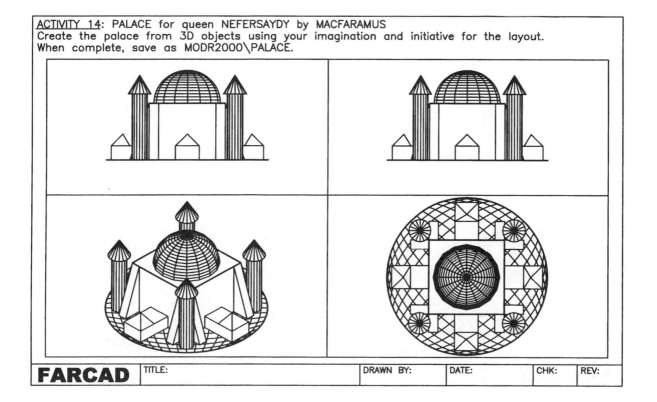

ACTIVITY 14: PALACE for queen NEFERSAYDY by MACFARAMUS
Create the palace from 3D objects using your imagination and initiative for the layout.
When complete, save as MODR2000\PALACE.

FARCAD | TITLE: | | DRAWN BY: | DATE: | CHK: | REV:

ACTIVITY 15
1. Recall the drawing layout MODR2000\CHESS
2. Design the other chess pieces
3. Save the completed layout for rendering.

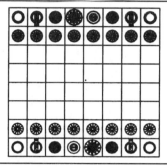

Chess set design produced by permission
of Craig Matthewman, student on the HNC
CADD course at Motherwell College, 1999–2000.

FARCAD | TITLE: | | DRAWN BY: | DATE: | CHK: | REV:

ACTIVITY 16
1. Open the saved edge surface layout MODR2000/HILL
2. Insert the MODR2000\PALACE model, centred on the top of the hill
3. Create viewports to display the complete model 'to perfection'

PALACE of Queen NEFERSAYDY
by
MACFARAMUS

VPOINT–Rotate at 50° and 20°

VPOINT–Rotate at 50° and 10°

FRONT

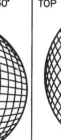

VPOINT–Rotate at 50° and 40°

VPOINT–Rotate at 50° and 60°

TOP

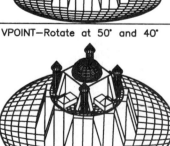

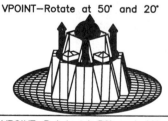

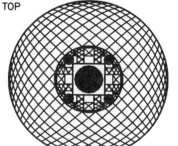

FARCAD | TITLE: | | DRAWN BY: | DATE: | CHK: | REV:

ACTIVITY 17

1. Recall activity 10
2. Make three new viewport specific layers eg DIMTR
3. Use the new viewport specific layers to add the dimensions as shown
4. Remember:
   a) restore the correct UCS
   b) make the correct layer current in the appropriate viewport.

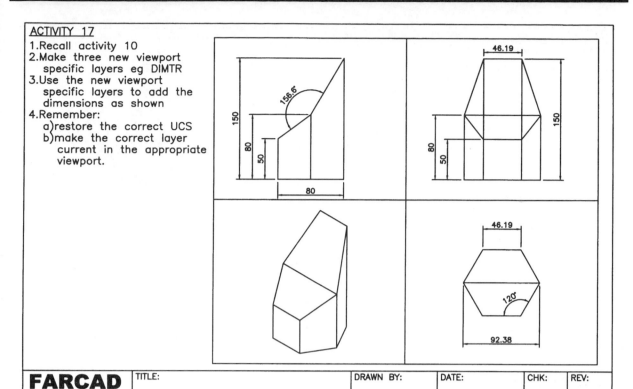

FARCAD | TITLE: | | DRAWN BY: | DATE: | CHK: | REV:

ACTIVITY 18

Create a layout of your own design using the six basic primitives.

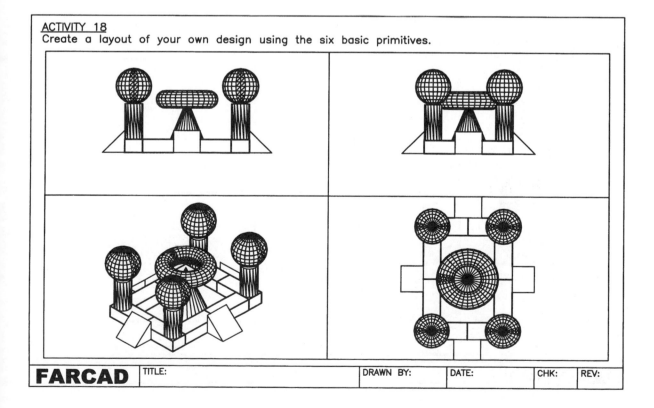

FARCAD | TITLE: | | DRAWN BY: | DATE: | CHK: | REV:

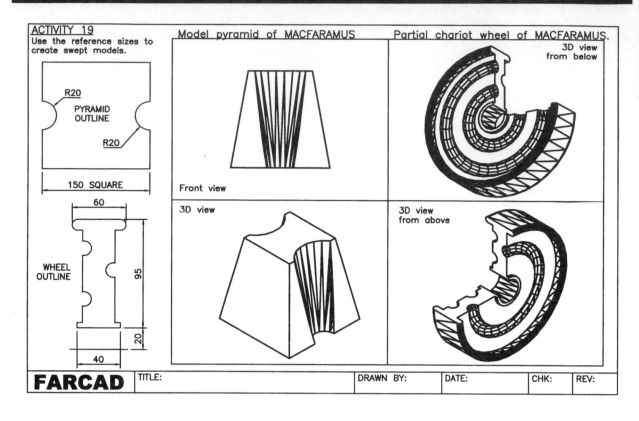

ACTIVITY 19
Use the reference sizes to create swept models.

R20
PYRAMID OUTLINE
R20
150 SQUARE

60
WHEEL OUTLINE
95
20
40

Model pyramid of MACFARAMUS

Front view

3D view

Partial chariot wheel of MACFARAMUS.

3D view from below

3D view from above

FARCAD | TITLE: | DRAWN BY: | DATE: | CHK: | REV:

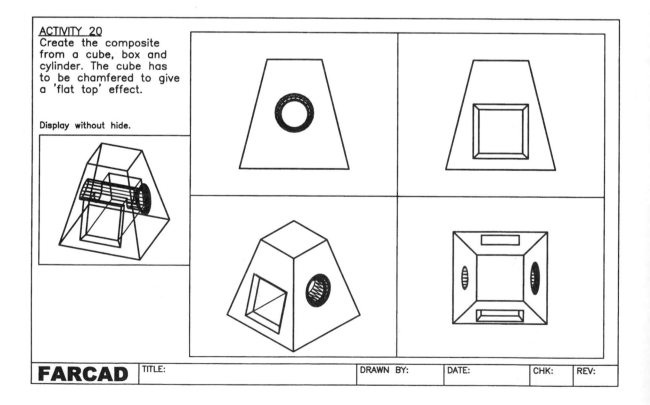

ACTIVITY 20
Create the composite from a cube, box and cylinder. The cube has to be chamfered to give a 'flat top' effect.

Display without hide.

FARCAD | TITLE: | DRAWN BY: | DATE: | CHK: | REV:

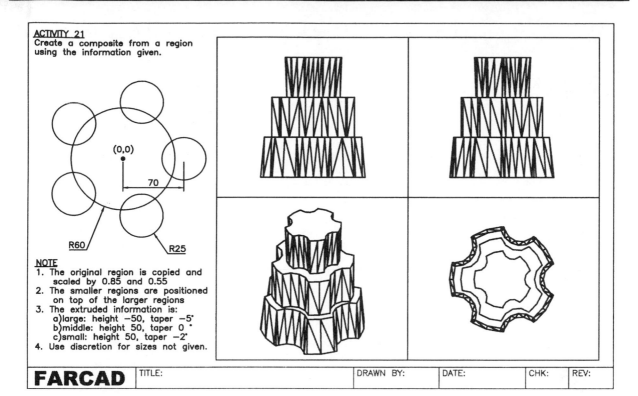

ACTIVITY 21
Create a composite from a region
using the information given.

(0,0)

70

R60   R25

NOTE
1. The original region is copied and
   scaled by 0.85 and 0.55
2. The smaller regions are positioned
   on top of the larger regions
3. The extruded information is:
   a) large: height −50, taper −5°
   b) middle: height 50, taper 0 °
   c) small: height 50, taper −2°
4. Use discretion for sizes not given.

FARCAD | TITLE: | | DRAWN BY: | DATE: | CHK: | REV: |

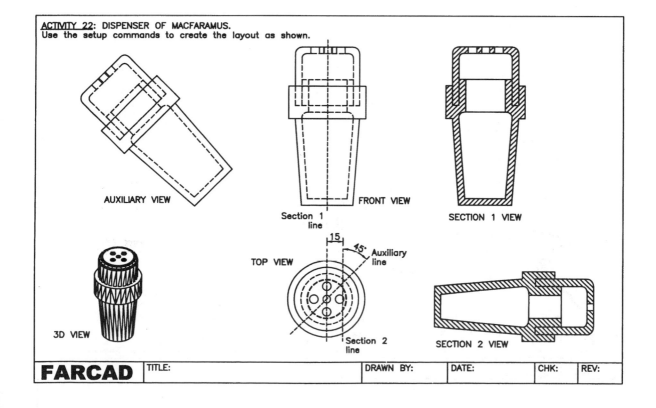

ACTIVITY 22: DISPENSER OF MACFARAMUS.
Use the setup commands to create the layout as shown.

AUXILIARY VIEW

FRONT VIEW

Section 1
line

SECTION 1 VIEW

3D VIEW

TOP VIEW

15

45° Auxiliary
      line

Section 2
line

SECTION 2 VIEW

FARCAD | TITLE: | | DRAWN BY: | DATE: | CHK: | REV: |

Index